THE MYSTERY
and
THE PASSION

A Homiletic Reading
of the Biblical Traditions

DAVID G. BUTTRICK

D1041713

FORTRESS PRESS | **MINNEAPOLIS**

THE MYSTERY AND THE PASSION
A Homiletic Reading of the Biblical Traditions

Scripture quotations, unless otherwise noted, are translated from the original languages by the author. Some translations are from the New Revised Standard Version of the Bible, copyright © 1989 by the Division of Christian Education of the National Council of Churches of Christ in the United States.

"Sunday Morning" from *The Collected Works of Wallace Stevens* by Wallace Stevens is copyright © 1923 and renewed 1951 by Wallace Stevens. Reprinted by permission of Alfred A. Knopf, Inc.

The diagram on p. 195 is adapted from *The Gospel According to Saint John,* vol. 2 by Raymond Brown (New York: Doubleday, 1970), and reprinted by permission of Doubleday, a division of Bantam, Doubleday, Dell Publishing Group, Inc.

"Fantasy on the Resurrection" by Vassar Miller from *Adam's Footprint* is copyright © 1957 by Vassar Miller and reprinted by permission of Wesleyan University Press.

Interior design: The HK Scriptorium, Inc.

Cover design: Patricia Boman

Cover art: Scala/Art Resource, NY, K 27659, Grunewald,
          Resurrection and Annunciation, Isenheim Altarpiece,
          Colmar, Musee Unterlinden

Library of Congress Cataloging-in-Publication Data

Buttrick, David, 1927–
    The mystery and the passion : a homiletic reading of the biblical
traditions / David G. Buttrick
        p. cm.
    Includes bibliographical references and index.
    ISBN 0-8006-2550-1 (alk. paper)
    1. Jesus Christ — Passion.   2. Jesus Christ — Resurrection.
3. Preaching. I. Title.
BT431.B84   1992
232.96 — dc20   91-36737
                                                                     CIP

The paper used in this publication meets the minimum requirements of American National Standard for Information Sciences — Permanence of Paper for Printed Library Materials, ANSI Z329.48-1984.   (∞)™

Manufactured in the U.S.A.   AF 1-2550
96   95   94   93   92   1   2   3   4   5   6   7   8   9   10

For sisters and brothers,
Ann and John, Edie and Bob

and in-laws,
Allaben, Farrell, Ives, Wales

especially,
Betty, Steve, Jenna, and Nathaniel

Contents _____

Preface

SOME CHAPTERS in this book have their origin in two lectureships that I gave in the spring of 1988. Before the beginning of Lent, I gave the McFadin Lectures at Brite Divinity School of Texas Christian University on "Preaching and Resurrection." I am grateful to Dr. Jack Suggs for a gracious welcome and to Dr. Joseph R. Jeter, Jr., an ace homiletician, for fine free time together.

Then after Easter, I gave the Lectures on Preaching at Wake Forest University where I was welcomed by Dr. Henry B. Stokes. Those lectures were entitled "Preaching the Passion of Christ." Dr. Stokes and his associate, Elaine Jack, were unusually kind.

Additional chapters have been drawn from courses taught at the Divinity School of Vanderbilt University where I have been much encouraged by Deans H. Jackson Forstman and Joseph C. Hough, Jr., not to mention faculty colleagues and a number of smart students who have tried to keep me somewhat alert.

I would like to acknowledge friendships. I have blundered around in theological education for some years: at Pittsburgh Theological Seminary (1961–1975), at the St. Meinrad School of Theology (1975–1982), and now at the Divinity School of Vanderbilt University. In each school I have had friends. But I am especially grateful to George at Pittsburgh, Brandon at St. Meinrad, and Ed, who, once on the faculty at Pittsburgh, is again a colleague since I have moved to Vanderbilt. They are all splendid thinkers and, of course, fine company. Grace is where you find it!

Two smart homileticians-to-be have worked with me: The Reverend L. Susan May has read the entire manuscript, checked references, and skillfully prepared the indexes. The Reverend Mary Alice Mulligan has chased down some sources, correcting my absent-minded memory. They have been most helpful.

As always I am intensely grateful to Betty More Allaben Buttrick, who, in addition to being a super copy editor, is a lady of courage, winsomeness, intelligence, and generous affection. I love her dearly.

The pages that follow contain both biblical exegesis and theological reflection. I am neither a guild exegete nor a licensed-to-practice systematician; unabashedly, I plead amateur status. I am, however, a practical theologian who enjoys serving the ministry of the church. I do hope these pages may be useful.

Passion, Mystery, and Faith _____

AN OLD HOMILETICS professor collected pictures of preachers. Through the years he amassed a bulky file: pictures of prophets — Moses, Elijah, Isaiah, Jeremiah, even wide-eyed Ezekiel dazzled by wheeling skies; a picture of Jesus perched on a hilltop declaiming the Sermon on the Mount; and other pictures too — Chrysostom, Francis, Luther — as well as more modern pulpiteers, Wesley, Whitefield, and passionate Charles Finney. Most preachers remain hidden in the anonymity of history; they come and go without much notice. But in every age since Christ, and in almost every place on earth, the gospel has been proclaimed. At a conservative estimate, three billion sermons have been preached over twenty centuries since that strange man, Jesus of Nazareth, strode a dry patch of earth in the Middle East.

In the Beginning

Although we may be jaded by sermons that chase Bible verses tediously for twenty minutes or more, original listeners heard the gospel as a huge excitement. If the Epistles are any kind of witness, the apostles announced a changed world. The human world, they claimed, has begun all over again; we are living now in a "new creation." They invited startled listeners to join God's new humanity. Did they use the word *salvation?* Yes, but when they spoke of salvation, they were not handing out stamped tickets to heaven or offering a happy armful of Jesus. Salvation certainly did not mean a cop-out from the wised-up, worldly world. No, for the apostles, salvation was a new social order,

1

forgiven and free, in the midst of a worn-out world.[1] Salvation was life, not self-destruction; love, not nagging self-interest; and freedom, true freedom for neighbors. Come, cried the apostles, come and be part of the world's new beginning. In a way, they continued the preaching of Jesus: "The time is fulfilled, and the kingdom of God has come near; repent, and believe in the good news" (Mark 1:15).

Was the early gospel christocentric? Yes and no. While the focus of the apostles' message was on God's new order, Jesus Christ was preached as its constitutive event; he was the "second Adam" of the new creation. The apostles claimed that Jesus Christ—his life and death and resurrection—was the means by which God had inaugurated a new state of affairs. So the "sermons" we find in Christian writings work two ways; either preachers begin with Christ and then speak of a new human situation or they announce the world's new order and then refer to the event of Jesus Christ. Christ is, if you will, the first cause, or creating event, or fount of newness. Early Christian preaching did not call people to a personal relationship with Jesus. Instead the gospel urged listeners to join a new humanity begun in Jesus Christ.

But Jesus was more than a founding father, was more than some George Washington type hanging around at the start of a new society. No, risen, Christ was also the regent of God's new aeon. Although he was the constitutive event, he was also Lord of God's new humanity. No wonder that the liturgical acclamation "Jesus is Lord," belted out like a pledge of allegiance, animated early Christian worship.[2] To live in God's new humanity was to be governed by Jesus Christ the liberator. The gospel was never an inwardness ("Come to my heart sweet Jeeeesus") but rather good news of a new social order inaugurated and led by the risen, once-crucified Jesus Christ.

What was the shape of the early gospel message? Listen: The promised new aeon has begun; its regent is risen to the right hand of God; and all people, even though under the sway of worldly ways, can begin to live as a new humanity. The gospel was future-present and not, as in our day, a reiteration of the biblical past.

---

[1] My approach here is consistent with many interpreters of Paul, as, for example, J. C. Beker, *Paul the Apostle* (Philadelphia: Fortress Press, 1980), who reads Paul within the framework of apocalyptic; W. D. Davies, *Paul and Rabbinic Judaism* (New York: Harper & Row, 1948); R. Scroggs, *The Last Adam: A Study in Pauline Anthropology* (Philadelphia: Fortress Press, 1966). See also L. Keck, "Paul and Apocalyptic Theology," *Interpretation* 38, no. 3 (July 1984): 229–41.

[2] C. F. D. Moule, *Worship in the New Testament* (Richmond, Va.: John Knox Press, 1961), chap. 5.

Something Has Happened to Us

The primitive gospel was future-*present:* It was never a dear dream not yet come true. Salvation was not in "the sweet by and by."[3] No, the gospel was firmly based on immediate experience. Early Christian communities could see that a new brand of redeemed life was showing up in their midst. The good news they announced was already taking shape in their life together. Salvation had happened to them and indeed was still happening to them. So they spoke of "what we have seen and heard" (Acts 4:20).

Retrospectively, they knew that they had "passed from death to life" (1 John 3:14). Had not the human Jesus somewhat hastily picked them out, twelve disciples to match the twelve tribes of Israel? Had he not instructed them like a latter-day Moses, trying to shape them up for the coming new order? But then, to their horror, there was mounting opposition on the way to Jerusalem. The sudden arrest, the trial, the crowd, the cross, and the dying — the end came so suddenly! With the death of Jesus, the community died as well; "strike the shepherd, and the sheep will be scattered" (Mark 14:27, from Zech. 13:7). Yet, three days later, Easter Day dawned. News of the resurrection drew them together again. They felt they had been recalled, indeed recommissioned as Israel's new beginning, for they had lived and died and were alive again. No wonder that some overenthusiastic Christians, such as a souped-up group in Thessalonica and a proud Petrine faction within the Markan community, guessed that they were already risen and that *parousia* had occurred.[4] Retrospectively, the early Christians knew that somehow they had died and been reborn.

But their experience was not merely retrospective. With wide-eyed astonishment they could see signs of a new order forming among them. Does not Paul talk of new life in the Spirit? He ticks off a list of new realities — peace, joy, courage, charity, to name a few. Conversely, Paul can draw up lists of sins he considers passé, the failings of an old, now supplanted humanity, the humanity of "the present evil age" (Gal. 1:4). Now admittedly Paul has an apocalyptic mind; he divides the human story into two aeons, aeons of old Adam and new Adam. But

---

[3] From "Sweet By and By," words by S. F. Bennett and music by J. P. Webster. Copyright 1910 by J. H. Webster.

[4] See 2 Thess. 2:2 for reference to the notion that the *parousia* had arrived. For a discussion of a faction within the Markan community, see W. H. Kelber, "Conclusion: From Passion Narrative to Gospel," in *The Passion in Mark,* ed. W. H. Kelber (Philadelphia: Fortress Press, 1976), 153–80.

we cannot write off Paul's language as apocalyptic exaggeration; he was writing to real people, and, presumably, his words described their actual experience to some degree. Early Christians were aware of a change in their lifestyles; they were living in a different, new way. What is more, their life together contrasted with the way of the world around them, and indeed was different from the life they themselves had once lived. They were startled by newness forming in the midst of their common life; good heavens, they were being changed! Although the Book of Acts may be given to exaggeration, it tells the story:

> All who believed were together and had all things in common; they would sell their possessions and goods and distribute the proceeds to all, as any had need. Day by day, as they spent much time together in the temple, they broke bread from house to house and ate their food with glad and generous hearts, praising God and having the goodwill of all the people. (Acts 2:44-47a, using the alternative reading "from house to house")

Let us be cautious. The tendency to romanticize early Christianity is an old habit, a chronic temptation that has been tagged "The Myth of Christian Beginnings."[5] If patterns of redeemed life were forming in Christian communities, they were showing up in the midst of usual tawdry human brokenness. The documents collected in our New Testament bear witness to divisions, power plays, hot party spirit, heresies, unsavory conflicts, triumphalism, dependencies, gossip, private greeds, not to mention sold-outness, small-mindedness, and some halfway hidden sexual gaming — all typical churchly stuff! The church then was as dismaying as the church now. Paul's Corinthian correspondence offers a sharp indictment of primitive Christianity, and the Pastoral Epistles are scarcely sweeter. The church, even in its halcyon days, bordered on dis*grace*ful.

Nevertheless, Christians were aware of being saved. They had passed from death to life and now, to their considerable surprise, the new life was enlarging; they were being made free and holy. We can suppose that individual Christians were experiencing some degree of inward liberation from both the burden of conscience and the strictures of "ought"; love can untie all kinds of psychic knots. But also, socially, they were evidently free for one another in a new, gleeful fashion as they had not been before. Perhaps their awareness of new life was mediated through what we now call the sacraments. Baptism into a new

---

[5] See R. L. Wilken, *The Myth of Christian Beginnings: History's Impact on Belief* (Garden City, N.Y.: Doubleday, 1972).

humanity was a powerful symbol,[6] and the Lord's Supper certainly displayed a "shape of things to come," as Jew and Greek, slave and free, men and women came together in a rehearsal of the great messianic banquet.[7]

So, in the early church, the preaching of the good news was matched in some way by a sense of God's new order happening in Christian communities: "Anyone in Christ is [of] the new creation."[8] Redemptive life was appearing in the midst of old-Adam brokenness.

A Story Reversed

How did it all start? Easter Day is Christianity's beginning. Both gospel and community came alive with the resurrection. The old chicken/egg arguments between Protestants and Catholics over which came first, faith or community, are bootless; the answer must be both/and. A proclaiming church came alive, neither a church per se nor a detached gospel. No wonder that virtually all the resurrection stories contain some sort of "go tell" commissioning. God had raised up Jesus Christ. As a result, a dead-to-the-world church came alive again, regrouped, and began to chatter good news.

Please note: The message of resurrection is a huge reversal. Jesus Christ was condemned to a cross; and, according to our Apostles' Creed, he was "crucified, dead, and buried." But on Easter Day, God turned the crucifixion upside down. Christ was approved, raised to life, and set free for the world. The cross, erected by the powers of ancient Palestine — temple priests, religious leaders, the patriotic populace, the Roman state — destroyed Jesus of Nazareth. He was branded a blasphemer and an insurrectionist; his message was labeled false, and his followers, fools. Nevertheless, God overturned the world's verdict. By resurrection, God certified the message Christ preached, endorsed his rebel life, and gave his movement impetus — Jesus Christ was obviously God's truth, life, and way. From the start, the structure of the gospel message was reversal: the indictment of the cross ("Jesus Christ of Nazareth, whom you crucified"); followed by an announcement of

---

[6] See R. Fuller, "Christian Initiation in the New Testament," *Made, Not Born: New Perspectives on Christian Initiation and the Catechumenate* (Notre Dame, Ind.: University of Notre Dame Press, 1976), 7–31.

[7] For a study of the eschatological dimension of the Lord's Supper, see G. Wainwright, *Eucharist and Eschatology* (New York: Oxford University Press, 1981).

[8] My reading of 2 Cor. 5:17. The NRSV has "If anyone is in Christ, there is a new creation."

vindication ("whom God has raised"); all set within the good news of human renewal ("there is salvation in no one else") (Acts 4:10-12). Such a pattern is still usual in preaching. Do we not hold up the cross and, in its reflection, see the terrible, tragic consequences of sin? More, do we not counter the sad facts of sin, law, and death with news of God's salvation? A huge reversal — death and resurrection — has shaped Christian preaching from the beginning.

But Christian preaching does not merely echo the past-tense miracle of Jesus' death and resurrection. No, preaching reads the same pattern of reversal on all human history. We pass along a promise of God's ultimate triumph. Now, make no mistake, Christian faith is not a Pollyanna grin that greets life with positive thinking come what may. No, we do not hand out tickets to a resurrection bash with unreserved glee; we speak of death and resurrection, and death is clearly crucifixion. Christian faith reads the world with grim realism. We know that sin is chronic and, like the plant that grows in *Little Shop of Horrors,* can enlarge and multiply; we know that law can be coercive and straitjacket the human spirit; we know that death is emphatically death, and will be the dead end of us all.[9] Life may be cruciform and, in fact, usually is, because the human urge toward self-destruction is large indeed. Nevertheless, God specializes in reversal: Whatever is love and life and light somehow will triumph in the end, that is, at the end of God's purpose. God's modus operandi is death and resurrection.

Nevertheless, the gospel is not a slice of pie-in-the-sky. We do not counter grim realism about the human enterprise with a puff of hereafter meringue. When Marx condemned Christianity for dispensing a put-up and shut-up message to the poor in view of a forthcoming heavenly payoff, he was appropriately outraged. No, the essence of the gospel is not payoff but a confidence in God, who with Christ was rejected and crucified. We are saying simply that God's impotent, modest, seemingly broken love is nonetheless ultimate. The death/resurrection analogy is built into the character of God. Of course, our gospel does not imply the triumph of church people either. We do not declare that the church, small-time in this world, will make it big in God's future — so join now and get in on the winnings. The sharp

---

[9] The plant, Audrey II, could be described as the "star" of A. Menken's musical play, *Little Shop of Horrors;* see *Little Shop of Horrors: A New Musical,* based upon the film by R. Corman; music by A. Menken; book and lyrics by H. Ashman (Garden City, N.Y.: Doubleday, 1982).

antitriumphalist critique of the Gospel of Mark is a helpful corrective.[10] The church, following Christ, must stumble toward crucifixion. But the gospel is news of God, a God whose sure but loving power raised up the well-known reject, Jesus. As any young Sunday School aficionado knows, God is love, love is all, and love specializes in reversals.

Preaching good news began with the resurrection.

Another Kind of Logic

Gradually another logic also determined the Christian message; call it "reading back." The logic is easy to follow: If God's power was on display in the resurrection of Jesus, then somehow God's power was also hidden in the crucifixion — after all, the two events are inseparable. Early Christians began to explore the mystery of Christ's death, looking for signs of God's "elusive presence."[11] In their search for meaning, naturally they drew on the scriptures, reading such texts as Psalm 22 and Isaiah 53 as well as celebrations of martyrdom found in the Maccabean literature.[12] So not only was the cross a mirror in which human sin was exposed, but the cross was also a clue to God's peculiar kind of saving love. Ever so slowly, the church began to develop primitive notions of atonement. Somehow the early Christians sensed that the cross was connected to the shape of new life they were experiencing together — forgiveness, freedom, and evangelical fervor. They saw the new order of their common lives as promoted by the death of Jesus, the risen Christ.

But their understandings were not systematic theology. Mostly they used conventional metaphors that were at hand, as most preachers do. They described the cross as a sacrifice or a ransom, as victory or as a spectacular display of selfless love.[13] But the metaphors they chose were not arbitrary; the metaphors were designed to bridge the mysterious gap between the event of the cross and their own current experience.

---

[10] Although the so-called Weeden Thesis has been much modified, most Markan scholars agree on the antitriumphalist aim of the Gospel; see T. J. Weeden, *Mark — Traditions in Conflict* (Philadelphia: Fortress Press, 1971).

[11] A phrase lifted from S. Terrien's brilliant *The Elusive Presence: Toward a New Biblical Theology* (San Francisco: Harper & Row, 1978).

[12] See B. Lindars, *Christian Apologetics: The Doctrinal Significance of the Old Testament Quotations* (London: SCM Press, 1961).

[13] For a recent study of the biblical metaphors and their relationship to experience, see P. S. Fiddes, *Past Event and Present Salvation: The Christian Idea of Atonement* (Louisville, Ky.: Westminster/John Knox Press, 1989).

They were not merely explaining the cross but trying to understand how the cross could result in the liberation of *being* saved. If they spoke of Christ's death as a sacrifice, it was because they were tying the cross in with their own sure sense of forgiveness and reconciliation. If they described the cross as a ransom, it was surely because they sensed that somehow they had been set free. Certainly the cross was a victory, because they were no longer intimidated by surly powers that be. The powers had been stripped down; they were no-powers now.[14] Classic metaphors of atonement in early Christian preaching do not merely expound the cross; they connect Christ's crucifixion with the experience of being saved in community.

Another dimension to the models and metaphors we find in scripture is that they probe God's own role in the death of Jesus Christ. What kind of God dies? How can sovereign God, the high and holy God of Israel, the God of the law and the prophets, be tangled up in a messy trial, tossed in a Jerusalem drunk tank, abused, humiliated, and put to death?[15] To use more modern lingo, early Christians were forced to rebuild their "God concept." Yes, they could see God's obvious power in the apocalyptic wonder of the resurrection. But how could God be mixed up in the disgrace, indeed the outright obscenity, of crucifixion? Was the death of Christ a necessary prelude to glory? Did tribulation inevitably precede exaltation? Or was God a self-giver by definition? In different ways, all the documents in Christian scripture struggle to comprehend the deep mysteries of the cross.

In time, the logic of reading back from the resurrection poked further into the past. If God was in on the resurrection, then surely God was involved in the passion; and if God was involved in the passion, then God was somehow busy in the life of Christ as well. Gospels were written.[16] Although the main moments of Christ's life are connected with history, the Gospels are not primarily historical documents. No, they explore the mystery of incarnation, God-with-us in the life of Jesus of Nazareth. So the Gospels are best described as theological portraits,

---

[14] On the powers, see my *Preaching Jesus Christ* (Philadelphia: Fortress Press, 1988), chap. 4.

[15] The problem has been addressed recently by J. Moltmann, *The Crucified God: The Cross of Christ as the Foundation and Criticism of Christian Theology* (New York: Harper & Row, 1974).

[16] W. Marxsen argues that stories of Jesus were circulating prior to the resurrection and that our Gospels contain some recollections uncolored by resurrection faith; see his *Jesus and Easter: Did God Raise the Historical Jesus from the Dead?* trans. V. P. Furnish (Nashville: Abingdon Press, 1990), chap. 1. I am somewhat skeptical.

somewhat impressionistic portraits, seeking to comprehend the logic of God's involvement in the life and teaching of Jesus Christ.[17] After all, resurrection clearly certified Christ's life as godly and his message as God's truth. The Gospels portray not merely a human being from Galilee at a particular juncture of history; no, the Gospels limn the shape of God's humanity and the mystery of God's word in human speech. The fundamentalist attempt to label the Gospels literal history is heresy precisely because it tends to annihilate theological mystery.

But reading back did not stop with the life of Christ. If God was involved in the resurrection, death, and humanity of Christ, then God was also doing something to bring Christ into life. Is it surprising that we get birth stories not to mention the somewhat labored genealogies that preface the Gospels of Matthew and Luke?[18] The event of resurrection had established a new mode of redemptive life, a second-Adam humanity; how could such a momentous event be a matter of momentary divine improvisation? No, God had been at work through long generations to bring Jesus Christ into being. The event of Jesus Christ was both continuous and yet somehow discontinuous with God's long love affair with sinful humanity. Birth narratives, as well as the massing of citations from the Hebrew scriptures, are an attempt to grasp God's purpose in bringing about the event of Jesus Christ.

In the light of Easter Day, early Christians rehearsed the event of Jesus Christ. They began to read back.

The Beginning and the End

Anselm laid down a dictum: True faith seeks understanding.[19] No doubt the statement rings true, for it describes a strong impulse in early Christianity—resurrection faith was seeking understanding. How did Christians seek understanding? In one way, they did so by reversing

---

[17] On the Gospel genre, see M. A. Tolbert, *Sowing the Gospel: Mark's World in Literary-historical Perspective* (Minneapolis: Fortress Press, 1989), chap. 4.

[18] "The addition of these stories to the Gospel proper is thus intelligible as part of a christological process—a process which explains why they appear in the later Gospels rather than in Mark" (R. E. Brown, *The Birth of the Messiah: A Commentary on the Infancy Narratives in Matthew and Luke* [New York: Doubleday, 1977], 31).

[19] The phrase "faith seeking understanding" is to be found in the preface to Anselm's *Proslogium*. Following Augustine, Anselm could write, "I long to understand in some degree thy truth, which my heart believes and loves. For I do not seek to understand that I may believe, but I believe in order to understand." The passionate, devotional quality of Anselm's own prose adds definition to the phrase. See *Saint Anselm: Basic Writings,* trans. S. W. Deane, 2d ed. (La Salle, Ill.: Open Court, 1962), 2, 7.

the pattern of scripture. The Hebrew scriptures begin in myth—the first eleven chapters of Genesis are mythic; then Hebrew scriptures turn to the "historical" stories of Israel, then to prophetic writings, to the Psalms and wisdom literature, and, finally, toward apocalyptic in Daniel and in the apocryphal documents. Early Christians almost seem to have reversed the sequence. Initially they explored the meaning of resurrection within an apocalyptic framework, but then they read back through wisdom texts, prophecy, and history toward the primal myths of creation.

Israel's self-understanding was bracketed by myth and eschatological vision, beginning and end, creation and consummation. Particularly in later writings we begin to see Christian communities dovetailing resurrection faith with creation and the eschaton. The so-called Christ hymns that appear in the first chapters of Colossians and Ephesians are witness to the endeavor. From the creation, they insist, God elected Jesus Christ, Lord and Savior, so that creation can be said to be through and for Christ. Likewise, the Book of Revelation, which may well be a rewritten Jewish apocalyptic, begins with a risen Christ announcing, "I am the first and the last" (Rev. 1:17). Christian understanding was moving toward something like a Johannine theology in which an eternal Christ descends to humanity and, risen, returns to the Godhead.[20]

In moving toward creation and eschaton, the resurrection faith of the early community was reaching beyond itself toward universal meaning. Because of the involvement of the early Christians in the death and resurrection of Christ, they were tempted to suppose that benefits of salvation were exclusively for Christians; the new humanity had a Christian trademark. We are still tempted by that notion; universalism remains a conservative Christian bugaboo. The tension between a determinate Christian community and the indeterminate gospel of God's salvation is unresolved in the documents of the Christian scriptures. Nevertheless, when resurrection faith connects with the great myths of beginning and end, of creation, fall, and consummation, the gospel message takes on universal significance and the story of the Christ event becomes a cosmic drama. The story is as yet unfinished. Although we read back trying to grasp the meaning of our faith, inevitably we read forward as well, looking toward a day when "God

---

[20] See J. Knox's helpful typology in *The Humanity and Divinity of Christ: A Study of Pattern in Christology* (London: Cambridge University Press, 1967), chap. 1.

may be all in all," and the event of Jesus Christ will be fulfilled (1 Cor. 15:28).

The Awesome Task of Preaching

In every age preaching centers on the life, death, and resurrection of Christ. But, properly, preaching is not obsessed with Christ. The demand that we preach nothing but "Jesus Christ, and him crucified" (1 Cor. 2:2), a test of conservative "kosher" homiletics, could lead to a perverse Christ-idolatry.[21] No, the gospel is still an invitation to join God's new humanity, to be a part of the world's new beginning. Salvation, in the broadest sense of that ever-changing word, is the promise of the gospel message.[22] But the possibility of redemptive, new-order life is somehow through Jesus Christ, his life, death, and resurrection.

Thus we preach the same patterned message that was articulated by prophets and apostles. In sermons we hold up the cross and in its reflection understand the width and depth of sin in the human world. And still we turn to resurrection as a witness to our hope in the promised power of God. Further, we explore the cross trying to connect the passion of Christ with our own experience of being saved. We search the whole Christ event trying to grasp the mystery of God's eternal love. Like the first Christian theological explorers, we investigate God's activity, tracing mysterious movements of grace through all human time and space. How can Christian preaching ever be glib? The gospel can be turned into trivia only by an act of deliberate homiletic sinfulness. To preach the gospel is to do theology at a profound, if quite practical, level.

In the chapters that follow, we shall probe some meanings of Christ's resurrection and death, examining the familiar texts that tell of passion and glory. Then, in the epilogue, we shall try to set our understandings within the promise of salvation.

---

[21] See the argument in E. TeSelle, *Christ in Context: Divine Purpose and Human Possibility* (Philadelphia: Fortress Press, 1975), chap. 3.

[22] For discussion, See E. Schillebeeckx, *Christ: The Experience of Jesus as Lord,* trans. J. Bowden (New York: Seabury Press, 1980), sec. 2.

PART ONE

The Mystery of Resurrection

CHAPTER 1

The Reality of the Resurrection _____

EVERY MINISTER visits graveyards, and, at grave side, every minister declares the same strange credo, "Christ is risen!" When it comes to death, Kübler-Ross does not quite do the trick; a minister has to reach back and once more declare the church's faith: "Christ is risen indeed!" But often, after a funeral is over, some family member will show up asking questions: "How do we know it's true? How can we believe that Jesus lives?" When tears cloud our eyes, and a gulp rises in our throat, and some unctuous undertaker slides a sealed box into the cold earth, we cling for dear life to the great proclamation: "Christ is risen!" But then, later, shadowy doubts steal into our minds: Is it true? Did it happen? How can Christ be risen?

Let us begin with *the* question: Is the resurrection true? Did Jesus Christ really rise from the dead? The question is bound to be asked, and not merely by the recently bereaved. No doubt we question because of the way in which the church celebrates the resurrection. We declare the resurrection in ancient creeds, "On the third day he rose from the dead, and is seated at the right hand of God the Father Almighty." We sing of the resurrection in soaring hymns, and hoist emptied crosses high in our church chancels. Do we not have a seasonal spring fling at Easter complete with bedecked buildings, Easter eggs, and bright discount-house clothes for the kids? So we appear to celebrate the resurrection as an annual cultic myth, a myth that, coupled with the tragic drama of Holy Week, provides some sort of meaning for our common lives.

Yet, at the same time, we appeal to factual history. In our sermons we treat the resurrection stories as if they were firmly fixed events; we tell what happened as if we were reciting past fact. The resurrection occurred in both Jerusalem and outlying rural Galilee in the year 28 C.E. We explain to our congregations exactly what happened: how risen Christ surprised Mary Magdalene in a garden — historical fact; how guarding soldiers were freaked out by a sudden earthquake — historical fact; how a brace of white-robed angels showed up beside an empty tomb — factual history all the way. On Easter Day we preach as if we were handing out facts from the past.

Well, no wonder our people have trouble believing. Although we talk history, we seem to venerate myth, a recurring cultic myth celebrated in song, creed, and story. Is it surprising that when Good Friday tears have dried and Easter lilies wilted, brains begin to function: Is it true? Did the resurrection actually happen? The questions are wonderful and can lead to faith, but, unfortunately, we do not stop to discuss questions much these days. Instead we hurry on to Pentecost where again we talk history (How high were the "tongues of flame"? How strong were the gale winds of the Spirit?) but celebrate the meaning of a myth.

Notice exactly what we are trying to do. We seem to be standing in our twentieth-century pulpits trying to certify the historicity of a past-tense event that has all the earmarks of a myth. We are preaching the resurrection as historical occurrence and graphically depicting the reality of what once took place; it is an impossible apologetic strategy. So we proceed in the usual historical way; we turn to sources, supposed eyewitnesses, ancient documents, and the like. We attempt to sift annals of the past to establish actual facts as we would with any historical occurrence. What happened during Washington's bivouac at Valley Forge? Did Nero actually scrape a fiddle during a five-alarm fire in ancient Rome? Did Jesus Christ truly rise from an empty tomb? We assume that some sort of happening happened, but like all such events, is over, and now is locked up in the historical past. All that remains is written records — a peculiar creed in 1 Corinthians 15 and a batch of odd stories that are bound to stretch the credulity of any alert child. Nevertheless, we stand in the present and attempt to validate a factual history of the resurrection for the in-church faithful.

Looking for the Future-present

But stop and think: In our preaching are we inadvertently reversing the mind of the first Christian witnesses? The first Christians did not look to the past but to the future. They understood the resurrection in the light of God's promises. What certified the resurrection for them was not an appeal to historical veracity, but that the resurrection fit a known scenario of God's planned future. No wonder that Ernst Käsemann could declare: "Apocalyptic . . . was the mother of all Christian theology."[1] At the time of Christ, people were short on hope; their recent history had been dismaying. They had grown weary of disruptive terrorism and a spate of "gates" to rival Irangate, Watergate, and worse. Clanking armies trudged their streets, and their economy, riddled by deficit spending, was quite beyond repair. Because their short-term future seemed undeniably grim, they had pushed hope past time; they dreamed of a new order, a new heaven and a new earth, including some sort of resurrection of the living and the dead. If you plow through the somewhat bizarre documents of the intertestamental period, you are bound to notice the rise of apocalyptic thinking.[2] If the people of Jesus' era had hope, it was a future-perfect hope that featured a new, second creation and a risen humanity. So the resurrection in its initial impact was interpreted not by sifting the historical past, but by recalling documents depicting God's future. Apocalyptic's prophesies interpreted the resurrection, not history. Is it any wonder that New Testament reports of the resurrection are so peculiar; they are crowded with apocalyptic allusions.[3]

Our problem, then, is how to get at the reality of the resurrection. We cannot write off the resurrection as did the early Karl Barth by labeling it a "non-historical happening" — whatever that would be.[4] Nor can we argue that the resurrection was so unique, so singular a happening that there was no language at hand to speak of its reality. Such an argument would explain mystic silence, but not the astonishing stories

---

[1] E. Käsemann, "The Beginnings of Christian Theology," in *Apocalypticism*, ed. R. W. Funk (New York: Herder and Herder, 1969), 40; and see also the other essays in the same volume.

[2] See the collection of apocalyptic materials in *The Old Testament Pseudepigrapha*, vol. 2, ed. J. H. Charlesworth (Garden City, N.Y.: Doubleday, 1983), which contains nearly a thousand pages of texts. For introductions to intertestamental apocalyptic thought, see J. J. Collins, *The Apocalyptic Imagination* (New York: Crossroad, 1984), and C. Rowland, *The Open Heaven* (New York: Crossroad, 1982).

[3] Recall white-robed angels, an earthquake, a monstrous grave stone tossed like a tiddlywink, appearances and disappearances, the wandering dead sprung from graves in Jerusalem, and so on.

[4] K. Barth, *The Resurrection of the Dead* (New York: Fleming H. Revell, 1933), 138, 150. Barth modifies his position somewhat in *Church Dogmatics*, vol. 4/2, *The Doctrine of Reconciliation* (Edinburgh: T. & T. Clark, 1958), 116–54.

we find in the pages of our Bibles. Nor can we leap into the skeptical minds of a now-outdated, nineteenth-century Feuerbach or Freud to suppose that primitive wishful thinking scribbled the resurrection accounts.[5] Wishful thinking does not dabble in stories that weave symbol, myth, and meaning together in such a stylish fashion. Besides, a culture as linguistically sophisticated as that in the Middle East in the first century can scarcely be tagged as primitive. What we can do is to view the resurrection narratives as products of a future suddenly present, and of a Christ not locked in past-tense obituary, but present and, indeed, exalted. Presence and a sense of the future taking place wrote the resurrection texts and, incidentally, wrote them with astonishing subtlety.

Is the Resurrection Historical?

Let us now ask an inevitable question: What is historical about the resurrection? Is there anything factual for us to seize? The Bible seems to offer a collection of creedal declarations, such as the formula to be found in 1 Corinthians 15:1-11, and a scatter of strange stories that conclude each of the Gospels. Some of the stories are elaborations of Mark 16:1-8, which is dubious history indeed,[6] while others such as the Emmaus Road narrative[7] and the sequence of episodes in John 20 are clearly symbolic in character.[8] For centuries scholars have tried to meld the stories into some kind of coherent historical account; but, to be blunt, we must admit that the stories are either contradictory or, at the least, filled with inner inconsistencies; they simply will not dovetail. All we can say is that there appear to be two traditions, one featuring

---

[5] L. Feuerbach, *The Essence of Christianity* (New York: Harper & Row, 1957), chap. 14; and S. Freud, *The Future of an Illusion,* trans. W. D. Robson-Scott (Garden City, N.Y.: Doubleday, n.d.), chap. 3.

[6] See analysis of Mark 16:1-8 on pp. 66–68 of this volume.

[7] The Emmaus Road narrative incorporates direct references to the church's preaching (v. 27) and eucharist (v. 30); see my article "Homiletic Resources for the Easter Season," *Quarterly Review* 6, no. 1 (Spring 1986): 65–85.

[8] There are four episodes in John 20: (1) the story of Peter and "the other disciple," which appears to relate to Peter's status in the Johannine community; (2) the story of Mary in the garden, which can be summed up by "Do not hold me, for I have not yet ascended to the Father"; (3) the story of the sealed room, which rehearses the conferred character of the church—its peace, its commission, its authority, and the gift of the Spirit; and (4) the story of doubting Thomas, which is a call to believe the word of preaching without any great sign of resurrection. See the study of these passages on pages 81–89 of this volume.

Galilee and the other Jerusalem, neither of which is entirely coherent.[9]

Now we can make an obvious move and point out that the resurrection tradition is itself in history. That is to say, we have Paul's first letter to Corinth as well as other Epistles, and we have the four Gospels, and they are all historical documents. We can date these writings, discuss their textual variants, their probable locations, their authorships, as we can with any other historical materials. Moreover, we can presume that behind these Letters and Gospels was an oral tradition, indeed some kind of Christian proclamation.[10] Further we can note that our documents give evidence of an early Christian conviction with regard to the resurrection, a conviction on display in creeds, liturgical texts, and sermons, all of which can be discerned form-critically within the Christian scriptures. In other words, we have historical documents and from them we can properly posit earlier proclamation—disciples did scurry about noising news of the resurrection. But can we probe materials so as to answer the question, What really happened? No, honestly, we cannot. Although we have testimony, we do not seem to have hard history.

Easter Sermon Strategies

Have we nothing that will serve as sure evidence of the resurrection? Is there any way we can say to congregations, "See, the resurrection must be true because . . ." and go on to point to some sure and convincing signs of truth? Many ministers will point to the existence of the church, insisting that the fact of the church is a witness to the actuality of Jesus' resurrection. We tend to argue that only a real resurrection could account for the emergence of the church after the devastating effect of Christ's death on a cross. The argument is only partially useful: (1) The church itself is not always a compelling image; it is often as limp and lifeless as a leftover Easter lily and a true comedown from the bold figure of Christ. As American church people, are we not chronically disappointed in ourselves, our small-time frightened faith, our sold-outness, our lust for institutional self-preservation, and the like? (2) As we survey the world, there seem to be other organizations built on someone's death that are surviving. For example, a dead Lenin still lies

---

[9] For a recent attempt to argue the essential historicity of the resurrection accounts, see an interesting work by G. O'Collins, *Jesus Risen* (New York: Paulist Press, 1987).

[10] Note the use of this assumption in F. Schüssler Fiorenza's *Foundational Theology: Jesus and the Church* (New York: Crossroad, 1985), pt. 1, chap. 2.

glass-coffined in Red Square, and yet the USSR seems very much alive. When preachers try to prove the resurrection from the existence of the church in the world, they cite duration—twenty centuries, count them, twenty!—or they wax triumphant and revel in the universality of the church, a church that has sprung up in every place on earth. But contemporary churchgoers, who may be well aware of the church's trivial pursuits and frequent tedium, merely yawn, saying "So?" or even "So what?" The church is not always an attractive body for the risen Christ.

Other ministers seem to assume that personal religious experience validates a living, potent Jesus Christ. Often they assume that Peter, Paul, James, and John all had separate but quite personal experiences— akin to the astonishing disclosure on the Damascus Road—that led them to the realization that Christ was risen indeed. Similarly, we too have (or should have) personal experiences of Jesus that lead us to our living faith. The gambit has been popular, particularly in regions of our land where tides of revivalism once ran strong. But the appeal is somewhat less than appealing for, again, two reasons: (1) There is almost no description of personal experiences in the resurrection accounts other than those covered by rather conventional storytelling terms— sad, glad, joy, astonishment. The inner experiences of the first supposed witnesses are simply not provided. The exception is the third-person account of the Damascus Road occurrence (Acts 9:1-9), which, long ago, scholars noted was at odds with Paul's own testimony in his letters.[11] As a result, historians of early Christianity are usually uneasy over the material in Acts; the word *legendary* often shows up in such studies. (2) Few sane contemporary Christians have reported vivid, visual revelations of the risen Christ. Thus, to argue that a personal experience of the risen Christ is basis for our faith can place a cruel demand on us; either we must admit a sense of failure because we have had no such experience or, to justify ourselves in faith, we must seek to generate vivid religious hysteria—or both!

Now, in a way, both gambits—appeal to the church and/or religious experience—may have a certain validity. Must we not suppose that the emergence of structures of redemptive life in the early Christian community did somehow align with the confession "Christ is Risen!"? We

---

[11] See the detailed argument in J. Knox, *Chapters in a Life of Paul* (Nashville: Abingdon-Cokesbury Press, 1950), 33-37 and chap. 7; and, more recently, G. Lüdemann, *Early Christianity according to the Traditions in Acts* (Minneapolis: Fortress Press, 1989), 106-16.

need not romanticize the primitive church in order to venture the claim. Structures of redemptive new life may well be disclosed amid the trivial, foolish, and blundering patterns of church life, as Paul remarks in 1 Corinthians 1:28-31. We do experience such disclosures in Christian life-together, and these disclosures may well be bolstered by surprising inner liberations as well. But such experiences must always be discerned along with the reality of our brokenness so that, as Paul observes, if we boast, we boast in the Lord. The problem for preachers is that, eager to prove the reality of the resurrection, we overstate both the triumphant nature of the church and the overwhelming character of personal experience. Redemption may well be true, but under the terms of our common sinfulness, it is seldom so obvious.[12]

A Second Look at the Scriptures

Let us turn and ask what the Christian scriptures offer as some assurance of the reality of the resurrection. Yes, basically, they appeal to the future of God's promises. But is there any attempt to marshal here-and-now evidence? Paul's sequence in 1 Corinthians 15 is instructive. The chapter begins with a kind of recited creedal tradition:

> For I handed on [*paredōka*] to you . . . what I in turn had received [*parelabon*]: that Christ died for our sins in accordance with the scriptures, and that he was buried, and that he was raised on the third day in accordance with the scriptures, and that he appeared to Cephas, then to the twelve. Then he appeared to more than five hundred brothers and sisters at one time. . . . Then he appeared to James, then to all the apostles. Last of all . . . he appeared also to me. (1 Cor. 15:3-8)[13]

Then, in the verses that follow, Paul tries to answer the problem of doubt in the Corinthian community: "How can some of you say there is no resurrection of the dead?" What does he put forth to convince his congregation? He speaks of the church's efficacious preaching, common faith, and knowledge of forgiveness. He appeals therefore to common, in-community Christian awareness.

If we examine the stories that conclude our Gospels, we find much the same pattern: brief creedal announcements are followed by allusions

---

[12] Is it possible that redemptive structures of life are always well hidden in our common humanness? Often, redemptive life appears to be disclosed sacramentally (still amid brokenness). Maybe the Protestant free-church tradition, notorious for its neglect of the sacraments, must overstate the nature and character of inward renewals.

[13] For my translation of the same passage, see p. 55.

to the church's common awareness — to preaching, Lord's Suppers, forgiveness (probably in some common ritual), shared life in faith, a sense of "calling," and so forth. Luke (24:47) and John (20:23) both allude to forgiveness. Matthew has a mountaintop Jesus mention baptism and the church's evangelical commission (Matt. 28:19). Luke depicts preaching (Luke 24:27, 47) and the Lord's Supper (Luke 24:30, 41-43). Mark has a white-robed (baptized?) Christian preaching ex cathedra (Mark 16:5-6), and, as Willi Marxsen has observed, all the stories seem to incorporate "go tell!" commissionings.[14]

Notice that the texts neither appeal to the existence of the church per se nor point to some kind of recurrent personal religious experience. No, they seem to refer to structures of meaningful activity happening in the common life of the early Christians — their preaching, teaching, forgiving, their sense of being commissioned, their celebrations of the Lord's Supper, and so on. These things are cited in connection with their confession of the risen Christ. Why are these things featured? They are singled out precisely because they are continuations of the activity of Jesus Christ among them. In life Jesus preached, taught, and forgave sins. In life he commissioned his disciples, broke bread with them at table, and formed them in common faith. Suddenly, these same activities were taking place among Christians in community; what once had been the work of Christ among them was now happening communally in his same Spirit. So the early Christians proclaimed Christ risen and, at the same time, were surprised to find his life and purpose continuing in community. The stories of the resurrection were scribbled in between confessions of faith (e.g., "He has been raised; he is not here" [Mark 16:6]) and an astonished communal self-awareness — his life is forming in our common life!

Now we must not reject the idea that the early Christians, as a community, sensed that they had corporately died with Christ's death and come alive with his resurrection. No doubt they did. But they did not seem to appeal to the duration, universality, or triumph of the church qua church. Instead, they acknowledged that the church was not obviously impressive:

> Not many of you were wise by human standards, not many were powerful, not many were of noble birth. But God chose what is foolish in the

---

[14] See W. Marxsen's controversial *The Resurrection of Jesus of Nazareth* (Philadelphia: Fortress Press, 1970); see also replies to Marxsen's position in C. F. D. Moule, ed., *The Significance of the Message of the Resurrection for Faith in Jesus Christ* (Naperville, Ill.: Alec R. Allenson, 1968).

world to shame the wise; God chose what is weak in the world to shame the strong; God chose what is low and despised in the world, things that are not, to reduce to nothing things that are, so that no one might boast in the presence of God. (1 Cor. 1:26-29)

But they also pointed to the continuation of Christ's own saving ministry in their midst. His word was in their broken, often inept preaching; his free Spirit was with their often cramped spirits. They could, and did, boast in the Lord *alone.*

Likewise, we must not cancel out the possibility that early Christians did have personal religious experiences that they may well have attributed to the risen Christ. Again, no doubt they did. Nevertheless, their focus was on the patterns of redemption forming in their common, interactional life together. Love was not a feeling in the heart so much as a way of exchange among them.[15] Peace was conferred and shared. They sensed not so much that they were new individuals inside of themselves but that they were part of God's new humanity, a new creation inaugurated by the risen second Adam.

So how can we support the reality of the resurrection? We cannot appeal to historical records of what took place on the first Easter Day. If we try to turn the resurrection stories into hard fact, objective history, we will convince no one and may well enlarge doubts. And we cannot propose that the resurrection was a felt event in the hearts of the disciples; we are given little or no information as to what Peter or John or Paul may have felt. Talk of a resurrection experience may fan feelings of religious inadequacy in the lives of our congregations. More, we cannot argue from the glorious presence of the church in the world because, if we do, we will stumble into a triumphalism that is ultimately antithetical to the gospel. Although denominations in a tumbling world are terribly insecure these days, and are prone to puff up terms such as *body of Christ,* we are emphatically not the risen body of Christ; instead we are a broken body animated by his risen power — there is a difference.[16] What we can do is to continue breaking bread, preaching good news, forgiving sins, and reaching out evangelically. What is more, with wide-eyed astonishment we can dare to name these things to each other as the work of the risen Christ among us. And we can

---

[15] I refer to something the late Charles Williams described with rare precision; see his *The Image of the City and Other Essays,* ed. Anne Ridler (London: Oxford University Press, 1958), 147–61.

[16] See the helpful essay by E. Käsemann, "The Theological Problem Presented by the Motif of the Body of Christ," in *Perspectives on Paul* (Philadelphia: Fortress Press, 1971), chap. 5.

sing, as we should sing, "Jesus Christ Is Risen Today" and even shout as we sing the word *today*.

Our Problem with the Resurrection

Time now to face facts: Why do we have such a struggle with resurrection fact today? Why do we strain to prove the resurrection? Why is it that we cannot seem to glance at what is going on in the church and, staggered by spectacular grace, believe? The problem can be stated bluntly: The church is all too human. We scarcely see some mystical vision of the "invisible" church marching through time and space "like a mighty army." No, to us the church is a human organization that lives in peculiar, mortgaged buildings, several of which are to be found in any American village competing like Wendy's and McDonald's for the American religious consumer. The church wears a human face; it breaks store-bought bread, preaches into microphones, sings remarkably trite poetry in hymns, and puts up signs to attract customers like liquor stores or gas stations. Was it not C. S. Lewis who had the devil remark that the best way to disillusion Christian people was to keep their minds flitting back and forth between high-sounding phrases, such as "the body of Christ," and the actual human faces of people in church pews?[17] What is dismaying about the church is not the zaniness of Oral Roberts or the soap-opera Bakkers or even the right-wing zealotry of a Pat Robertson; it is us.[18] We have somehow managed to turn our full-service churches into trivial pursuit with classes on parenting, white-gloved bell choirs, and pulpit psychologizing. Church affairs are seldom soul-sized; they are simply tedious. Although we strain to jazz up church services with storytelling sermons and so-called creative worship, trivial is still trivial. Perhaps in South Africa or in regions of South America martyrs may blaze, but here in America we seem to be stuck with what Søren Kierkegaard described as "the caricature of Christianity."[19] The church we see is all too human.

So we have tended to locate miracles of grace within the hidden hearts of believers. If the overt church is anything but a testimony to

---

[17] C. S. Lewis, *The Screwtape Letters* (New York: Macmillan, 1948), 15–16.

[18] For a truly perceptive study of the Bakkers and, indirectly, other televangelists, see F. FitzGerald, "Reflections: Jim and Tammy," *The New Yorker,* April 23, 1990, 45–87.

[19] S. Kierkegaard, *The Point of View for My Work as an Author,* trans. W. Lowrie (London: Oxford University Press, 1939), 77.

grace, then the trick has been to locate grace in the unseen, invisible regions of the heart.[20] If the church seems to bear no resemblance to God's new order, at least we can presume people have been made new inside of themselves. We suppose true resurrection is a personal miracle — a new feeling or wholeness inside of us.[21] And there are plenty of nineteenth-century hymns to provide background music for the notion.

But a problem has emerged. Once upon a time, taught by *Pilgrim's Progress,* we could believe that every twist or turn of our inner experience was part of a godly pilgrimage, a struggle of soul on the way to salvation; but these days our lives are interpreted not by Bunyan but by *Psychology Today.* We struggle not with the devil but with inhibiting factors and developmental blocks. The inner world is no longer a province of grace requiring spiritual direction, it is an arena for psychological dynamics. John Bunyan has given way to Erik Erikson and, when all else fails, to Kübler-Ross. So here we are left as psychological selves to struggle for meaning in an all too human church.

Some years ago, the playwright Arthur Miller penned a smart essay. He argued that it is exceedingly difficult to write great tragedy these days when there are neither gods nor heroes and life has been domesticated.[22] We live, he suggested, in a Willy Loman America. The problem for preaching is not dissimilar. When church is reduced to church management and the soul is scaled down to psychological promptings, who can speak of resurrection or spot surprising signs of redemptive power among us? No burned martyrs light our skies; ministers burn out instead. No Christians are persecuted; they merely perish from boredom.[23] Where there is no significant cross, how can resurrection have meaning?

---

[20] Certainly R. N. Bellah et al., *Habits of the Heart* (Berkeley: University of California Press, 1985) documents the internalization of religion in America.

[21] For a fairly intelligent version of the strategy, see H. A. Williams, *True Resurrection* (New York: Harper & Row, 1972).

[22] A. Miller, "Tragedy and the Common Man," in *Tragedy: Vision and Form,* ed. R. W. Corrigan (San Francisco: Chandler, 1965), 148–51. Reprinted from *New York Times,* February 27, 1949.

[23] Walker Percy depicts our predicament. He has one of his fictional characters complain that he has trouble with believers and unbelievers: "Take Christians. I am surrounded by Christians. They are generally speaking a pleasant and agreeable lot, not noticeably different from other people. . . . But if they have the truth, why is it the case that they are repellent precisely to the degree that they embrace and advertise the truth. . . . And if the good news is true, why are its public proclaimers such assholes and the proclamation itself such a weary used-up thing? . . . As unacceptable as

To be sure, we can quickly ask, What else is new? Has not the church always been staggeringly human and, to be blunt, evidently sinful? Flip the pages of the Epistles and what do you find? Conflicts in Corinth, intellectual corruption in Galatia, proto-Gnostic nonsense in Colossae, and in the "Catholic Epistles" a recurrent twist toward heresy. Where there is not perverse factionalism, there is banality. How does Paul put it? He says, in effect, "Not many of us are smart, not many are V.I.P.s, not many have cash." Obviously primitive Christian communities were not featured on "The Lifestyles of the Rich and Famous." But what a blessing. Our all too human humanness is a gift, Paul argues, so that we may more readily spot the grace of our Lord Jesus Christ at work among us.

Do you sense the suggestion of a strategy? In preaching the reality of resurrection today, we must begin by being scandalously honest about the church. It is not merely a matter of not being smart, prominent, or wealthy — we may have all of these types in our congregations. But certainly we stumble along at the brink of apostasy and would sell out Jesus Christ for a good deal less than thirty pieces of silver any day. We may make biblical noises, but are usually bored silly by biblical study. We praise the Lord but, increasingly, long for leisurely Sunday bathrobed brunches with coffee, fruit, and the ponderous *Times*. [24] We must begin with an open-eyed acknowledgment of our corrupted Christian communities.

Then, just maybe, we can be surprised by the life of Christ living in the midst of our common lives. Look, we continue to break bread — women and men, labor and management, black and white — at the table of the Lord. We preach, and oddly enough the good news seems to be heard through our inept testimonies. And once in a while, backed up against the wall, we are forced to speak for peace or justice. To be honest, we know everything is happening in spite of our natural

---

believers are, unbelievers are even worse. . . . The present day unbeliever is crazy. . . . We are stuck with two alternatives: (1) believers, who are intolerable, and (2) unbelievers, who are insane" (W. Percy, *The Second Coming* [New York: Farrar, Straus & Giroux, 1980], 188–90).

[24] Complacencies of the peignoir, and
   Coffee and oranges in a sunny chair,
   And the green freedom of a cockatoo
   Upon a rug mingle to dissipate
   The holy hush of ancient sacrifice.
Wallace Stevens, "Sunday Morning," in *Poems of Wallace Stevens* (New York: Vintage Books, 1959), 7.

inclinations. We can begin to name grace in the midst of our brokenness, and sense, even today, that the risen Christ continues ministry among us.

How do we prove the resurrection? We cannot. All we can do is to confess our broken infidelity and then, with eyes of faith, name evident grace in our common life. Christ is risen indeed!

CHAPTER 2

A Risen
Crucified Christ _____

SOME YEARS AGO one of the religious publishing houses printed a bulletin for Easter Day. The bulletin cover showed a healthy looking Jesus standing before Mary Magdalene in a garden with his hands outstretched in triumph. He was risen. Now admittedly the picture, painted in pastel shades, was awful — Mary Magdalene looked strangely like a young Natalie Wood and Jesus like a devout, if demented, Kirk Douglas. But style was not the real problem. An old church janitor took one look at the picture and saw the trouble at once: "No nail holes," he said. Jesus' outstretched hands were uncut. No nails had pierced him; no thorns had scratched his brow. He was serene, glorious, but not the crucified Christ. How different from the Christian scriptures. In the Bible, the risen Christ is the crucified Christ. Today, let us ask the odd question: What does it mean to say that the *crucified* Christ is risen?

The Glory and the Wounds

When we read through the strange resurrection stories that end our Gospels, we are bound to notice that the risen Christ is different. In the stories, we are handed a bodily resurrection, but somehow the body is different. Paul uses a seemingly odd phrase, *sōma pneumatikon* (a body by the agency of the Spirit), to distinguish the resurrection body from our ordinary flesh and bones (1 Cor. 15:44).[1] He rallies a metaphor to

---

[1] See the discussion by M. E. Dahl, *The Resurrection of the Body* (London: SCM Press, 1962); and also by J. A. T. Robinson, *The Body* (London: SCM Press, 1952). For a discussion of philosophical issues, see T. Penelhum, *Survival and Disembodied Existence,*

underscore the difference: The resurrection body is as different from our old-Adam flesh as a bright blossom from an ungainly dead seed (1 Cor. 15:37).[2] Even Jesus himself, when quizzed about marriage and resurrection, pointed to the unimaginable difference between our social order and the newness of resurrection (Matt. 22:23-33). Maybe the resurrection stories are underlining the same paradoxical difference between the human and the risen, glorified Christ. In these stories, Jesus seems to transcend bodily limitation — he drifts through walls, he appears and disappears, he is sometimes unrecognizable, and yet he invites touch, he chews fish, and he apparently enjoys a beachfront breakfast. Probably the Bible would join W. H. Auden in snarling, "I wouldn't be caught dead without a body," because resurrection must involve the whole self and not merely a truncated soul.[3] Nevertheless, the resurrection tradition seems to affirm that the risen Christ is different. If Christ is risen bodily, then his body is a *sōma pneumatikon,* something as paradoxical as "a body by the agency of the Spirit" — whatever that would be. Maybe all we can do is to throw up our hands, bow our heads, and say the single word *Glory!* The risen Christ was revealed in glory.

Yet again and again we are told that the risen Christ is the crucified Christ. Risen Jesus stands among disciples in the Gospel of Luke, and the first thing he says is "Look at my hands and my feet" (Luke 24:39). In the Gospel of John, when stubborn Thomas refuses to credit news of the resurrection and demands proof, an angry Jesus backs him to his knees by daring him to jam his fist into the wounds (John 20:24-29). Now we can argue that these odd texts have been inserted for apologetic purposes to demonstrate that the risen Christ was not some imposter but was in fact the same Jesus who was "crucified, dead, and buried,"[4] but we find the same theological emphasis in the little confessions that are featured in the sermons in Acts: "Jesus Christ of Nazareth, whom you *crucified,* whom God raised from the dead" (Acts 4:10; emphasis

---

ed. R. F. Holland (London: Routledge & Kegan Paul, 1970). For a theological approach, see J. H. Hick, *Death and Eternal Life* (New York: Harper & Row, 1976).

[2] It may be important to notice that the first century regarded agricultural growth as a *discontinuous* miracle, involving a dead seed and the sudden appearance of a glorious flower. Thus, in 1 Cor. 15, Paul is stressing difference, not identity.

[3] See the famous essay by O. Cullmann, *Immortality of the Soul or Resurrection of the Dead? The Witness of the New Testament* (New York: Macmillan, 1958).

[4] Most commentaries suppose an apologetic rather than a theological purpose; for example, see discussion in I. H. Marshall, *The Gospel of Luke: A Commentary on the Greek Text* (Grand Rapids, Mich.: William B. Eerdmans, 1978), 900-03.

added). We are dealing then not so much with an apologetic strategy as with a theology. The Christ who was raised up by the power of God is the Jesus Christ who was nailed to a cross. The crucified Christ is risen!

Incidentally, whenever the church overlooks the cut hands of the risen Christ, the church courts triumphalism. The statue of Jesus that towers over Eureka Springs, Arkansas, has no scars. When the statue was completed, Gerald L. K. Smith crowed, "The world comes to us at Eureka Springs."[5] There is the motive. We want to picture Jesus as a winner, able to conquer every adversity, on top of the world. No wonder we smooth over the cuts and the scars. The same impulse lives in our churches. If our unruffled Christ is throned in glory without a single scar, then surely our churches can be steepled success stories, guaranteed "bus 'em in" winners. All our hours will be "hours of power." All we have to do is to erase the agony, wipe the sweat away, and empty the tomb. But the odd few texts are still in scripture to embarrass us — "Look at my hands and my feet." The one whom God has exalted is precisely the nailed-down, judged, impotent Christ who was crucified. To a church that positively lusts for power, Christ still says, "Look at my hands and my feet."[6]

The Great Reversal

What are we suggesting? We are arguing that the basic structure of the resurrection message is reversal, a reversal that cannot, indeed

---

[5] See A. Whitman, *Christian Occasions* (Garden City, N.Y.: Doubleday, 1978), 14–31.

[6] A truly fine poet, Vassar Miller, offers a commentary in "Fantasy on the Resurrection":

Flaws cling to flesh as dews cling to a rose:
The cripples limp as though they would prolong,
Walking, a waltz; the deaf ears, opened, close
As if their convolutions hoard all song;
The blind eyes keep half shut as if to fold
A vision fast men never glimpse by staring;
Against their will the mute lips move that hold
A language which was never tongue's for sharing.
Shocked shag of earth and everything thereunder
Turned inside out — the nail-gnarled have caught Heaven
Like a bright ball. Not in their reknit wonder,
But in their wounds lies Christ's sprung grace engraven —
Not in the body lighter than word spoken,
But in the side still breached, the hands still broken.
In *Wage War on Silence* (Middletown, CT: Wesleyan University Press, 1957), 17.

must not, be forgotten: The risen Christ *is* the crucified Christ. The judge is the one who was judged. The pardoner is the one condemned. The justifier is the one who was rejected. The life-giver is the Christ who was done to death by cruel capital punishment. The basic structure of the resurrection is reversal, a reversal of God and the world.[7] The Jesus whom we have betrayed, denied, and crucified, God has raised up. Resurrection is not restoration — the story of a dead person brought back to life; that would mean we revere a Christ of the living dead, and zombies do not easily qualify as saviors. No, resurrection means nothing less than exaltation. The Jesus who was put down by the human world, God has raised up to be Lord of lords. But, raised up, the nail scars still define Christ's character, his status in the world. So if we wish to explore the meaning of resurrection, we must study the reversals of meaning, the bold ironies of God.

The Irony of Freedom

IRONY: Jesus Christ, who was judged under the law, is our freedom from the law.[8] Let us make no mistake: Jesus the Nazarene was repudiated. He was hauled before human courts, was judged, condemned, and executed. Yes, in all likelihood there was some conniving; justice may well have been circumvented as justice frequently is by human will to power. And, yes, there was "police brutality" — soldiers abused Jesus as soldiers have been known to do. Probably there was an almost erotic denigration of flesh — crucifixion was an obscene, X-rated custom. So sin was clearly involved as sin always is in judgment — Calvinists are scarcely surprised. Nevertheless, we must not forget that there was a legal process; capital punishment is seldom cavalier. Jesus Christ was judged, condemned, and put to death under due process of law. What is more, law was regarded as much more than a stack of precedent cases; it was The Law. All law was viewed as divinely ordained for human good. Whether Roman or Jewish, it was surely

---

[7] No wonder that the teaching of Christ features reversals of status as in the Beatitudes and, of course, in many, many parables such as the rich man and Lazarus, the Pharisee and the publican, the great feast, the last judgment, and so on. See my article "On Preaching a Parable: The Problem of Homiletic Method," *Reformed Liturgy & Music* 17, no. 1 (Winter 1983): 16–22; see also a splendid study of the parables by B. B. Scott, *Hear Then the Parable: A Commentary on the Parables of Jesus* (Minneapolis: Fortress Press, 1989).

[8] I have previously dealt with the ironies of resurrection; see "Preaching on the Resurrection," *Religion in Life* 45, no. 3 (Autumn 1976): 278–95.

understood as God's law, for in the ancient world law was essentially religious. Jesus, then, was judged and sentenced with religious zeal under the law of God. We must never write off the trial of Jesus as a put-up job, manipulated by hiss-and-boo villains. Instead, let us affirm that Christ was crucified by the best impulses of the human world — respect for religion, the desire to preserve society, regard for values — under God's law.

What is more, God seemed to endorse the condemnation of Jesus Christ. Everyone was bound to concur with the judgment of the courts and the rightness of the sentence, for it was common knowledge that cruel and unusual death was a sign of divine displeasure — "Cursed is everyone who hangs on a tree" (Gal. 3:13, from Deut. 21:23). If a cruel death was allowed, then clearly the sovereign God had concurred. No wonder that the crowd at the crucifixion could call out, "If you are the King of the Jews, save yourself!" (Luke 23:37). If Christ could not save himself from suffering and death, then, obviously, God permitted his death and, in effect, agreed with the verdict rendered. The law that condemned Jesus Christ was divine law, and the sentence was uncontested by God.

So, do you see what resurrection signified? Acquittal. The world's verdict was reversed and its divine endorsement was refuted. For if Christ was risen, then he had already passed through the judgment and had been vindicated by God. And not only was Christ vindicated; he was exalted — "Jesus Christ of Nazareth, whom you crucified, whom God has raised. . . ." Notions of resurrection existed before the time of Christ, but in the majority of such texts, resurrection is closely tied to the Day of the Lord and the idea of God's righteous judgments. Resurrection was either a resurrection of the righteous or the sign of a divinely certified righteousness that had cleared ultimate judgment.[9] So if Christ had been raised, then he was righteous and his righteousness was approved by God. Although condemned under the law of God by religion and state, he was divinely acquitted. He was, in fact, an embodiment of God's true law, a new and living Torah.[10] Suddenly God's law of love displayed in the life, death, and resurrection of Jesus

---

[9] On resurrection to judgment, see M. Barth and W. H. Fletcher, *Acquittal by Resurrection* (New York: Holt, 1964), 185ff.; see also S. G. F. Brandon, *The Judgment of the Dead: The Idea of Life after Death in the Major Religions* (New York: Charles Scribner's Sons, 1967), chaps. 2, 4, and 5.

[10] See W. R. Davies, *Paul and Rabbinic Judaism: Some Rabbinic Elements in Pauline Theology* (New York: Harper & Row, 1948), chap. 7, and also his *Torah in the Messianic Age and/or the Age to Come* (Philadelphia: Society of Biblical Literature, 1952), chap. 5.

Christ reinterpreted the true intent of divine law. The reversal of judgment is radical.

No wonder early Christianity seems almost antinomian. Christians could live in freedom-to-love, liberated from the law's condemnation. And no wonder the gospel tradition is so emphatic in its exhortation, "Judge not!" Christ who was free for neighbors in love had been raised up by the Holy Judge of Israel. The only way we can possibly understand Paul's sense of freedom from law—from the legal impositions of religion and from what Karen Horney termed "the tyranny of the should"[11]—is to remember that resurrection was nothing less than a verdict reversed. Christian moral liberty begins in the resurrection of Jesus Christ. Yes, the law given at Sinai and urged by prophets was God's good law, but in the figure of Christ the true purpose of God's law is redefined, not as circumscribed self-interest or as a religious project, but as freedom-to-love in the Spirit, the same Spirit that was in Christ Jesus. The odd, almost inexplicable antithesis between law and Spirit in the Epistles can be understood only in light of the declaration, "Christ is risen!"

The Irony of Mercy

IRONY: Jesus Christ, who was labeled a sinner, is our declaration of pardon. The most surprising thing about the Christian scriptures is freedom from guilt. The Christian scriptures seem to have an unshakable sureness with regard to absolution; we are forgiven. Early Christians appeared to be altogether free from pangs of guilt, which, if you consider their behavior, is astonishing. After all, had they not run from their Jesus in frightened self-preservation? Had not one disciple betrayed the Lord and another denied him point-blank? What is more, had not their world—a world they had internalized, a world of meanings in which they lived—condemned and crucified Christ Jesus? How could they live with the finality of the cross? Their personal infidelities were carved in memory like a stony epitaph. Yet the Christian scriptures appear to be written in the midst of an Assurance of Pardon that was reiterated and sure. Probably early Christian worship featured a kiss of peace that was much more than down-home friendliness—"How

---

[11] K. Horney, *Neurosis and Human Growth: The Struggle toward Self-realization* (New York: W. W. Norton, 1950), chap. 3.

are you? How are you doing? Nice to see you again."[12] The kiss of peace was an act of reconciliation within The Mercy, a mutual recognition of Christians' common status as baptized, forgiven sinners. How can we come to terms with a gleefully forgiven people who were so obviously guilty?

Listen to the resurrection texts: "He appeared to Cephas." So Paul lines out his resurrection credo in 1 Corinthians 15. "The Lord has risen indeed, and he has appeared to Simon"—Luke 24:34 underscores the event. And the Gospel of John contains a strange absolution in which the risen Christ asks three times "Simon son of John, do you love me?" to cancel Peter's previous three cockcrow denials (John 21:15-17). Evidently the resurrection was understood as a huge Declaration of Pardon. No wonder that Paul can state the blunt alternative, "If Christ has not been raised, your faith is futile and you are still in your sins" (1 Cor. 15:17). But Christ is risen and, therefore, the obvious contrast applied: We are no longer locked up in our sins. What else could resurrection mean but that Jesus—who himself was judged, condemned, and crucified—was disclosed to sinners, the same sinners who had been involved in his death. Obviously God's covenant faithfulness could not be broken but was reaffirmed. Although the human world may deny, desert, and even betray God, God will not desert humanity. The resurrection, like Noah's stunning rainbow, arches the world as a sure pledge of God's eternal love. No wonder we get an offbeat creed in 2 Timothy 2:13: "If we are faithless, he remains faithful—for he cannot deny himself." Even as Christ had called disciples into a community with himself, so in the resurrection Christ came to his chosen ones in spite of their awesome indiscretions. "He appeared to Cephas," the phrase is filled with the mercy of God.

But the trouble with God's mercy is that we must receive it from the one whom we have crucified. "Jesus Christ of Nazareth, whom you crucified, whom God raised. . . . There is salvation in no one else" (Acts 4:10-12). We are not forgiven by some heavenly therapist who polishes up our self-esteem or murmurs only one half of a famous Tillichian formula, "You are accepted."[13] No, we are forgiven by the

---

[12] On the history of the kiss of peace, see Dom G. Dix, *The Shape of the Liturgy* (London: Adam & Charles Black, 1945), 105–10; and also, G. Wainwright, *Doxology: The Praise of God in Worship, Doctrine and Life* (New York: Oxford University Press, 1980), 31–32, 402.

[13] P. Tillich, "You Are Accepted," in *The Shaking of the Foundations* (New York: Charles Scribner's Sons, 1948), 153–68. Tillich argued that the message of our acceptance by God comes to us in the midst of estrangement and self-rejection. As sinners, we are unacceptable; but by grace alone we are accepted.

risen crucified Christ. With nail-cut hands, Christ announces our absolution: "You are forgiven even though you have denied, betrayed, and, yes, crucified me." In the midst of mercy, we see the staggering enormity of our sin; in the midst of judgment, we hear the high, holy absolution of God. The Reformers grasped the strange paradox. So Calvin argued that faith and repentance were simultaneous. And Luther framed his famous equation: *Simul iustus et peccator* (simultaneously justified and a sinner). They were not handing out Camus's "little ease," a torture box in which captives could neither stand up straight nor fall asleep.[14] No, they were getting at the true character of a Christian life — "While we still were sinners Christ died for us" (Rom. 5:8). Although we are judged as sinners, nevertheless, God's mercy is certain and liberating. We can stand up straight or sleep the sleep of the justified. Our mercy is not from an undamaged Christ, but from the risen Lord who still confronts us with his broken hands.

The Irony of Life

IRONY: Jesus Christ, who was put to death, is Lord of life. Surely the resurrection sings a song of triumph: "Go down death!"[15] Christ risen bears witness to a power of God that is greater than the sheer self-destruct of death. Now we must be cautious. The Christian gospel is never a denial of death; we are incurably mortal, we die, and that is that. I shall never forget watching as a grandmother attempted to comfort a four-year-old whose pet security-blanket cat had been run over, improbably, by a steam roller. As the child stared with horror at her flat cat, the grandmother fluttered about saying, "Kitty isn't dead. Kitty's happy with God." The child, quite sane, looked back with utter disbelief and, no doubt, has grown up to be a thoroughgoing atheist. No, if death is an illusion, then the resurrection means nothing. Death is emphatically death. Although we are conscious of having to die, there is no evidence that consciousness is greater than death; consciousness cannot be postmortem because consciousness is mortal. Ultimately death is deadly. So resurrection is sheer gift, a miracle of grace from

[14] A. Camus, *The Fall,* trans. J. O'Brien (New York: Alfred A. Knopf, 1957), 109–10.

[15] J. W. Johnson, "Go Down Death — A Funeral Sermon," in *God's Trombones: Seven Negro Sermons in Verse* (New York: Penguin Books, 1972), 27–30. Johnson is quoting from a well-known spiritual.

God, whose love is eternally forthcoming. The resurrection is a promise, never a proof, a promise of a free, forgiven, new life toward God.

The reversal of death is more dramatic than we know. Death is extensive. Death is in all things. Lift Mother Nature's leafy wig and death's head is underneath; unseen rot, rust, and decay eat away all brief beauties. But death pervades the social world as well.[16] Not only do we self-destruct, but the power of death rules in our social order. Why do we tolerate out-of-control military spending when there is hunger on earth? Because we suppose that death is power, and power is more important to us than compassion. Why do many people support capital punishment even though Jesus Christ himself was crucified? Because they suppose that the death penalty is a powerful deterrent against social misconduct. Some months ago an airline magazine ran a profile of a successful corporate president who was admired because, said the magazine, "he seems to have a killer instinct." Our whole world assumes that death is power, the power of control. Certainly, the power of death was operative in Jerusalem nearly two thousand years ago. How do we human beings dispose of a God who threatens our sovereign self-will, a neighbor who gets in our way, the true self within us who condemns our chronic falsity? "Crucify him," cried the carnival crowd in Jerusalem, "Crucify him."

What does the resurrection mean? The resurrection is nothing less than a demonstration of God's power, the power of life. The resurrection is not therapy for our death-fears; Jesus Christ was not an early-day Jewish Kübler-Ross. Nor is the resurrection news of personal survival; we do not survive.[17] No, instead, resurrection is a witness to the power of God-love that gives life in the midst of a deadly world. Ultimately resurrection brands the power of death as no-power. There is no power in the Pentagon budget, no power in capital punishment, and no power in a terrifying corporate killer instinct. God-love is greater than death. Can we see why early Christians seem to have been somewhat cavalier about dying? They defied persecution, thumbed their noses at the threat of sword, and, of all things, partied at funerals. God-love is greater than death; that is the good news of Easter.

Law, sin, and death—these are Paul's list of enemies (1 Cor.

---

[16] For a brilliant theoretical discussion, see E. Becker, *The Denial of Death* (New York: The Free Press, 1973).

[17] Anyone who has watched someone well-loved linger, broken, in a nursing home for months and years, can wonder why death is regarded as a threat when, perhaps, it is paradoxically a good gift.

15:55-57). Law, sin, and death are not simply destroyed by the resurrection of Jesus Christ; they are radically reversed, ironically reversed. Now, in Christ Jesus, we live in mercy, in freedom-to-love, and in what the Bible calls eternal Life, spelled with a capital "L." Why? Because "Jesus Christ is risen today!"

A Nail-cut God

The greatest irony of all is hidden in the mystery of God. Who is God if the crucified one, risen, is taken into the Godhead, is raised up "to the right hand of God," as our creed announces? How does risen Jesus Christ redefine the mystery of God? Scholars suppose that, originally, Easter Day was not merely a celebration of resurrection, but of exaltation and the gift of the Spirit as well. At one time, Easter, Ascension Day, and Pentecost were packed into a moment. We find such a primitive pattern lurking in John 20. But, in Luke, Easter, Ascension, and Pentecost are stretched out and historicized, perhaps to coincide competitively with Jewish festivals. So Easter is not primarily concerned with death to life, so much as with down to up—the crucified Christ is exalted; he is Lord and regent of God's new aeon. What does it mean to say that Christ is taken up into the mystery of God?

We tend to define God by absolutes. Remember the rolling words of the Scot's Confession?[18] God is "eternal, infinite, immeasurable, incomprehensible, omnipotent, invisible," to which we usually tack on "omniscient" as well as "perfect in truth, goodness, and beauty." Many of us memorized some such list of attributes when we were young. Now all that the Scot's Confession is doing is defining God as the opposite of our own all too obvious finitude. We are frequently incapable, obviously visible, peculiarly limited, perishable, imperfect, time-swept, and beset by a chronic "cloud of unknowing." But, fortunately, God is our opposite. God never faces unpleasant dying or frightening change. Our God is a do-all, see-all, know-all sort of God.

But, watch out; although we cram our definitions with rolling Latinate words to label God, the words must be understood. When it comes to definitions we are seldom as objective as a dictionary. A hermeneutic shaped by sinful desire warps our understanding. Remember how, back in Eden's apple orchard, our first mythic parents were tempted to "be like God." Well, rather obviously, we have not

---

18   *The Scot's Confession: 1560,* ed. G. D. Henderson (Edinburgh: Saint Andrew Press, 1960), 58-80.

become like God, perhaps because we are always striving to be like our fantasy of God. What does "omnipotence" mean to us? Omnipotence is being able to do anything we want to do; it is the unlimited power of personal will. And what is omniscience? Omniscience is being in on everyone else's secrets; if we know all, perhaps we can control all. Being "eternal" means we can possess ourselves forever. Being perfect means we never need to change. If we are infinite, then there is no limit to our outstretched will to power. Hand us a handful of absolutes and we will pack them full of our own will to be God. Thus, we define God by our own sinfulness.

Do you see now why the nail holes are so embarrassing? They are a sign that Christ who died in utter helplessness, bawling for a drink, shouting his doubt, is somehow risen into the very nature of God. Repeat: The sheer nailed-down impotency of Jesus Christ must be aligned with the attributes of God. Well, we have not yet begun to wrestle with that theological gambit, particularly in our preaching. In sermons, we will celebrate the unlimited power of God in one sentence and then, in the next sentence, observe that in Christ God dies in humble weakness for our sins. As a result we end up with a slightly schizoid God—strong as a clenched fist but tender as a dying man's last breath. We cannot seem to reconcile God to God. Like the hero of Tennessee Williams's *The Night of the Iguana,* we have a God whose unlimited power fills heaven like thunder and, at the same time, a God whose mercy in Christ is as gentle as a silvery rain.[19] As a result we tumble into strange theologies. We end up with God sacrificing God to satisfy God; or maybe God's love dying to appease God's inflexible justice, a conflict between the left and right brains of a divine absolute.[20] Something is clearly wrong.

But watch out. What happens if we take the broken figure on the cross seriously? What if we say point-blank that the impotent, dying Christ *is* the disclosure of God? Then the attributes of God are up for grabs.[21] Omniscience? Well, omniscience can only mean to know through suffering and dying the full depth of the human condition. And omnipotence? God's power must be defined entirely by suffering,

---

[19] T. Williams, *The Night of the Iguana* (New York: Signet Books, 1961), 61, 83.

[20] I do not mean to suggest that notions of vicarious atonement are inappropriate, but merely that some metaphors, such as penal substitution, are not without theological difficulty.

[21] Philosophers and theologians have sensed the problem for some time; see, for example, C. Hartshorne, *Omnipotence and Other Theological Mistakes* (Albany: State University of New York, 1984), chap. 1.

nonviolent, self-giving love; it can no longer be conceived of as unlimited domination. If somehow the crucified Christ is taken into the Godhead, our conceptions of God must be transformed. How will we preachers ever explain to our people that God is not a can-do God, a God for the "hour of power," but rather is defined by the thorns and the nails and the lone crying on the cross? Can we dare to preach a crucified God? What is the greatest irony of all? The crucified Christ *is* the image of God!

Who Is in Charge Here?

The confession "Jesus is Lord," associated with resurrection faith, is more awesome than we know. Not only is the crucified Christ taken into the nature of God, but the confession announces that the crucified Christ is Lord of the whole wide world. Is it possible that a God of domination, an enthroned God of unlimited power, has prompted in turn the will to domination among us? Perhaps. But suppose that instead God is like Christ Jesus the crucified one — what then? Then the sovereignty that sways the universe is not domineering force but self-giving love calling us all to a similar freedom-in-love for one another. Obviously the ambitions that have driven us — getting ahead, being somebody, having something — are suddenly undercut. We live for self-giving, not getting. What is more, the threat of death, the only power we human beings know, is not threat at all because nonviolent, self-giving love is risen over death. Christians are never meant to drop out of the world, a world of power politics and corporate killer instincts. No, Christians are meant to live in world. But, as citizens of God's new order, with bemused laughter, high courtesy, and love, they are called to a lifestyle that reflects God's own self-giving. To reverse a dictum put forth once by football coach Vincent Lombardi: "Winning isn't everything, it's *nothing!*" The symbolic figure of Christ crucified, a loser by anyone's standards, has disclosed the character of God and of the sovereignty in which "we live and move and have our being."

Prompted by resurrection faith, we say "Christ is Lord." Our confession is an ethical statement.

CHAPTER 3

Resurrection and God's New Order _____

ONE OF THE astonishing moments in 1987 occurred in connection with the New Age movement in California. In mid-August, more than fifty thousand people were perched on top of Mount Shasta waiting to be swept by New Age consciousness — termed "harmonic convergence." Well, nothing seemed to happen. So, when people stumbled down from the mountain, jokes and jibes and obvious disappointments were heard. By all normal expectations, the New Age movement should have drifted rapidly into forgotten history. Yet, although struggling, it survives. Perhaps the movement is something more than usual West Coast lunacy. Perhaps the New Age movement expresses longings that live in most weary American souls at the ragged end of the twentieth century. In a time of cultural fatigue, do we long for the dawning of some sort of new age? Such longing is not new. The dream of a coming new order, God's new order, animated the apocalyptic mind of the first century.[1] Perhaps it shaped the message of Jesus and the hopes of his disciples. Do not Christians still voice the prayer, "Your kingdom come"? Let us consider the resurrection of Jesus as a sign of God's new order.

God's New Order Is at Hand!

The hope of a new order, a kingdom of God, was a feature of the world in which Jesus lived. The dream of a new Israel, indeed of a

---

[1] R. A. Horsley with J. S. Hanson, *Bandits, Prophets, and Messiahs: Popular Movements at the Time of Jesus* (San Francisco: Harper & Row, 1985).

transformed humanity, was alive in the land.[2] Of course, the message was not exactly new. If we trace our way through the pages of scripture, we find eschatological vision forming all along. At first Israel's hope focused on a dream of land, of a people of God in a promised land. That was followed by a vision of kingship: A king as righteous as David and as powerful as Solomon would appear as God's regent in a new golden age. During exile, the dream enlarged and fixed on the symbol of Zion, a glorious, restored Zion, city of God. In the days when exiles stumbled back to Jerusalem, the vision was refurbished to compensate for a stringent economy and a patchwork temple. Someday, somewhere, somehow God would usher in a bright future for Israel — and indeed for the whole wide human world. For as long as God is God, and God is redemptively at work among us, there will be hope of a transformed humanity and the renewal of nature — swords will be beaten into John Deere tractors, the lion and lamb will bed down together, and everyone will know the Lord! *Mañana,* someday.

During the intertestamental period, the vision of God's new order got hooked up with the notion of resurrection. Israel had suffered political and religious disillusionment; its kings were less than regal and its priests corrupt. Israel's fortunes were ebbing, at best. The only solution seemed to be a new beginning for the human enterprise. Apocalyptic revisionists nudged hope into an eschatological future that would be heralded by terrors on earth, a "great tribulation," leading up to a Day of the Lord.[3] Then, with a resurrection of the living and the dead, the promised new age would begin. The slightly vague "someday" of prophecy turned spooky and, not only spooky, but cataclysmic. Because the present age was condemned, God would pull off a new creation. So, during the time of Christ, the mind of Israel was marked by both human pessimism and radical eschatology. The hopeless human world would be transformed, cataclysmically; by resurrection God would usher in a whole new social order — perhaps under some sort of messianic figure.

To what extent is Jesus' message apocalyptic? Certainly Jesus seemed to announce a new order: "The time is fulfilled, and the kingdom of God has come near; repent, and believe in the good news" (Mark 1:15). The message of Jesus, as Albert Schweitzer noticed years ago, was

---

[2] D. E. Gowan, *Eschatology in the Old Testament* (Philadelphia: Fortress Press, 1986), 4–29, 93–96.

[3] See D. C. Allison, Jr., *The End of the Ages Has Come* (Philadelphia: Fortress Press, 1985), chap. 2.

clearly eschatological;[4] surely it was a call to enter the new aeon proleptically, joining God's new humanity. No wonder that Jesus announced a general amnesty for sinners as well as a call to excessive righteousness. And no wonder Jesus' teachings seemed filled with a reversal of values, woes, and blessings: the poor would be exalted and the socially successful ultimately demoted; the misfits would be in and the self-righteous emphatically out. Certainly the parables of Jesus seem to "deconstruct" our everyday world with its everyday God and then to confront us with the mystery of another order, a new order in which most of our common human values are tossed topsy-turvy.[5] Was Jesus' partying with sinners rehearsal for a banquet of the new age? Was his temple prophecy a gesture toward an eschatological Zion with a new temple? The old shibboleth that Jesus was prophetic but emphatically not apocalyptic no longer looks sure; there was, if nothing else, an apocalyptic urgency to his words. Jesus came preaching the new order of God.

"Crucified, Dead, and . . ."

Then, what happened? Crucifixion happened. Jesus was hauled before courts, condemned to death, and systematically executed. He was "crucified, dead, and buried," as the creed affirms. But the crucifixion of Christ was not merely the execution of a popular Galilean visionary preacher; it was the killing of a dream. Is there a more pathetic line in scripture than the idle remark by two disciples trudging toward Emmaus, "But we had hoped that he was the one . . ." (Luke 24:21)? Note, the phrase is in the past perfect tense—"had hoped." They no longer harbored the dream because, obviously, Jesus was judged guilty by reputable priests, sent to his death by a Roman official, and branded with God's own repudiation, for, as we have noted, it was commonly held that cruel death was a sure sign of divine displeasure.[6] It is almost impossible for us who view the cross in retrospect to conceive the degree of disillusionment that must have swept the disciples: "We had thought he was the one to redeem Israel." Caitlin Thomas,

---

[4] A. Schweitzer, *The Quest of the Historical Jesus* (London: Adam and Charles Black, 1911), esp. 348–401.

[5] The attempt by E. P. Sanders (*Jesus and Judaism* [Philadelphia: Fortress Press, 1985]) to deny the radical character of the parables in order to view them within the Pharisaic tradition is not, I think, convincing.

[6] J. Moltmann makes much of divine rejection in his *The Crucified God: The Cross of Christ as the Foundation and Criticism of Christian Theology* (New York: Harper & Row, 1974), 145–53.

Dylan Thomas's widow, has a phrase that captures the same anguish. She had thought Dylan was God, but then suddenly he was gone. So she wrote a book entitled *Leftover Life to Kill.*[7] The early Christian movement, twelve disciples for twelve new tribes of Israel, was shattered by the death of Jesus. The disciples were utterly disillusioned; they had leftover lives to kill. With the crucifixion of Jesus, the fledgling Christian community also perished.

Let us look more deeply into the disaster of the cross. Christ's death, like the death of a dramatic tragic hero, reinforced both the nature of transcendence and the structures of society. In other words, the death of Christ ratified the "as is" human world. Let me explain. In great tragedy, for example *Oedipus Rex* or *King Lear,* an assertive, self-willed hero is destroyed and, although an audience may weep and be purged by pity and fear, no audience would have it otherwise.[8] Think of how we would react if at the end of *Hamlet,* when the stage is literally strewn with bodies, Hamlet were to rise, rub his hands together, and cheerily stride off the stage remarking, "There's a job well done!" We would be absolutely appalled. Why? Because our moral universe would be threatened and our "gods" rendered impotent. The reason tragedies always seem to end with a sense of "the world will go on" is because that is precisely what we want to affirm; our "gods" are in heaven, are in control, and the social order is safe—life can go on. So, in a way, the death of a tragic hero reaffirms our common faiths. Hamlet must die to confirm transcendent meaning, the "sacred canopy" of the social order.[9] The death of Christ therefore served to reaffirm the religion of the temple as well as the status quo of the powers that be; the world would go on in its usual way. Temple sacrifice was reinforced. Economic patterns were firmly ordained. The social order, even the Roman occupation, was re-established. As the high priest remarks, "It is better for you to have one man die for the people than to have the whole nation destroyed" (John 11:50).

So what did the resurrection signify? The resurrection of Jesus Christ was nothing less than a sign of God's new order. God's new order had

---

[7] C. Thomas, *Leftover Life to Kill* (Boston: Little, Brown and Co., 1957).

[8] The notion of a tragic catharsis goes back to Aristotle, *Poetics,* 5.2. For discussion, see F. Fergusson's introduction to *Aristotle's Poetics,* trans. S. H. Butcher (New York: Hill and Wang, 1961), 32–36.

[9] The phrase "sacred canopy" is from P. L. Berger, who argues that cultures regard their own social projections as sacred; see his *The Sacred Canopy: Elements of a Sociological Theory of Religion* (Garden City, N.Y.: Doubleday, 1967); and also his book with T. Luckmann, *The Social Construction of Reality* (Garden City, N.Y.: Doubleday, 1967).

arrived in spite of all appearances, for Christ was risen, Lord and King. The present age was swept into past tense; the new creation had commenced. "Anyone in Christ is [of] the new creation!" Paul announced gleefully. The early Christian message was a bold proclamation of the new order begun. Christian apostles preached the reality of a new creation and called people, by baptism, to join a new humanity. Although the old-Adam world might have seemed firmly in place, the new, second Adam had been raised up and, with him, the world had begun all over again. We cannot write off Pauline theology as an odd, idiosyncratic, apocalyptic aberration; it was good news — Christ had passed through the "great tribulation" and a new age had dawned. The resurrection cannot be reduced to one man dead and one man risen. No, the resurrection was a great sign imprinted on cosmic history. All that Jesus preached — "The time is fulfilled, and the kingdom of God has come near" — was ratified; God's new order, a new covenant, had commenced. In a word, God's new order *is*.

Where in the World
Is God's New Order?

The problem for preaching can be stated bluntly: Where on earth is God's new order? As far as any of us can see the world is still spectacularly unredeemed. The powers that be are still firmly in place. Military budgets enlarge while the famished squeeze dust for nourishment. The rich appear to get richer while the poor multiply as a worldwide, resilient "cockroach culture." Injustice has become a way of life, and every human choice seems to involve a choosing of lesser evils, with the lesser evils becoming less and less morally viable. If there is a kingdom of God somewhere around it is certainly well hidden. So we preachers are clearly embarrassed. If we do not solve the problem by an appeal to personal piety (the kingdom *is* invisible because it is hidden in the hearts of individual believers who are personally renewed), we buy into Reinhold Niebuhr's Christian Realism and end up endorsing a kind of Christian casuistry.[10] Yes, Jesus did say, "Love your enemies," but in our world, a world of power politics, the injunction is simply not practical. Are we supposed to aid and abet the drug

---

[10] See, for example, R. Niebuhr, "The Ethic of Jesus and the Social Problem" and "When Will Christians Stop Fooling Themselves?" in *Love and Justice: Selections from the Shorter Writings of Reinhold Niebuhr,* ed. D. B. Robertson (New York: World Publishing, 1967), 29–46.

lords of Colombia or actively support the Iraqi menace? No, let us adopt a little Christian Realism; enemies are enemies, but perhaps we can learn to be moderate in our felt enmity. Or, again, the Sermon on the Mount is explicit, "Judge not!" But in our kind of world moral judgments must be made, so let us understand the injunction to mean we ought to be sensitive in our judgments or, perhaps, suspend final, fixed judgments. In our sermons we constantly temper the teaching of Christ. We suppose that Jesus, living in an age of high-pitched eschatology, was culturally a bit loony; he actually thought God's new order was about to appear. But the kingdom has not come, so surely Jesus himself would want us to adapt and take the edge off his overexcited, obviously overstated "interim ethic" lest his church appear kooky and become socially isolated. As any sane, realistic human being can see, there is no new order of God anywhere around our world these days. In our kind of society, Jesus' kind of message is inappropriate, not to mention downright impractical. Where is his new order of God?

What we are doing must be seen clearly: We are writing off the eschatological demands of the gospel so that our congregations may get along in the world as is, be personally adjusted, and, possibly, have some degree of self-esteem. Although the church is not meant to be of the world, realistically it is in the world, and there is no other social order available except among utopian dreamers. Thus, we regard the hard demands of the gospel as a first-century error that inevitably colored Jesus' own thinking, but that has to be corrected in view of political and social practicalities. So we modify the social dimension of the gospel and endorse a personal, often psychologically defined inward kingdom of faith for converted individuals. Yes, Jesus did preach, "The time is fulfilled, and the kingdom of God has come near; repent and believe in the good news," but we simply excise the first two clauses, and announce, "Repent and believe in Jeeeesus." We buff our fingernails on the sleeves of our pulpit robes and preen ourselves for being christological. After all, talk of the kingdom is the stuff of theological liberalism, and nobody but nobody wants to be a liberal anything these days in the land of the Bush and the Quayle. Besides, chatter about a coming new order sounds suspiciously Marxist to our all-American, chronically Republican, Protestant, middle-of-the-road congregations. So let us promise a heart transformation and leave the social order alone. All that exaggerated stuff about God's new order must be regarded as a first-century aberration and not central to the gospel of love.

Yet, how can we get rid of the resurrection? For if Christ is risen — that is, raised to the "right hand of God" — then the "King" is enthroned and, in some sense, the kingdom has been inaugurated. Although we may regard "seated at the right hand of God" as a dispensable, quite dated myth, it is still in the creeds and, before the creeds, is a claim underlined in scripture. Must we not assume that, if nothing else, the image of Christ, including his message of the new order, is somehow risen into the very nature of God? God is a God who promises a new order that, because God is God, shall be — indeed is. If such is the case, then Christian Realism is a form of faithlessness and our preaching is a counsel of outright compromise. Yes, the world in its falsity has yet to acknowledge the rule of Christ, but we who are church presumably have. Are we not commissioned to announce a forming new humanity and, what is more, in some fashion to live as a sign of the new order in the world? All Christian Realism does is to base common behavior on the world's patterned sinfulness, which does not appear to be a solid basis for anything like a Christian ethic. The Bible seems to suggest that, Christ risen, a new order has begun and that, therefore, those who will not live in the new order — the powerbrokers, the movers and shakers of the world — are choosing to live in illusion. Resurrection *is* Christian realism.

How Can We Preach God's New Order?

How can we announce God's new order in an empirically old-order world? How do we explain that when we repent, we do not merely feel a little Jesus in our hearts, but deliberately live contrapuntally as interacting citizens in God's new aeon? Obviously, the biblical gospel is thoroughly wrapped up in the myths and thought forms of a first-century world. As Luther long ago remarked, we cannot portray Jesus as literally perched on a heavenly throne directing the business of earth.[11] In spite of a Southern Baptist lust for inerrancy these days, and mainline Protestant pumping-up of "Word of God" triumphalism, biblical literalism is a form of nonsense — not to mention, heresy. Two-story universes are no longer viable models, and two-aeon time frames are scarcely creditable even in an emerging "new physics." Moreover, our world is still evidently under the domination of sin and law and death. So, preached, news of God's new order is bound to sound like

---

[11] Luther's works, Weimar ed. 23:131.

a fluffed-up fairy tale at best. No wonder that many preachers, chasing after Harry Emerson Fosdick, prefer to address personal problems with therapeutic problem-solving moralisms; at least we can be this-worldly and practically helpful. After all, if this world is all there is, we might as well encourage healthy adjustment in the name of a once-upon-a-time Jesus. How on earth can we announce God's new order?

Let us line out some specifics: We can call people to join a new humanity. At present we live between the ages in the cultural "sense of an ending."[12] People do sense dimly that somehow the social construct of the Enlightenment is gone, that the Protestant Era may well be over, that an age dominated by Western thought is giving way to rising Third and Fourth Worlds; they sense something is going down with a thud like the curtain in a theater. In such an epoch, we are peculiarly able to announce the coming of God's new order.

> There will be signs in the sun, the moon, and the stars, and on the earth distress among nations confused by the roaring of the sea and the waves. People will faint from fear and foreboding of what is coming upon the world, for the powers of the heavens will be shaken. Then they will see "the Son of Man coming in a cloud" with power and great glory. Now when these things begin to take place, stand up and raise your heads, because your redemption is drawing near. (Luke 21:25-28)[13]

We can speak of new life, not merely inside individual psyches but for the social world; we can declare a new world-a-coming in the midst of our worn-out society. People nowadays are peculiarly aware of being trapped in worn-out, no longer workable systems — the political, economic, and social patterns in which we all live. And many people long to break out of the systems into something like a new world because, after all, Yuppie dreams are ultimately tedious. So a call to be part of the world's new beginning can be strangely stirring and much more compelling than the somewhat Gnostic nonsense of "You can be a new you inside of yourself" even in the same old in-a-rut world. In a recent science fiction short story, after some sort of great catastrophe, a little

---

[12] The phrase is borrowed from F. Kermode's *The Sense of an Ending: Studies in the Theory of Fiction* (New York: Oxford University Press, 1967). Kermode's thesis is relevant for theology.

[13] P. S. Minear argues that the shaking of the earth and the heavenly luminaries are symbols of the shattering of the social order, and specifically of the "powers that be," so that the Son of Man coming on a cloud may usher in a new day. See his *Christian Hope and the Second Coming* (Philadelphia: Westminster Press, 1954), esp. chaps. 6, 8, and 12.

band of remnant people are left to rebuild human society on earth. "With us," cries their leader, "with us the world begins all over again!"[14] The gospel does announce that with the resurrection of Jesus Christ a new being-saved order of humanity has appeared that, by God's grace, will widen out through time and space to transform the world — a theological notion that has animated Eastern church thinking for ages. The concept of a new creation in the midst of a withering old-order world is still a viable message of hope.

Of course, if we preach the promise of a new humanity, we will have to supply eschatological images of God's future. People will not venture toward C. S. Lewis's fairy-tale worlds.[15] So we will have to study prophetic and apocalyptic poetry all over again, particularly those passages that envision a new order with peace and justice and mutual service among us all. We may have to feed on the strange, often exotic images that clutter the Book of Revelation and once more catch sight of the Holy City, free of pain and crying, into which the nations and races parade, dipping their ensigns and dropping their arms, a city filled with the joy of festivity that circles the throne of the Lamb. Although such visions are poetic, they do portray a new world. And poetry has a certain virtue; it is made up of vivid, often quite concrete images drawn from our world, thus conveying a sense of reality, yet poetry is imprecise enough to leave room for the sweet improvisations of God. Walter Brueggemann urges prophetic preachers "to penetrate despair so that new futures can be believed in and embraced."[16] Only with a vision of God's future, the new order God intends, can people let go of their as-is social order. At present, America is still wallowing in a kind of cultural nostalgia, chasing old-time States' rights; old-time free enterprise; old-time "big stick," Pentagon-style foreign policy; and old-time American folk religion. We will let go of ourselves only if we are drawn by some compelling vision of God's liberating future. Today, we preachers may be called to announce once more the coming kingdom to a fading, ultimately shattered social order.

Perhaps we can do more than paint word pictures. Maybe we can

---

[14] I have been unable to locate the source of this quotation.

[15] I have always been unsure of casting Christian apologetics in a fairy-tale form, which, I suspect, is what happens in much of C. S. Lewis; the technique may encourage a sense of the gospel's unreality. By contrast, at his best, Charles Williams portrayed awesome eschatological realities breaking into common life, as for example in his stunning *Descent into Hell* (New York: Pellegrini & Cudahy, 1949).

[16] W. Brueggemann, *The Prophetic Imagination* (Philadelphia: Fortress Press, 1978), 111.

turn ritual around to recover the eschatological dimension of the sacra-ments.[17] In early Christianity, the sacraments were not so much repre-sentations of the past as celebrations of the in-breaking of God's future; they were eschatologically oriented.[18] In baptism, early Christians did not so much join a church as they entered the new humanity. And, in the Lord's Supper, they ate and drank proleptically in the banquet of the new aeon. For what greater sign of God's promise is there than to see people gather as one family of God at table, serving one another in the name of Jesus Christ? The church is always ambiguous; it is seldom if ever a clear sign of God's new order. But the Lord's Supper can demonstrate the shape of God's promises, the coming of a new order. So in our preaching we can announce the new aeon and then, in sacraments, show the gospel we proclaim. In the American Southwest a remarkable congregation meets in an abandoned school building; the congregation is approximately one-fourth Indian, one-fourth Chicano, one-fourth black, and one-fourth Anglo. And most Sundays, after they have heard the gospel preached, they are apt to press together around the table, and sing: "Our eyes have seen the glory of the coming of the Lord, / He is bringing in the kingdom according to God's word." You hear the song and look around at the gathering and, yes, you see the promise of the gospel coming true. Baptism is neither instant conver-sion nor a church growth device; it is entering the world's new begin-ning. Likewise, the Lord's Supper is not a guilty, grief-stricken recol-lection of the cross, and it certainly is not a mere heartfelt get-together between Jesus and believers; the Lord's Supper is nothing less than a living sign of God's promised new order.

The Dangers of Preaching the Gospel

A word of caution: We must not suppose that preaching God's new order will be popular. Such a gospel will be rejected by both the church and the world. American churches are still gripped by conservatism, by

---

[17] For a study of sacramental eschatology, see G. Wainwright's important *Eucharist and Eschatology* (New York: Oxford University Press, 1981); see also G. Martelet, *The Risen Christ and the Eucharistic World* (New York: Seabury Press, 1976).

[18] Just as the notion of revelation in history has tended to rivet our preaching to a recital of past tense "mighty acts of God," so since Dom Odo Casel sacraments have been understood as making present and potent past salvific events. As a result, recent eucharistic liturgies, although containing obligatory gestures toward eschatological consummation, are basically oriented toward anamnesis, a recitation of the past, along with somewhat triumphalist declarations of presence in the ecclesial body of Christ.

orthodoxies or neoorthodoxy, and therefore will regard the message of
the kingdom as a return to a watery theological liberalism from the past
or as a dangerous shift toward a thinly veiled Marxist Liberation
Theology. Of course, denominations tend to have a stake in the status
quo. Clearly the message of the kingdom is bound to include the demise
of separate ecclesial loyalties — after all, there are no more churches in
the Holy City. And, these days, all old-line denominations are patho-
logically into self-preservation. Frightened churches will not readily
welcome the gospel of God's new order.

Neither will a frightened America. America has been clutching
nostalgic illusions of power and affluence for the past decade — we refurbished the Statue of Liberty and bred a generation of spectacularly
careless, conspicuous-consumer yuppies. America's political life has
been dictated by a profound aversion to social change; we think we
possess cash and power and do not want to let go in a turbulent time
of political alteration. One thing we do not want to hear from our clergy
is the message of a new order. After all, we have bet our economic lives
on the old order. If Americans — and in particular American, old-
money Protestants — have invested themselves in things as they are,
they will not receive word of social change gladly. Likewise, if we have
based psychological adjustment on a world that *is,* news of its displacement will be threatening indeed. So if we preach the peace of the
kingdom, will we not bump into America's defense-spending economy?
And if we declare justice, will we not collide with the nation's deliberate
policy of benign neglect? Let us be candid: The Preaching of God's new
order will almost inevitably be refused by both the national mind and
the conservatism of white Protestant churches.

Yet, in spite of obvious resistance, news of a new order is bound to
be good news for the poor, the alienated, the ill-adjusted, and the
broken people of earth. And news of a new order may also address
weary levels within the American soul at the tag-end of an era. There
may be a kind of pendulum swing to the preaching of the gospel; we
can preach the preaching of Jesus Christ — namely, the coming of God's
kingdom — in a narrative structure, or we can preach Christ in a
vertical triumphalism to individual souls hankering for social-security
salvation. Now, between the ages, preachers may be called to once
more join in Jesus Christ's announcement of God's new order, calling
America to let go of itself and repent. To do so will mean we must align
ourselves with international government, an ecumenical church, and

the macro-economics of shared wealth — none of which is currently in vogue in the American mind.

We are Christ's ministers. We were Christ's ministers long before we signed on to be ordained within our separate traditions. Jesus came preaching, "The time is fulfilled, and the kingdom of God has come near; repent, and believe in the good news." So must we. Once more we who are ministers are called to speak news of God's new order. If Christ is risen, the new order *is,* in some sense, inaugurated. Certainly the new order as an eschatological mode of consciousness is here.[19] How can we dare to break loose as preachers? How can we be free of our own terrifying, competitive denominational games? Deeper still, how can we risk disapproval in our home communities? Actually it is easy. At least it is a lot easier than to keep on playing small-scale church games or offering therapeutic adjustment in an ill-adjusted world. So we can trust grace, live in the free laughter of our Lord, and preach the wild surmise of the gospel. We can be sure of the Lord, risen. And, at the least, our lives will be interesting.

Why do we preach the new order of God? Not because we are continuing the preaching of Jesus Christ — although he called us to do so. We are preaching God's new order because it *is;* it is the reality in which our world lives. Christ is risen! The resurrection is news of God's new order. We say to an exhausted, end-of-an-age world, Come join the new order of God.

---

[19] If the "lived-world" is patterned in consciousness, cannot the "kingdom" be here and now as a structure in Christian communal consciousness?

CHAPTER 4

The Resurrection Tradition _____

PREACHERS HAVE a huge stock of texts with which to preach the resurrection. After all, resurrection faith underlies the entire body of the Christian scriptures. Nevertheless, there are texts that, again and again, have been associated with the Easter message, notably the fifteenth chapter of 1 Corinthians and, of course, the several stories that conclude our Gospel narratives.

These materials can be arranged to demonstrate an emerging tradition.[1] They can be layered from early to late. Moreover, they can be divided into two flows of tradition: a Galilean/Pauline pattern and a Jerusalem/tomb/women tradition. They cannot, however, be harmonized into a consistent history.

I will not attempt any reconstruction of a resurrection history. Nor will I try to arrange texts into separate traditions. Instead, for homiletic analysis I will select the major texts that preachers preach.

---

[1] There are several fine studies of the resurrection tradition, among them, N. Perrin, *The Resurrection according to Matthew, Mark, and Luke* (Philadelphia: Fortress Press, 1977); R. H. Fuller, *The Formation of the Resurrection Narratives* (New York: Macmillan, 1971); X. Léon-Dufour, *Resurrection and the Message of Easter,* trans. R. N. Wilson (New York: Holt, Rinehart, and Winston, 1974); U. Wilckens, *Resurrection: Biblical Testimony to the Resurrection: An Historical Examination and Explanation,* trans. A. M. Stewart (Atlanta: John Knox Press, 1978); R. H. Smith, *Easter Gospels: The Resurrection of Jesus according to the Four Evangelists* (Minneapolis: Augsburg, 1985); P. Perkins, *Resurrection: New Testament Witness and Contemporary Reflection* (Garden City, N.Y.: Doubleday, 1984). See also the remarkably helpful studies by C. F. Evans, *Resurrection and the New Testament* (Naperville, Ill.: Alec R. Allenson, 1970) and Peter Selby, *Look for the Living: The Corporate Nature of Resurrection Faith* (Philadelphia: Fortress Press, 1976).

Elsewhere I have argued that the resurrection texts do not tell us what happened. They do not describe the moment of resurrection or the actual appearance of the risen Christ. Nor do they disclose the true experience of the disciples. But all the resurrection texts feature (1) creedal/liturgical confessions; (2) allusions to the common life of the Christian community; and (3) apocalyptic symbols.[2] I will try to underscore these elements within the several texts.

Although I will present brief exegetical information, I will not document such information extensively. Through the centuries, exegesis tends to be a cumulative wisdom, so that commentators agree on much exegetical detail. I will note items of controversy and sharply divergent positions if such occur. As for homiletic help, readers may find that, at times, I assume some familiarity with my *Homiletic*.[3]

The exegetical sections do not seek to establish historicity; they will not study historical settings, historical custom, and the like in lengthy detail. Instead I am seeking to get at a word to be preached. Sermons are not Bible study lessons. They are not a talking about the Bible, but a preaching of the gospel from the Bible. So I will limit exegesis to the homiletically necessary.

A word about the translations provided: Although I have tried to represent the syntax and standard vocabulary of the texts, I have also tried to bring out the *koine* flavor of the texts. I have replaced the term *kingdom of God* with *God's new order,* and whenever the term *brothers* occurs have added *sisters* so as to endorse inclusiveness. Readers will wish to consult Greek texts or other translations, in particular the New Revised Standard Version, the New International Version, or, perhaps, the careful translations by Richmond Lattimore.[4]

THE WITNESS OF PAUL

The Pauline letters predate the Gospels and, therefore, may offer the earliest witness to the resurrection. Of all the Pauline writings, 1 Corinthians 15 contains the most developed presentation of the resurrection message.[5]

---

[2] See my *Preaching Jesus Christ* (Philadelphia: Fortress Press, 1988), chap. 5.

[3] See my *Homiletic* (Philadelphia: Fortress Press, 1987).

[4] R. A. Lattimore, *The Four Gospels and the Revelation* (New York: Farrar, Straus & Giroux, 1979), and idem, *Acts and Letters of the Apostles* (New York: Farrar, Straus & Giroux, 1982).

[5] There are several useful commentaries on 1 Corinthians, among them: C. K. Barrett, *A Commentary on the First Epistle to the Corinthians* (New York: Harper & Row,

1 Corinthians 15:1-19

The first half of 1 Corinthians 15 divides into two large sections, vv. 1-19 and 20-34; each includes an argument (vv. 12-19 and 29-34), and each concludes with quoted sayings.

An Early Creed

Most scholars agree that the creedal recitation in 1 Corinthians 15:1-11 is no doubt the earliest testimony to the resurrection. Although the resurrection is assumed and referred to in Paul's previous letters (e.g., 1 Thess. 1:9-10), the recitation in 15:1-11 is a primitive tradition that Paul is passing along (*paredōka*) to his Corinthian congregation. Notice its formal, almost creedal character, built out of a series of "that" (*hoti*) clauses:

> [3]I handed on to you as most important what I myself had received; namely,
>   that Christ died for our sins
>   as in the scriptures;
> [4]that he was buried, and
>   that he was raised on the third day
>   as in the scriptures;
> [5]that he was disclosed to Cephas,
>   then to the twelve,
>   [6]and later to more than five hundred [people]
>   at once, most of whom are still around,
>   although some have "fallen asleep."
> [7]He was then disclosed to James,
>   then to all the apostles,
>   [8]and, lastly, as if to someone born unexpectedly,
>   he was also disclosed to me.
> [9]For I am the least of the apostles, and not worthy to be called an apostle because I persecuted the church of God. [10]But I am what I am by the grace of God, and God's grace has not been in vain, for I have worked harder than all, though not I but the grace of God with me. [11]But, whether I or they, so we have preached and so you have believed.

See some features of the creedal formula:

1. Resurrection is God's mighty act; God discloses (*ōphthē*) the risen

1968); Hans Conzelmann, *1 Corinthians,* trans. J. W. Leitch (Philadelphia: Fortress Press, 1975); and Jean Héring, *The First Epistle of Saint Paul to the Corinthians,* trans. A. W. Heathcote and P. J. Allcock (London: Epworth Press, 1962). J. C. Beker (*Paul the Apostle: The Triumph of God in Life and Thought* [Philadelphia: Fortress Press, 1980]) offers an extended discussion of 1 Cor. 15. I have previously reviewed portions of 1 Cor. 15 in *Epiphany,* a volume of *Proclamation 3: Series C* (Philadelphia: Fortress Press, 1985).

Christian.[6] Moreover, the resurrection is not a departure from God's eternal purposes, but a fulfillment of God's plans for humanity. The phrase "as in the scriptures" establishes the connection.

2. Resurrection establishes the character of the church; thus there is mention of church leadership, Peter (Cephas) and the Twelve, followed by James and "all the apostles." The formal arrangement is almost hierarchical.

3. Resurrection creates a new humanity born of the forgiveness of sins ("for our sins"), establishes witnesses, and commissions an apostolic ministry such as Paul's own missionary enterprise.

Our problem is how to preach a creed. Perhaps we begin where we are — that is, as people to whom news of the resurrection has been passed. The resurrection comes to us in creeds ("On the third day he rose again from the dead") and, if not creeds, then hymns and sermons and Easter celebrations. The tradition is passed down century on century. But how do we take the good news of resurrection into our own lives? Perhaps the phrase "for our sins" offers a clue. When we sense that Christ died because of our sins, then we can hear the resurrection message as very good news indeed. Our sins are not chiseled in the gravestone past, but are canceled in the power of God, who raised up Jesus. Is the message hard to grasp? Yes, but we can trace meaning through the scriptures. When we do that, we, like Paul, can say, "he was disclosed to me."

An Odd Argument

What is the problem? Apparently some folk in Corinth were denying the likelihood of a general resurrection. Were they clinging to notions of immortality, or did they suppose that the resurrection would apply to the living but not to those already shoveled into graves? Evidently they believed that Christ was risen and that they themselves, baptized, were beyond death, yet they doubted that the previous dead would rise.

Paul replies by connecting a general resurrection with Christ's resurrection. He views Christ's resurrection as the forerunner of a soon-to-be general resurrection — "If there is no resurrection of the dead, then Christ has not been raised." With reverse English (perhaps I should

---

[6] See discussion of *ōphthē* in W. Marxsen, *The Resurrection of Jesus of Nazareth* (Philadelphia: Fortress Press, 1970); see also the subsequent debate in *The Significance of the Message of the Resurrection for Faith in Jesus Christ,* ed. C. F. D. Moule (Naperville, Ill.: Alec R. Allenson, 1968).

say, reverse Greek), he proceeds to argue that if Christ has not been raised then the Corinthians' common experiences are a deception — namely, the experience of forgiveness, the power of the liberating gospel message, and the hope of the community, all of which derive from a risen Jesus Christ.

> [12]Now, if Christ is preached as raised from the dead, how can some of you say there is no resurrection of the dead? [13]If there is no resurrection of the dead, then Christ has not been raised. [14]And if Christ has not been raised, our preaching is emptiness and your faith also! [15]What is more, we are shown up as false witnesses for God, because we testified that God raised Christ, whom God has not raised if the dead are not raised. [16]If the dead are not raised, Christ has not been raised: [17]your faith is illusion, you are still stuck in your sins, [18]and those who have fallen asleep in Christ are gone forever! [19]If in our Christian lives we only have hope, we are more to be pitied than anyone.

Some features of the passage:

1. Notice that underlying the passage is the conviction that a new age has dawned. The new age has two foci, the resurrection of Jesus and a general resurrection yet to come. These foci are connected; they are part of a great apocalyptic salvation event that, now begun, will inevitably be concluded. We think of Christ's resurrection as past event and the possibility of a general resurrection as future. For Paul they are one event now in process of unfolding.
2. The appeal to experience is crucial. Here Paul is taking note of the congregation's common experience of redemptive life: They know the gospel has been liberating and is thus true; they know they are forgiven and, indeed, are living interpersonally in mercy; they know their faith is somehow real and valid. These common experiences testify to the power of risen Christ. The experiences are sure and, therefore, sure testimony to the reality of Christ's resurrection. The final statement in v. 19, "If . . . we only have hope, . . . we are more to be pitied than anyone," is probably the quotation of a saying with which the congregation is familiar.

Obviously, many twentieth-century people have trouble believing in resurrection. Not only are we skeptical about our own life after death, but we may find it difficult to credit the annual Easter rumor of Christ's resurrection. The answer to our doubts is not to be found in historical verification; the biblical resurrection stories may well seem fanciful. Nor is there much point in offering the existence of the church as a proof. The church can be dismaying indeed. No, Paul's strategy is not passé. We are obviously a gaggle of sinners; our brokenness is spectacular. Yet through us good news is spoken, and people are reconciled, and human lives are salvaged. Christ is continuing his saving work among us. The surprising fact of grace among us is a witness to the risen power of Jesus Christ.

1 Corinthians 15:20-34

The passage may be broken down into two sections: (1) vv. 20-28, a vision of the fulfilled work of Christ; and (2) vv. 29-34, which contain a peculiar reference to baptism for the dead, whatever that custom may mean, before concluding with a personal reference (as in v. 11) and the quoting of some familiar adages.

A Final Triumph

20But, now, Christ has been raised from the dead, the first fruits of those who have fallen asleep. 21For since death came through a human, resurrection of the dead is also through a human; 22for as in Adam we all die, so in Christ we will all be made alive, 23but each in proper order; the first fruits, Christ, and afterwards, at his coming, those in Christ. 24Then comes the End when he hands over the kingdom to God the Father, having nullified every ruler, and every authority and power; 25for he will reign until he has brought all enemies under his feet, 26the last enemy being death, for "all things will be brought as subjects under his feet." 27When it says, "all things will be brought as subjects," it means all except the one who causes all things to be subject to him. 28But when all things are subject to him, then the Son himself will be subject to the one who caused all things to be subject to him, so that God may be all in all.

The passage is difficult to translate and even more difficult to interpret. In part, difficulties are caused by uncertainty. Exactly what concept of resurrection is Paul espousing? He obviously believes Christ is risen, inaugurating an imminent new age that, apparently, will involve a general resurrection of the living and the dead. What is more, the risen Christ "will reign" until the whole universe is conquered. Is Paul projecting an interim messianic age? And exactly what does he have in mind when he speaks of every "ruler," "authority," and "power"? The passage, full of mythic stuff, is a tough one for preachers — or anyone else.

The use of "first fruits" in v. 20 probably works from a harvest image; in the biblical world, the first gleaning was customarily offered to God (Lev. 23:10-20). The term implies the special character of Christ's resurrection but also the notion of a coming harvest, that is, a general resurrection. In the following verses (vv. 21-22), Paul sets up a two-part, rhetorical contrast. First, he draws on similarity: "Since death came through a human [the word 'ādām means human], resurrection of the dead is also through a human." Second, Paul introduces a temporal argument: "For as in Adam we all die, so in Christ we will all be made alive." Here the idea is that death has been introduced into human generations by Adam's disobedience, but now being "made alive" is possible in Christ. Paul will return to the first-Adam/second-Adam pattern later.[7]

With v. 23, Paul introduces sequence into the unfolding drama of resurrection. We will be raised "each in proper order" (*tagma,* rank), first Christ and then, with the coming of Christ, those who belong to him. There is scholarly debate over vv. 22-24. When Paul says "all" in v. 22, does he mean all humanity? And when he says "those in Christ" in v. 23, does he exclude those who are not in Christ? Could the word *kingdom* in v. 24 imply all humanity?[8] Throughout the chapter, Paul has been speaking of a general resurrection of the full humanity that Christ has chosen.[9]

The passage moves toward a cumulative triumph. In v. 24, Paul widens out from Christ, to Christians, to the whole universe that will be handed over to God in "the End" (*telos*), after the taming of rulers, authorities, and powers. Here we bump into Paul's notion of the powers that be.[10] Although the powers may well be otherworldly cosmic

---

[7] For discussion of the concept, see the following: C. K. Barrett, *From First Adam to Last: A Study in Pauline Theology* (New York: Charles Scribner's Sons, 1962); R. Scroggs, *The Last Adam: A Study in Pauline Anthropology* (Philadelphia: Fortress Press, 1966); as well as older works by K. Barth, *Christ and Adam: Man and Humanity in Romans 5,* trans. T. A. Smail (New York: Collier Books, 1962), and R. Bultmann, *The Old and New Man in the Letters of Paul,* trans. K. R. Crim (Richmond, Va.: John Knox Press, 1967).

[8] For a summary of positions, see Héring, *First Epistle,* 165-68.

[9] So argues Beker, *Paul the Apostle,* 170-73.

[10] What are the "principalities and powers"? Some scholars seem to identify them with earthly powers (G. B. Caird, *Principalities and Powers* [Oxford: Clarendon Press, 1956]). Others focus on inner oppression — the law, fear, death (H. Schleir, *Principalities and Powers in the New Testament* [London: Burns and Oates, 1966]). G. H. C. MacGregor seems to combine both approaches ("Principalities and Powers: The Cosmic Background in Paul's Thought," in *New Testament Sidelights,* ed. H. K. McArthur [Hartford: Hartford Seminary Foundation, 1960]). Still other scholars look to Jewish apocalyptic sources. Most scholars of late seem to argue that the powers are heavenly "spiritual rulers" who are, nonetheless, influential in human affairs (C. Morrison, *Powers That Be* [London: SCM Press, 1960]). For an exegetical study of the passages, see R. Leivestad, *Christ the Conqueror* (London: S.P.C.K., 1954). I am much indebted to a fine thesis by J. D. Small, III, "Principalities and Powers in the Pauline Epistles" (Princeton Theological Seminary, 1970). Most recently see volumes by W. Wink, *Naming the Powers* (Philadelphia: Fortress Press, 1984) and *Unmasking the Powers* (Philadelphia: Fortress Press, 1986).

forces, they are clearly connected to unacknowledged social dominations—political attitudes, conventional wisdoms, denominational
loyalties, and goodness knows what else. Perhaps they are social projections that, divinized, turn and control us.[11] The risen Christ will defuse
the powers and bring them into subjection. Mention of death as "the
last enemy" is not surprising; although Christ has risen, human beings
are still dying.

Paul suddenly corrects his own rhetoric. Although he has raised up
a triumphant Christ whose redemptive work will be done in the End,
he adds an unexpected demur. Christ may be God's own saving outreach into the world, but ultimately Christ himself, the Son, will bow
before God's sovereignty, so that God will be "all in all." The verses are
not venturing into incarnational theology, but describing step by step
the redemption of the world.

How on earth are we to preach an apocalyptic vision these days? We
should certainly not turn Paul's understanding into a literal history of
"this is what is going to happen to us in the following 1-2-3 order." We
need not dive into some sort of crypto-fundamentalism; we are dealing
with the stuff of myth. But we can begin with the resurrection of Christ
as a great sign of God's ultimate power over the force of death and the
human demonic. We can affirm that, ultimately, God's redemptive
purpose in Christ will be done. A renewed humanity will be set free
from social dominations—racism, power politics, and so on—and from
its own deathward bent, and will be brought into communion with
God. To use a troublesome word, we can *demythologize,* and we can
declare good news to our twentieth-century congregations.

Baptisms for the Dead

Rather abruptly, there is a turn in Paul's thought. Once more he
addresses the original problem: "How can some of you say there is no
resurrection of the dead?"

> 29Otherwise, what about those who are baptized on behalf of the dead? If there is
> no resurrection of the dead, why are they baptized on behalf of them? 30Also, why
> do we risk danger every hour? 31I die daily—just as I boast you do, my family in
> Christ Jesus our Lord. 32If, from a human point of view, I fought wild beasts at
> Ephesus, what good did that do? If the dead are not raised, "Let us eat and drink,
> for tomorrow we die!" 33Do not be misled: "Bad company corrupts good morals."

---

[11] See my *Preaching Jesus Christ,* chap. 4.

³⁴Come to your senses, be virtuous, and do not sin, as do some who have no knowledge of God. I speak in this way to your shame.

Paul drifts into a chain of ad hominem arguments to correct those who suppose there is no general resurrection: (1) He refers to those who are baptized for the dead; (2) to Christians who willingly risk their lives; and (3) to a connection between convictions and behavior. The arguments are scarcely compelling.

First, Paul refers to a group within the Corinthian congregation who apparently are undergoing baptisms on behalf of those who have died. We have no other reference to such a custom in the biblical writings, although Chrysostom (c. 347–407) claims it was practiced by Marcionites.¹² In essence, he asks, Why bother if there is no resurrection? Second, Paul seems to argue that Christians who risk their lives as he did in Ephesus ("I fought wild beasts") are idiotic if there is no resurrection promise. People might as well settle for less: "Eat and drink, for tomorrow we die!" (Isa. 22:13). But, third, Paul says that such moral aimlessness would be corrupting. He then urges the Corinthians to shape up and act like Christians rather than like pagans who have no knowledge of God.

Because we live in a post-yuppie culture, given to "eating and drinking, for tomorrow we die," the passage may still be preachable. Moreover, we have had a long history of Christians who are willing to risk martyrdom — and that long history extends to recent martyrdoms in Central America, South Africa, and elsewhere. If there is no hope of resurrection, all martyrdoms are simply a misguided masochism. Yet, we do espouse such hope and display it in behavior. The hope we have is based on Christ, crucified and risen.

1 Corinthians 15:35-58

The second half of 1 Corinthians 15 contains three units: vv. 35-44, on the resurrection body; vv. 45-49, on the first and second Adam; and vv. 50-58, which might be described as a coda.

The Resurrection Body

³⁵But, someone may ask: How are the dead raised? With what body do they come? ³⁶How silly, what you sow does not come to life unless it dies; ³⁷and when you sow,

---

¹² The text from Chrysostom is included in Conzelmann, *1 Corinthians,* 276 n. 117.

you do not sow the body that is to be, but a bare grain of wheat perhaps or something else. ³⁸God gives it a body as [God] chooses; to each seed, its own body. ³⁹Not all flesh is the same; one kind is human flesh, another is animal flesh, another is bird flesh, and another is fish. ⁴⁰There are heavenly bodies and earthly bodies. There is a glory of the heavenly body, and a glory of the earthly body; ⁴²there is glory of the sun, glory of the moon, and another glory of the stars; and stars differ from stars in glory.

⁴²So also is the resurrection of the dead; it is sown perishable, it is raised imperishable; ⁴³it is sown in disgrace, it is raised in glory; it is sown in weakness, it is raised in power; ⁴⁴it is sown a natural body, it is raised a spiritual body. If there is a natural body, there is also a spiritual one.

When we think of agricultural growth, we think of a continuous process of germination. Paul and his contemporaries did not. Agricultural growth was a discontinuous miracle; a dead seed is tossed into the earth and then, miraculously, there is suddenly a blossom. We may view seed as a potential blossom, but to first-century people, the blossom after dead seed was a sheer gift of God: "God gives it a body as [God] chooses." So preachers must be cautious. The discussion of bodies here does not imply continuity; resurrection is always a gift of God by the power of God. We are not immortal. Like "bare" seed, we are emphatically mortal.

Thereafter, Paul launches into a somewhat labored digression on the subject of bodies, different kinds of bodies.¹³ In my translation, the word *glory* (*doxa*) might be translated better as "splendor" or "luster."¹⁴ The burden of his argument is that there are many different kinds of bodies, all with their own peculiar "glory," and that, therefore, the resurrection body will be different, indeed, of a different order.

Certainly, Paul says that the resurrection body will be entirely new compared to our natural body. Naturally, our bodies are "sown" in weakness and disgrace;¹⁵ we are perishable. But we will be raised in splendor, imperishable. If, says Paul, "there is a natural body, there is also a spiritual body." The word translated "spiritual body" is *pneumatikon,* a "body by the agency of the Spirit." Thus Paul is not describing a quality, ephemeral rather than material, but is speaking of

¹³ On the resurrection body, see M. E. Dahl, *The Resurrection of the Body* (London: SCM Press, 1962), and J. A. Schep, *The Nature of the Resurrection Body: A Study of the Biblical Data* (Grand Rapids, Mich.: William B. Eerdmans, 1964).

¹⁴ Charles Williams somewhere refers to the "geometry of glory" in human flesh. See his essay, "The Index of the Body," in *The Image of the City and Other Essays,* ed. Anne Ridler (London: Oxford University Press, 1958), 80–87.

¹⁵ I have translated *atimia* as "disgrace"; the word can mean dishonor or meanness. Paul uses it in contrast to *doxa,* "glory" or "splendor." Perhaps "shabby" might do, but disgrace (that is, without grace) will have to suffice.

sources — our natural body is from nature, but the risen body is given by the Spirit. No doubt J. A. T. Robinson is correct in suggesting that even here in a discussion of bodies, Paul is concerned with a social resurrection, a resurrection of the "body of Christ."[16] The whole passage stresses the newness of resurrection and the power of God. We do not continue, thank heavens. Instead, we are to be made different by the Spirit of God.

First and Second Adam

Continuing his discussion, Paul reintroduces the notion of the two Adams, which he has previously employed in vv. 21-22.

> [45]Thus, it has been written: "The first human, Adam, became a living being"; the last Adam became a life-giving Spirit. [46]It is not the spiritual first; but first the natural, and then the spiritual. [47]The first human was from the earth, earthly; the second human is from heaven. [48]Like the earthly human, so are the earthly; and like the heavenly, so are the heavenly. [49]As we wear the image of the earthly one, so shall we wear the image of the heavenly one.

We can sum up the argument by saying: We shall be like the risen Christ. But the content is much more complex, for we are dealing with a two-aeon theology. Paul divides the story of God and humanity into two cosmic space-time ages, the age of Adam and, now, the new age of Christ. Paul is an apocalyptic thinker. So in v. 45, he quotes a modified version of Genesis 2:7: "The first human, Adam, became a living being."[17] To the brief quote, he adds a parallel, "The last Adam became a life-giving Spirit." If the first Adam generated our mortal, broken humanity, the second Adam, Christ, begins a new aeon, filled with the power of the Spirit.[18] Note that the first Adam is from earth (i.e., is made from earth as in Gen. 2), whereas the second Adam is from heaven, as is the promised "Son of Man" in apocalyptic literature.[19] Paul, however, may be thinking of a second coming as in 1 Thessalonians 4:16, a verse that depicts a general resurrection in

---

[16] J. A. T. Robinson, *The Body: A Study in Pauline Theology* (London: SCM Press, 1952).

[17] For Genesis 2:7c, the NRSV has, "the man became a living being." The Hebrew word for "man" is *'ādām* ("earthling"), which relates to *'ădāmâ,* soil or ground.

[18] Verse 46 stresses proper sequence, first the natural and then the spiritual. Paul may be countering a notion that in Gen. 1:27 there is a human created in the image of God, whereas in Gen. 2:7 there is a human from the dust — first the archetype and then the type. Such an exegesis is found in Philo. Paul sharply rejects the idea and, instead, stresses historical sequence.

[19] See, for example, Dan. 7:13; 1 Enoch 46:1ff.; and 4 Ezra 8:1ff.

which all humanity will be redeemed. Final redemption is sure: We *shall* "wear the image of the heavenly one" (v. 49).

In preaching we cannot simply discard two-aeon thinking as a rather bizarre apocalyptic blip that will not play in Peoria or anywhere else in the twentieth century. The idea that Christ has inaugurated some sort of change in the human condition is, I think, basic to the gospel message. We cannot relegate both nature and history to stage scenery for one-by-one soap operas of individual salvation. We do live in an old-Adam world, mortal and misguided. But, Christ has come, and in some manner God's new order has begun. The new humanity, generated by Christ, is spreading and, therefore, we look for the consummation of God's good purpose. As Christians in community, although we live in an old-Adam world, we also live in the sphere of the Spirit, looking to the future of God.

A Coda

Paul completes his discussion of the resurrection triumphantly in a kind of apocalyptic coda.

> [50]I say this to you, brothers [and sisters], flesh and blood cannot inherit God's new order, neither can the perishable inherit the imperishable.
>
> [51]Look, I will tell you a mystery: We all will not fall asleep, but we all will be changed [52]in an instant, in the wink of an eye, at the last trumpet. For a trumpet will sound, and the dead will be raised imperishable, and we will all be changed. [53]For this perishability must put on imperishability, and mortality put on immortality. [54]When perishability puts on imperishability, and mortality puts on immortality, then, as it is written, "Death has been swallowed up in victory."
>
> > [53]"Where, O death, is your victory?
> > Where, O death, is your sting?"
>
> [56]Now the sting of death is sin, and the power of sin is the law. [57]But thanks be to God for giving us the victory through our Lord Jesus Christ.
>
> [58]So, my loved brothers [and sisters], be firm, unmovable, always eager in the work of the Lord, knowing that in the Lord, your labor is not empty.

In vv. 50-52, Paul is referring to a general resurrection of the living and the dead. With the coming of Christ, both those alive and those who previously have died will be transformed. Thus in v. 50, he mentions both groups—"flesh and blood" (those alive), and "the perishable" (those who have died)—neither of whom can inherit the kingdom.[20] The same distinction shows up in v. 52 with "the dead will be raised"

---

[20] The distinction has been made quite clear by J. Jeremias, "Flesh and Blood Cannot Inherit the Kingdom of God (1 Cor. XV 50)," *New Testament Studies* 2, no. 3 (February 1956), 151–59.

and "we all will be changed." In v. 51, Paul explicates the idea: "We all will not fall asleep, but we all will be changed." Apparently he means that some Corinthians can expect to be alive with the coming of Christ and be transformed, along with those who have "fallen asleep," in a great resurrection of the living and the dead. The notion of a last trumpet comes from both the Hebrew Bible (Joel 2:1; Zeph. 1:16) and, particularly, intertestamental apocalyptic literature (4 Ezra 6:23).

In vv. 54-55, Paul rallies some rather loose translations of scripture: from Isaiah 25:7, "Death has been swallowed up in victory," and from Hosea 13:14, "Where, O death, is your victory? / Where, O death, is your sting?"[21] But he works off the quotes in a typically Pauline way: "Now the sting of death is sin, and the power of sin is the law" (v. 56). Probably he sees death as causally following from sin, and sin as revealed by God's law. We need not shy away from the verse. Not only is much death caused by human exploitations, such as war and poverty, but, obviously, there is a kind of self-destruction in us all. So, although we may not wish to regard death as an imposed divine punishment, we can see that the "wages of sin is death." Moreover, sin is surely connected with the inescapable fact of death; in dying, we know it is too late to rectify the damage we have done. For those who believe in God's bottom-line moral demands, which are expressed in the law, sin is all too self-evident.

Paul's coda ends with a wonderful flourish: "But thanks be to God for giving us the victory through our Lord Jesus Christ." Christ, who was put to death under the law by us sinners, has been raised up by the power of God. Therefore, our victory over sin and law and death is sure. So, Paul concludes by urging his Christian congregation to be "eager in the work of the Lord," that is, in witness and charity. Notice "the work of the Lord" does not earn resurrection in Paul's thought. But we can work with cheer and confidence, knowing that God's purposes will be consummated, that the new age has begun, and that our hopes will be fulfilled.

Can we hand out the notion of a resurrection of the living and the dead at the second coming to contemporary Christian people? Probably not. On the one hand, fundamentalists who churn out Pauline expectations as a literal timetable do not serve faith well. On the other hand, we need not preach personal survival to quiet the death fears of our congregations every Easter. Personal survival is not a biblical idea;

---

[21] The NRSV for Isa. 25:7c reads, "He will swallow up death forever"; and for Hos. 13:14 has, "O Death, where are your plagues? O Sheol, where is your destruction?"

resurrection is. The hope of a general resurrection is connected with God's ultimate purpose for humanity—namely, a whole world reconciled and in communion with God. Easter faith hooks up with such a hope. Christ is risen, and now, as Paul exclaims, *now* is the day of salvation. We live in a time when God is at work to bring about the redemption of the world, a work begun in Christ, a work that will be done. The resurrection proposes not merely an end to death, our last enemy, but to sin and law and demonic powers that be.

We have looked at 1 Corinthians 15, which expresses Paul's understanding of the resurrection. It is a good place to begin. Although there are gospel stories of the resurrection, behind them all is a cosmic theology not unlike Paul's. All the accounts of resurrection anticipate the consummation of God's purpose, a new heaven, a new earth, and a glorious new humanity.

THE WITNESS OF MARK

Mark 16:1-8 is a strange conclusion to the Gospel of Mark.[22] The verses are often described as "problematic," for they are historically suspect and they end in midsentence. The so-called longer ending of Mark (vv. 9-20) is not found in earlier and better manuscripts of Mark and, therefore, is footnoted in some Bibles. We will not discuss the longer ending.[23]

Look at the first eight verses:

[1]When the Sabbath was over, Mary Magdalene, and Mary of James, and Salome came with spices in order to anoint him. [2]Very early on the first day of the week, they came to the tomb, after the rising of the sun. [3]And they were saying to each other, "Who will roll away the stone from the tomb for us?" [4]And looking up, they saw that the stone had been rolled back, for it was tremendously huge. [5]Going into the tomb, they saw a young man dressed in a white robe sitting to the right, and they were very alarmed. [6]So he said to them, "Don't be so alarmed. You are looking for Jesus the Nazarene, who was crucified. He has been raised; he is not here. See! Here is the place where they put him. [7]But, go tell his disciples and Peter, that he is going on ahead of you into Galilee. There you will see him as he told you." [8]And, going out, they ran from the tomb for they were beside themselves and shaking. No one said anything; they were afraid for . . .

Let us face the historical difficulties, verse by verse. In v. 1, three women are mentioned. They are faithful in contrast to the disciples

---

[22] On Mark 16:1-8, see an impressive reading by M. A. Tolbert, *Sowing the Gospel: Mark's World in Literary-historical Perspective* (Minneapolis: Fortress Press, 1989), 288–99.

[23] For discussion, see V. Taylor, *The Gospel according to St. Mark* (New York: St. Martin's Press, 1966), 610–15.

who have scattered.[24] But the names do not match up with women mentioned in 15:40 or in 15:47. They bring spices, presumably to embalm the body of Christ; however, embalming a body after three days in the climate conditions of Judea would be a pointless endeavor. Moreover, Mark has already reported an anointing at Bethany: "She has anointed my body beforehand for its burial" (14:8). Plus, according to 15:43-46, Joseph of Arimathea has provided a proper burial. Verses 1-2 seem to mention three different times: "when the sabbath was over" (sundown), "very early on the first day" (before sunrise), and "after the rising of the sun." Do the different times demark three days, or is the reference to "the rising of the sun" a symbolic allusion? In v. 3, a conversation about moving the grave stone is somewhat ludicrous. The women had seen the tomb sealed (15:47) and knew that a strong work crew would be needed. So probably vv. 3-4 are included as a tribute to the awesome power of God.

In v. 5 we encounter "a young man dressed in a white robe sitting to the right." Is the young man an angelic messenger (e.g., 2 Macc. 3:26, 33), or is Mark engaging in a woven symbolism? Earlier, when Jesus is arrested in the Garden of Gethsemane, an unknown young man, losing his robe, runs away; the passion strips away pretensions of righteousness (Amos 2:13-16). Here we have a similar young man, clothed in a white (baptismal?) robe, seated in a preaching posture, declaring good news. His message appears to be a kind of "creedlet," an affirmation that may have been featured in early Christian worship: "He has been raised; he is not here."[25] Several scholars argue somewhat convincingly that the young man functions as a symbol for the death and evangelical rebirth of the Christian community and, therefore, is scarcely historical.[26]

The next verse, v. 7, appears to be a somewhat clumsy insertion,

---

[24] E. Schüssler Fiorenza, *In Memory of Her: A Feminist Theological Reconstruction of Christian Origins* (New York: Crossroad, 1983), 138-39.

[25] "He has been raised; he is not here" may seem to jar much popular Jesus piety. In a remarkable book, T. W. Jennings, Jr., argues that Christian worship begins with the absence of Christ and is filled with eschatological longing; see *Life as Worship: Prayer and Praise in Jesus' Name* (Grand Rapids, Mich.: William B. Eerdmans, 1982), chap. 1.

[26] For discussion, see R. Scroggs and K. I. Groff, "Baptism in Mark: Dying and Rising with Christ," *Journal of Biblical Literature* 97 (1973): 531-48; J. D. Crossan, "Empty Tomb and Absent Lord," in *The Passion in Mark,* ed. W. H. Kelber (Philadelphia: Fortress Press, 1976), 147-48; and, a more recent summary, R. H. Smith, *Easter Gospels: The Resurrection of Jesus according to the Four Evangelists* (Minneapolis: Augsburg, 1983), 33-35. See also F. Kermode, *The Genesis of Secrecy* (Cambridge: Harvard University Press, 1979), chap. 3.

disrupting a natural flow between v. 6 and v. 8; and, in the Greek, grammatical seams show. Why is the verse included? Does it tie together two resurrection traditions, Galilee and Jerusalem? Or is the verse symbolically meaningful, picturing Jesus going before a re-grouped discipleship, leading out into a wider Gentile world with evangelical purpose? Or, again, does the verse refer to an expectation of coming *parousia?*[27]

The final verse, v. 8, is a huge problem. Why does it break off in midsentence, ending with a preposition, "for" (*gar*)? Has the conclusion been lost, or is the break deliberate? Is the ending left unended for us, who are subsequent disciples, to conclude?[28] All in all, Mark 16:1-8 is a mystery. But, verse after verse, if history is uncertain, the symbolic options multiply. Maybe the text is a passage for preachers and not for historians.

Certainly the passage is preachable. Look at the symbolic pattern of the passage:

1. The passage begins with the fact of death—Jesus Christ is dead and emphatically buried. The faithful women, who come to embalm the body, underscore the reality of death.
2. Yet, the huge grave stone is tossed aside, as a sign of God's triumphant power over death and, not only death, but over sin's power to crucify.
3. As a result, we preach good news of resurrection—"He has been raised; he is not here." Christians, exposed by the cross as sinners, are now new people, who declare the gospel of Jesus Christ.
4. So where is Christ? Christ is alive in the world, leading the church into every land with the good news. He is still "going on ahead" of us.
5. But, like the women at the tomb, we are frightened and often silent. Yet we are called to speak, to "go tell" a death-filled, hopeless world, "He is risen!"

The risen Christ does not appear in Mark 16:1-8. No, instead, the resurrection message is preached at the tomb. So, in a way, Christ comes as a word, a word that we in turn may speak.

---

[27] So argue Perrin, *The Resurrection*, 25-27, and W. Marxsen, *Introduction to the New Testament: An Approach to Its Problems* (Philadelphia: Fortress Press, 1968), 142.

[28] On the peculiar ending in v. 8, see some options: Fuller, *Formation of the Resurrection Narratives,* 52-53; N. Petersen, "When Is the End Not the End? Literary Reflections on the End of Mark's Narrative," *Interpretation* 34 (1980): 151-66; Smith, *Easter Gospels,* 40-45; W. Kelber, *The Oral and the Written Gospel* (Philadelphia: Fortress Press, 1983), 127-29; and Tolbert, *Sowing,* 295-99.

THE WITNESS OF MATTHEW

Matthew's resurrection story is told in three rather distinct episodes: the women at the tomb (28:1-10), the bribed guards (28:11-15 [with 27:62-66 and 28:4]), and, finally, Christ's appearance on a mountain in Galilee (28:16-20).

Women at the Tomb

Presumably, Matthew has altered Mark's account by adding and subtracting material.[29] Matthew drops mention of Salome, the second of the references to time (i.e., "early on the first day of the week"), and Mark's mention of spices for anointing. In Matthew, the women simply go "to see the grave," which of course is guarded by soldiers. The question "Who will roll away the stone?" is skipped and, instead, Matthew adds an earthquake and an angel whose appearance is "like lightening and his clothing white as snow." References in Mark to "the Nazarene" and to Peter disappear. In Matthew, the women are not silent; instead they go with joy to tell disciples the good news. Of course the big change in Matthew is a direct appearance of the risen Christ to the worshiping women.

[1]Late on the Sabbath, as daylight grew on the first day of the week, Mary Magdalene and the other Mary came to see the grave. [2]And, look, there was a great earthquake; for an angel of the Lord came down out of heaven and, drawing near, rolled away the stone and sat on it. [3]His appearance was like lightning and his clothing white as snow. [4]Afraid of him, those on guard were shaken and became as if dead. [5]Speaking, the angel said to the women: "Don't be afraid. I know you have been searching for Jesus, who was crucified; [6]he is not here for, as he said, he has been raised. Come see the place where he lay. [7]Then, quickly, go tell his disciples that he has been raised from the dead and, look, he is going before you to Galilee. You will see him there." [8]Leaving the tomb quickly, with fear and great joy, they ran to tell the disciples about him. [9]And, look, Jesus met them, saying, "Hail." Coming near, they held on to his feet and worshiped him. [10]Then Jesus said to them, "Don't be afraid. You go tell my brothers that they can go off to Galilee and they will see me there."

At the outset, notice that Matthew has enlarged apocalyptic detail: the earthquake (see Exod. 19:18; Ps. 68:8; as well as Isa. 13:13; Ezek. 38:19-20; Hag. 2:6), the angel whose appearance is described with heightened apocalyptic language, and an earlier (27:51-52) reference to tombs of the dead sprung open in Jerusalem. In a similar fashion,

---

[29] For studies of Matthew's elaboration of Mark 16:1-8, see F. W. Beare's useful *The Earliest Records of Jesus* (Nashville: Abingdon, 1962), 240–42; and, more recently, J. L. Houlden, *Backward into Light* (London: SCM Press, 1987), chap. 3.

Matthew 24 has elaborated the apocalyptic "sermon" provided in Mark 13, heightening spectacular supernatural wonders to come.

Mark's resurrection story is filled with ambiguity; it does not end on a note of triumph. But Matthew resolves ambiguities and, indeed, underscores God's decisive triumph. More, he moves the resurrection into public history—thus, many graves are opened, and there are soldiers guarding the tomb. As J. L. Houlden puts it, there is "a loss of purity, but a gain in sheer power."[30] While Mark seeks to portray the character of God's secret, suffering, self-giving power, Matthew stresses the power of God over all earthly powers. No wonder that, finally, Jesus gleams on a mountain and is filled with authority. Matthew looks forward to the ultimate triumph of God. Preachers will want to stress a contrast between the destructive and dishonest forces that have crucified Christ and the overthrow of such earthly powers by almighty God in the resurrection of Jesus Christ the Lord. In a world dominated by powers that be, the message of the resurrection is very good news indeed.

Some scholars suggest that the scene in vv. 9-10, where Jesus himself appears to the women, is redundant, merely an echo of the angel's earlier message. But the scene adds an important detail, namely, "they held on to his feet and worshiped him." At Jesus' birth the Magi bowed in worship, and here, at the triumphant conclusion to the Gospel, both the women and the disciples (v. 17) worship. They greet the risen Son appropriately.

The Guards at the Tomb

The story of the guards at the tomb is unique to Matthew. The account begins in chapter 27 and continues in chapter 28:

27:62On the next day, after the Day of Preparation, the chief priests and the Pharisees gathered before Pilate, 63saying, "Sir, we remember how that impostor while he was alive said, 'After three days, I will rise up.' 64Therefore, order the grave to be secured until after the third day, lest his disciples come and steal him, so as to tell the people, 'He was raised from the dead'—and the last fraud be worse than the first." 65Pilate said to them, "Take a guard. Go, and secure it if you can." 66They went and with the guard secured the grave with a stone. . . .

28:4Afraid of him [i.e., the angel], those on guard were shaken and became as if dead. . . .

---

[30] Houlden, *Backward,* 36.

28:11As they [i.e., the women] were leaving, look, some of the guard went into the city and told the chief priests all that had happened. 12They met and, consulting with the elders, gave the soldiers some money, 13saying, "Say, 'his disciples came at night and stole him while we were sleeping'; 14and, if the governor hears about it, we will reason with him, so you don't have to worry." 15They took the money and did as they were told. And the report has been spread among the Jews to this day.

Many scholars suppose that the story of the guards has been inserted to counter a rumor current among Jewish opponents during Matthew's time.[31] But the story should not be dismissed as apologetic strategy; it is theologically profound. The passages contain two different contrasts: (1) a contrast between the restrictive power of the guards and the free, liberating power of God; and (2) a contrast between the women's obedience and the guards' duplicity.[32]

Certainly the dispatching of the guards is filled with irony. In 27:62, note that the chief priests and Pharisees, guardians of the Sabbath day, are desecrating the Sabbath by meeting with Pilate. They address him as "Sir" (*kyrie*), which can also be translated "Lord." They are concerned, as was King Herod at the time of Christ's birth, with a loss of social power. If news of a resurrection gets out, their authority among the people is lost. So they suggest the tomb be sealed and a guard set in place, lest "the last fraud be worse than the first." In essence, they beg power to thwart God's resurrection purpose. Pilate, who seems to have a penchant for irony in the Gospels, orders a guard, but adds, "Go, and secure it if you can."[33]

The plot is laughable, for how can any earthly power block the power of God, particularly when God's redeeming purpose has already commenced (27:52-53)? So when the life-giving power of God arrives, along with an earthquake and a visiting angel, the soldiers faint and "became as if dead." Surely Matthew is playing with a contrast: God raises Christ to life, and the soldiers faint dead away.

But the contrasts continue. Although the women are badly frightened, they hear the angel's reassuring word: "Don't be afraid." While

---

[31] Both Justin Martyr (c. 150), *Dialogue with Trypho,* 17.108, and Tertullian (c. 200), *On Spectacles,* 33, allude to a similar rumor in their own times.

[32] D. Patte, *The Gospel according to Matthew* (Philadelphia: Fortress Press, 1987), 392–402, brings out these contrasts brilliantly.

[33] The apocryphal Gospel of Peter (in *The Apocryphal New Testament,* trans. M. R. James [1924; reprint, Oxford: Clarendon Press, 1972]) intensifies the story. In the Gospel of Peter 8:23-33, the Pharisees, along with elders and scribes, slap the gravestone in place, sealing it with seven seals, and then remain in a tent nearby to guard the scene themselves.

the soldiers lie in a dead faint, women hear a message of life. The
angel's words are full of imperatives: "Don't be afraid," "Come see the
place," "Go tell." The women obey and, along the way, meet the risen
Christ.

Then ironies are heightened: As the women obey and "go tell," so do
the soldiers. The guards go and tell the chief priests "all that had happened," even though they had been in a faint. Then the chief priests,
meeting with the elders, decide to bribe the soldiers to spread a false
story. If the soldiers should get in trouble with the governor, why, they
would go to Pilate and "reason with him." So the soldiers take the cash
and do as they are told.

The women obey and declare truth, whereas the soldiers lie and obey
a devious command. The conjunction of the two stories poses a choice:
Will we obey and tell the truth of the gospel or, co-opted by earthly
powers, will we be false?

Risen Christ on the Mountain

Here we have the famous Matthean commissioning of disciples by
the risen Christ. The passage, familiar to most of us, is puzzling.
Scholars have debated its form: Is it a "ritual of enthronement," a "cultic
I-saying," a "revelation speech," a "farewell discourse," a "Shema," a
"foundation myth," a "commissioning," a "Royal Decree"?[34]

> [16]Then the eleven disciples went on into Galilee, to the mountain Jesus had desig-
> nated, [17]and, seeing him, they worshiped him; but some doubted. [18]Coming near,
> Jesus talked with them, saying, "All authority in heaven and on earth has been given
> me. [19]Go out, therefore, and make disciples of all the nations, baptizing them in the
> name of the Father and the Son and the Holy Spirit, [20]teaching them to observe all
> that I have commanded you; and, look, I am with you all the days until the end of the
> aeon."

Although the passage is historically doubtful (Would Jesus cite a
Trinitarian baptismal formula, "Father, Son, and Holy Spirit"?), it is
nevertheless theologically meaningful. Matthew perches the risen
Christ on a mountain. For Matthew, a Jewish-Christian, Jesus is the
new Moses for a new Israel. So, like Moses, Jesus delivers his key
sermon from a mountain (5:1); he prays on a mountain (14:23); he
glows, transfigured, on a mountain (17:1); and, finally, he appears
risen on a mountain, waving toward a promised land of evangelical
opportunity.

---

[34] See Smith, *Easter Gospels,* 75–76.

The disciples, like the women at the tomb, fall down and worship (*prosekynēsan*) their Lord. That "some doubted" (v. 17) is not inconsistent, for although Matthew does not debunk disciples as does Mark, nevertheless they often display "little faith." Moreover, Matthew stresses the mixed character of the faithful; they are "wheat" and "tares," "sheep" and "goats." The fact that they worship, however, reflects a high, Matthean christology; after all, to Matthew, Jesus is Messiah, the Son of Man and the Son of God.[35] More, he is the one to whom God has given "all authority in heaven and on earth" (v. 18). In Jewish circles, authority was ascribed to Torah. So, here, Jesus is acknowledged as a new, regnant, living Torah for the new cosmic Israel.[36] Notice the repetition of "all" throughout the passage — "all authority," "all the nations," "all that I have commanded," "all the days."

There is some debate over what is meant by *ethnē*, "nations" (v. 19). Is Matthew's Jesus sending disciples to Jews of the diaspora or to the wider Gentile world? In view of the "all," the answer must be both/and. The use of the word *teaching* (*didaskontes*) is significant. Here, for the first time, Matthew suggests that the disciples will teach. Previously, Jesus has been the teacher. In the first half of the Gospel, he teaches Israel, and in the second half, he instructs disciples; now he tells the eleven to continue his teaching ministry in the wider world. The phrase "all that I have commanded you" echoes God's repeated injunction in the Hebrew scriptures (e.g., Exod. 7:2; Deut. 1:3; 2 Chron. 33:8; Jer. 1:7).

The final statement, "Look, I am with you," is again a matter of some conjecture. To some interpreters the clause means that the word of Christ will be with his disciples. While obviously the words of Christ's teaching are important to Matthew, it is possible that "I am with you" parallels assurances that have been given to the prophets (e.g., Exod. 3:12; Jer. 1:8). A Jewish statement, "Where two or three are gathered in Torah, there the Shekinah will be with them," may be even more to the point.[37] Thus, disciples will speak the words of the new Torah, Jesus Christ, and will be enabled by his Spirit, which is the Spirit of God. The final phrase, "until the end of the aeon," gives a clue to Matthew's eschatology. He believes that risen Christ will rule between

---

[35] On Matthew's christology, see J. D. Kingsbury, *Matthew: Structure, Christology, Kingdom* (Philadelphia: Fortress Press, 1975); and also J. P. Meier, *The Vision of Matthew: Christ, Church, and Morality in the First Gospel* (New York: Paulist Press, 1978).

[36] See W. D. Davies, *The Setting of the Sermon on the Mount* (Cambridge: Cambridge University Press, 1966), chap. 3.

[37] See D. Daube, *New Testament and Rabbinic Judaism* (London: Athlone Press, 1956), 27–32.

the resurrection and the *parousia,* when the nations will be judged by a Christ returned. "Until the end of the aeon" is, therefore, a time of evangelical opportunity for the new Israel; the church is to be a beacon light to the nations.

The passage describes the church. Because of the risen Christ, we worship. And, obeying the Lord's command, we go out into the world with good news. We baptize those who hear the message into the worshiping community. Although we must not claim to be Christ, we continue his ministry of teaching, passing on his ethical commands. And, certainly, we do not lose heart. After all, he has promised us his Spirit: "Look, I am with you."

THE WITNESS OF LUKE

We will divide Luke's resurrection narrative into four units: (1) the women at the tomb; (2) the Emmaus Road story; (3) the Jerusalem gathering; and (4) Jesus' final speech. Of course, in contrast to Mark and Matthew, Luke intends to continue his story. Therefore, his conclusion is not really a conclusion; he is also preparing the way for a new narrative to follow in the Book of Acts.[38]

Many scholars suppose that, originally, the resurrection included exaltation, ascension, and the gift of the Spirit; Luke has spread these meanings out and turned them into separate historical moments. Therefore, his notion of resurrection is somewhat circumscribed.

Women at the Tomb

Luke treats the Markan source quite differently from Matthew:

23:56bThey rested on the Sabbath, as is commanded;

24:1but, at the crack of dawn on the first day of the week, they came to the tomb, bringing spices they had prepared. 2They found the stone rolled away from the tomb 3and, going inside, they did not find the body of the Lord Jesus. 4As they were puzzling over this, look, two men stood beside them in dazzling clothes. 5They were terrified and bowed down to the ground. But [the men] said to them, "Why do you seek the living among the dead? 6[He is not here; he has been raised.] Remember, while he was still in Galilee, 7he told you 'Humanity's Child must be turned over to sinners and be crucified, and on the third day, rise.'" 8Then, they remembered his words.

---

[38] For a study of connections, see C. H. Talbert, *Literary Patterns, Theological Themes, and the Genre of Luke-Acts* (Missoula, Mont.: Scholars Press, 1974), 58–61; see also Smith, *Easter Gospels,* 130–43.

> 9Returning from the tomb, they told everything to the eleven and all the rest. 10Now the women, Mary Magdalene and Joanna and Mary, James's mother, and others with them, kept telling the same story to the apostles. 11But the words seemed humbug to them, and they did not believe. 12But Peter got up and ran to the tomb; bending down and looking in, he saw the linen clothes by themselves; and he came back, wondering about what had happened.

Luke has radically altered the account of the empty tomb in Mark 16:1-8. Briefly: He has enlarged the circle of women and detailed their experience — the risen Christ himself does not appear at the tomb. Luke doubles the angels and recasts their message; he alone has "Why do you seek the living among the dead?" He deletes mention of going on to Galilee, perhaps because of a literary pattern he has imposed on Luke-Acts; in the Gospel Jesus comes to Jerusalem, whereas in Acts the good news goes out from Jerusalem. Many manuscript versions of Luke do not contain the confessional formula, "He is not here; he has been raised." Likewise, some manuscripts do not have v. 12, but manuscript evidence for its inclusion is strong. The account of Peter running to the tomb may parallel the language of shepherds running to the manger.[39]

The women do have a prominent role in the Lukan story. They have been with Jesus from the beginning of his ministry and have been listed previously in 8:13. Moreover, they have witnessed the crucifixion (23:49) and the burial: "The women who had come with him from Galilee . . . they saw the tomb and how his body was laid" (23:55). Now they arrive on Easter Day to find the tomb open and emphatically empty. Suddenly two dazzling persons are on hand as earlier at the Transfiguration (9:30); two witnesses are regarded as reliable.[40] The women are terrified (see Dan. 10:9). Whereupon the two messengers declare the resurrection by citing an edited version of an earlier prediction, also from the Transfiguration narrative. Please notice the word *must* in their recitation, a word that is crucial in Luke's understanding of the passion and the resurrection; *must* is a testimony to the purposes of God.

The women then return to tell the eleven what had happened. Over and over they recite their experience, but to no avail. The eleven refuse to believe (women were regarded as fuzzy-headed witnesses in the first-century world) and dismiss the story as nonsense.[41] Peter then runs

---

[39] See Smith, *Easter Gospels,* 111-12.

[40] See Deut. 17:6 and 19:15, as well as John 8:17.

[41] Josephus advises, "Let not the testimony of women be admitted, on account of the levity and boldness of their sex" (*Antiquities of the Jews,* 4.8.15). The statement is not untypical and reflects the widespread sexism of the ancient world. The fact that women

off to the tomb and, as a second witness, corroborates the women's discovery; he returns "wondering about what had happened." A key clause in the account is "they remembered his words." Luke is suggesting that the resurrection makes sense in relation to the life and teaching of Christ.

Luke's story begins where we begin—with a message that some believe and others find humbug. The story, however, finds meaning when it is connected with the life and words of Christ, as well as with some sense of God's moving purposes in human events.

The Emmaus Road

The story of the walk to Emmaus,[42] found only in Luke (24:13-32), has been a favorite among preachers for centuries.[43] As a story it unfolds in a series of well-defined episodic units:

> [13]Look, on the same day, two of them were going to a village named Emmaus, about seven miles from Jerusalem. [14]They were talking to each other about everything that had taken place. [15]And, it so happened that, as they were talking and debating, Jesus himself came up and went along with them; [16]but their eyes were stopped from recognizing him.
>
> [17]He said to them, "What's this you're saying back and forth to each other as you walk?" They stood still, frowning. [18]Answering, the one whose name was Cleopas, said, "Are you the only stranger in Jerusalem who hasn't heard about what's been happening these past few days?" [19]And he answered, "What's that?" They said, "About Jesus the Nazarene, a prophet who was powerful in word and deed in sight of God and all the people. [20]And how both the chief priests and politicians handed him a death sentence and crucified him. [21]We had been hoping he was the one to liberate Israel, but now it's three days since everything happened. [22]But then, some of our women astonished us; at dawn, they went to the tomb, [23]but they didn't find his body. They came back to us saying they had seen a vision of angels who told them he was alive. [24]But some of us went to the tomb, and though it was as they had reported, we didn't see him."

---

are mentioned as first witnesses to the resurrection gives historical credence to the Jerusalem/empty tomb/women tradition. Luke is usually considered to be more open to the role of women in Christian community—both his Gospel and Acts feature women significantly—but he still provides males to support their testimony; see E. Schüssler Fiorenza, "You Are Not to Be Called Father: Early Christian History in a Feminist Perspective," in *The Bible and Liberation: Political and Social Hermeneutics,* ed. N. K. Gottwald (Maryknoll, N.Y.: Orbis Books, 1989), 401-2.

[42] I have previously studied the Emmaus Road narrative in "Homiletic Resources for the Easter Season," *Quarterly Review* 6, no. 1 (Spring 1986): 65-85.

[43] The only parallel to the Emmaus Road story is an odd reference in the longer ending of Mark: "After this, he appeared in another form to two of them, as they were walking into the country."

²⁵Jesus said to them, "Oh, you blockheads, and slow of heart to believe all the words of the prophets, ²⁶how it was necessary for the Christ to suffer in order to enter glory." ²⁷And, beginning with Moses and all the prophets, he expounded for them everything in scripture that related to him.

²⁸As they neared the village they were heading toward, he acted as if he were going on. ²⁹They pleaded with him, saying, "Stick with us. The sun has set and it's getting late." So he went in to stay with them. ³⁰And it happened that as he was at table with them, he took bread and blessed it and broke it and gave it to them. ³¹And their eyes opened up and they recognized him. But he disappeared. ³²Then, they said to one another, "Didn't our hearts blaze when he spoke to us on the road and opened the scriptures for us?"

The story of the Emmaus Road is beautifully told and is filled with subtleties. Notice that "on the same day" ties in the Emmaus narrative with the earlier story of the women at the tomb. In v. 15, the word translated "debating" can refer to rabbinic counterquestioning. The same idea shows up in v. 17, "saying [lit., tossing] back and forth," which might better be translated by the neologism, "rapping." There has been much speculation about Cleopas (v. 18). If "Cleopas" could be a version of "Clopas," who is mentioned in John 19:25 ("Mary the wife of Clopas"), then perhaps we have a couple walking toward Emmaus.[44] Notice that the two disciples do not recognize Jesus because "their eyes were stopped" (*ekratouto*), a term sometimes used to describe sleight-of-hand tricks. The verb, however, is a "reverential passive," indicating that God had prevented their seeing.

In v. 19, the crucified Jesus is described as "a prophet who was powerful in word and deed." Perhaps Luke is alluding to some popular messianic expectations (see Deut. 18:18; also Mal. 4:5), for earlier he has had a crowd, dazzled by a miracle, declaring "a great prophet has risen among us" (7:16). The mention of "chief priests and politicians" is consistent with Luke's tendency to blame the crucifixion on Jewish leadership. Verse 21 is poignant, "We had been hoping . . . "; they were past hoping now. Perhaps they had been hoping for a liberator, a political messiah who could free Israel from Roman occupation.

Verses 22-24, which seem to be inserted into the account, reiterate the events reported earlier in vv. 10-11. Notice the failure of the disciples to believe the *word* of resurrection, possibly because it has been delivered by women.

In v. 27, we suddenly realize that Jesus is preaching a formal sermon

---

⁴⁴ Although confusion of the two names is unlikely (see J. A. Fitzmyer, *The Gospel according to St. Luke (X–XXIV)* [Garden City, N.Y.: Doubleday, 1985], 1563–64), the usual identification of the strollers as two males is probably sexist.

in the middle of the road — "beginning with Moses and all the prophets, he expounded [*diermēneusen*] . . ." The phrase "Moses and all the prophets" may refer to the Torah/Haftarah Jewish preaching tradition that seems to have been a pattern in the worship of early Christian communities.[45] Of course, Jesus' sermon voices a Lukan theme, namely, "It was necessary for the Christ to suffer in order to enter glory"; that is, "necessary" in the purposes of God.

In v. 28, Jesus appears to be "going on" further, a phrase that may function symbolically. Instead, the three gather at table; whereupon "he took bread and blessed it and broke it and gave it to them." Luke often pictures Jesus eating and drinking. Frequently he uses some version of the same formula — taking, blessing, breaking, giving (see 9:16 and 22:19; also Acts 27:35). So Luke, having referred to preaching, now hands out an obvious eucharistic phrase. The disciples at Emmaus knew Christ in the breaking of bread. And they remembered how fired up they were by his preaching.

As a story, the Emmaus Road narrative is designed around two foci, Jesus' "sermon" on the road and the Lord's Supper that concludes the passage — a pattern of word and sacrament. For preachers, the story poses a choice. Do we cling to historicity, preaching the passage in a "now this is what happened" style, or do we fulfill Luke's evident purpose and line up the reality of resurrection with preaching and eucharist? We are meant to acknowledge that Christ is risen through the power of the word and the mystery of sacrament. In our own day, we still can.

An Appearing to the Gathered Disciples

Although Luke 24:33-43 is connected to the Emmaus Road narrative, the passage draws on a separate tradition, a tradition that may also underlie John 20:19-23 and 24-29. Here the risen Christ appears to disciples who are gathered somewhere in Jerusalem. Verses 33-35 bridge the two accounts.

33They got up that same hour and returned to Jerusalem, where they found the eleven, and others gathered with them, 34saying, "It's true. The Lord has been raised

---

45 While all scholars seem to spot the reference to the Lord's Supper in v. 30, few seem to recognize the allusion to preaching in v. 27. In synagogue practice, two lections were used, one called Seder, from the Pentateuch, and the other called Haftarah, from the Prophets and Writings.

and has appeared to Simon." [35]And they told about the happenings along the road and how he was known to them in the breaking of bread.

[36]While they were still talking of these things, he himself stood among them [saying, "Peace to you"]. [37]Astonished and terrified, they thought they were seeing a ghost. [38]He said to them, "Why are you shaken and why do such thoughts rise up in your hearts? [39]Look, my hands and my feet; I am myself. Touch me and see; a ghost does not have the flesh and bone you see I have." [40]So saying, he showed them his hands and his feet. [41]Because they still did not believe due to joy and amazement, Jesus said to them, "Have you anything here to eat?" [42]They handed him a piece of cooked fish, [43]and he ate it in front of them.

Although the two people at Emmaus had previously remarked the late hour (v. 29), they get up at once and return to Jerusalem. There they find the eleven disciples and others already rehearsing news of the resurrection: "The Lord has been raised and has appeared to Simon." The declaration seems to be another "creedlet," a brief confessional formula similar to Paul's "he appeared to Cephas" in 1 Corinthians 15:5. So the two people from Emmaus add their testimony of how "he was known to them in the breaking of the bread." As many commentators have noted, "the breaking of the bread" is used repeatedly in Acts to refer to the Lord's Supper.[46]

Suddenly, Jesus stands in their midst and says, "Peace."[47] The disciples are terrified, supposing that they are seeing a disembodied "spirit." To reassure them, Jesus calls attention to his hands and feet. Some scholars suppose that mention of Jesus' hands and feet underscores his bodily state in contradistinction to the idea of a spooky presence, but the mention of hands and feet also bears witness to the crucifixion; the risen Christ *is* the crucified Christ. The eating of cooked fish is somewhat baffling—Is it a leftover scrap of Galilean tradition? Is it a eucharistic symbol as in John 21?[48] In context, it is still another demonstration of corporeality contra Docetic notions.[49] But please

---

[46] For recent discussion, see I. H. Marshall, *Last Supper and Lord's Supper* (Grand Rapids, Mich.: William B. Eerdmans, 1980), 123–33; and X. Léon-Dufour, *Sharing the Eucharistic Bread: The Witness of the New Testament,* trans. M. J. O'Connell (New York: Paulist Press, 1987), 21–31.

[47] Although the phrase is not found in some manuscripts, it is fairly well attested. Peace, of special interest to Luke, is not so much an inner feeling as a communal way of life. On the meaning of the biblical word *peace,* see the brief but helpful summary by C. F. Evans in *A Theological Word Book of the Bible* (New York: Macmillan, 1952), 165–66. A recent study by J. L. Stotts, *Shalom: The Search for a Peaceable City* (Nashville: Abingdon, 1973) is also helpful.

[48] O. Cullmann, *Early Christian Worship,* trans. A. S. Todd and J. B. Torrance (London: SCM Press, 1953), 14–16.

[49] C. H. Talbert, *Luke and the Gnostics: An Examination of the Lucan Purpose* (Nashville: Abingdon, 1966), 30–32.

notice the ambiguity of Christ's risen body in the Lukan tradition; although he may munch cooked fish, he also appears and disappears at will.

Theologically the passage contains the resurrection message, a conferral of peace (*šālôm*) and the testimony that the crucified one is vindicated by God — all of which rest on the reality of the risen Christ.

The Final Speech

Tacked on to the appearance before the assembled disciples is a final speech by Jesus prior to his ascension. Here Luke's theological themes emerge rather clearly.

> [44]Then he said to them, "These words I spoke to you while still with you—everything written about me in the law of Moses, the prophets, and the psalms must be fulfilled." [45]Then he opened their minds to understand the scriptures. [46]And he said to them, "Thus it is written that the Christ is to suffer, and to rise from the dead on the third day, [47]and that repentance and forgiveness of sins is to be preached in his name to all nations, beginning with Jerusalem. [48]You are witnesses of these things. [49]Look, I issue my Father's promise to you: Remain in the city until you are clothed from above with power."
>
> [50]And he led them out as far as Bethany, and lifting up his hands, he blessed them. [52]And it so happened that as he blessed them, he left them and was carried up to heaven. [52]They returned to Jerusalem with great joy, [53]and were continually in the temple blessing God.

Here we have a version of the Great Commission that concludes Matthew, except that Luke stresses a somewhat different theological agenda. Luke speaks of preaching, repentance, and forgiveness; he calls the disciples "witnesses"; he inaugurates the church's missionary activity in Jerusalem; and he promises the empowering gift of the Holy Spirit. Instead of having Christ high on a mountain, Luke concludes with a bodily ascension into heaven. Nevertheless, here we have a final commissioning.

In v. 44, Christ recalls previous instruction he has given, although it is difficult to locate exactly what passages may be intended. Essentially he claims that his own life and teaching, as well as his death and resurrection, are in line with the purposes of God that are recorded in scripture. As he did on the Emmaus Road (v. 27), he opens the disciples' minds to understand the true meaning of scriptural testimony. Then, in v. 46, he rehearses a passion prediction similar to the angelic message at the empty tomb (v. 7). Both of these verses reinforce the idea that Christ's death and resurrection are "necessary" in God's plan for humanity, namely, the forgiveness of sins. Thus does the risen Christ instruct his disciples for their universal ministry.

The disciples are also a part of God's plan. They are chosen witnesses who will preach the gospel from Jerusalem out into the wide world (see 9:1-6 and 10:1-12).[50] Their ministry will fulfill prophecy: "The word of the Lord shall go out from Jerusalem" (Isa. 2:3; Mic. 4:2). To them, Christ promises the "clothing" of the Spirit, which will be given them in Acts 2. Like Elijah clothing Elisha, Christ promises the disciples the gift of his own Spirit. Finally, he leads the disciples out to Bethany, near the Mount of Olives, where he had begun his entry into Jerusalem (19:29). There he blesses them, completing a gesture left undone by mute Zechariah at the beginning of the Gospel (1:21-22).[51] There are, of course, many farewell blessing stories in the Hebrew scriptures: blessings by Jacob (Gen. 48:20), by Moses (Deut. 33:1), by King Solomon (1 Kings 8:54ff.), and, in the apocryphal Book of Tobit, a blessing by the angel Raphael before an ascension.[52] Luke has, however, effected a kind of closure; blessings fill both the first and the last chapters of his Gospel.

The ascension of Christ is full of mystery: Ascension recognizes the lordship of the crucified/risen Christ, his absence from the earthly sphere, and his entrance into the nature of God-for-us.

THE WITNESS OF JOHN

The resurrection stories in the Gospel of John are crowded into chapter 20. Although the Gospel originally concluded with the last verse of chapter 20, we have an additional chapter that begins with a resurrection "fish story" (21:1-14). Thus we will discuss four units of chapter 20—the empty tomb (1-10), Christ's appearance to Mary in the garden (11-18), the locked room episode (19-23), and the story of "doubting Thomas" (24-29)—as well as the fishing story in chapter 21.

The Empty Tomb

[1]Now on the first day of the week, while it was still dark, Mary Magdalene came to the tomb and saw that the stone had been removed. [2]So she ran back to Simon

---

[50] For discussion, see P. S. Minear, *To Hear and to Reveal: The Prophetic Vocation according to Luke* (New York: Seabury Press, 1976).

[51] See Smith, *Easter Gospels,* 129–30.

[52] For discussion, see U. Wilckens, *Resurrection: Biblical Testimony to the Resurrection: An Historical Examination and Explanation,* trans. A. M. Stewart (Atlanta: John Knox Press, 1978), 67–73.

Peter and to the other disciple, the one whom Jesus loved, and said to them, "They've taken our Lord from the tomb, and we don't know where they put him."

3Then Peter and the other disciple got up and went to the tomb. 4The two ran together, but the other disciple, running faster, got to the tomb first. 5Bending down, he saw the wrappings lying there, but he did not go in. 6Following him, Simon Peter came up and went into the tomb. He looked at the sheets lying there 7and the napkin, which had been on his head, not lying with the sheets, but separately, rolled up in a different place. 8Then the other disciple, who had come there first, entered the tomb. He saw, and he believed. 9They did not yet know the scripture, that he must rise from the dead. 10The disciples then went back, each to his own home.

Here John offers his version of the empty tomb tradition, an account that seems to parallel the Lukan tradition in some respects. But, obviously, John offers a number of different touches to express a very different theological understanding. In John, there is only one woman who goes to the tomb, Mary Magdalene — although note the peculiar use of "we" in v. 2. She goes "on the first day of the week," that is the Lord's Day, but "while it was still dark," not at dawn. She discovers that the stone has been removed and immediately runs back to "Simon Peter and to the other disciple, the one whom Jesus loved," with the news. Thereafter the story involves the two disciples.

Who is the beloved disciple? We need not chase down the many possible guesses?[53] Suffice it to say he functions in two ways: (1) according to 21:24, he has some role in the production of the Gospel itself, if not as an author, then as a guarantor of the tradition; (2) more importantly he may function symbolically, for he seems to epitomize the "ideal disciple," at least according to the Johannine community. Often he appears in concert with Peter but not, as some suggest, as Peter's rival.[54]

Peter and the other disciple go to the tomb, the other disciple out-racing Peter to get there first. Bending down, the unnamed disciple spots the linen wrappings. Catching up, Peter enters the tomb itself to see not only the linens, but the bandannalike head wrapping rolled up in a separate place. Quite likely mention of the head napkin draws a contrast between the resuscitation of Lazarus and the resurrection of Christ. When Lazarus emerges from his grave, his face is still wrapped (11:44).

---

[53] For a survey, see R. Schnackenburg, *The Gospel according to St. John,* vol. 3 (New York: Crossroad, 1987), 375–88.

[54] R. E. Brown suggests that the notion of a rivalry between Peter and the beloved disciple is a product of Catholics/Protestant tensions; see *The Gospel according to John (xiii–xxi),* in *The Anchor Bible* (Garden City, N.Y.: Doubleday, 1970), 1004–7; see also R. E. Brown, "Peter in the Gospel of John," in *Peter in the New Testament,* ed. R. E. Brown, K. P. Donfried, and J. Reumann (Minneapolis: Augsburg, 1973), 129–47.

Verse 8 is important; the other disciple "saw, and he believed." Was Peter an observer, whereas the "beloved disciple" was a believer because of *love?* Perhaps, for throughout the Gospel, John connects faith and love in a profound way. The following verse, v. 9, is peculiar: "They did not yet know the scripture, that he must rise from the dead." Does the "they" refer to Mary and Peter? Is the verse a somewhat unassimilated remark from John's source? In Luke, the risen Christ interprets the scriptures, pointing out references to his own death and resurrection. Likewise, Paul's recited creed contains the phrase "according to the scriptures." The verse may simply mean that they had not yet put the empty tomb together with the prophecies of scripture. When faith seeks understanding, then scripture becomes important.

In praising the other disciple's faith, does John endorse believing without seeing, as in 20:29b ("Blessed are those who haven't seen, but believe")? No, in 20:29, those who believe without seeing do so on the basis of the *word* they hear. But the other disciple in the empty tomb narrative does see; he bends down and sees the linen grave wrappings. Evidently, he believes out of love — a first-stage faith that, later, will be confirmed.

Mary Magdalene in the Garden

The story of Mary and the risen Christ (John 20:11-18) is poignant and, therefore, has been a preaching favorite for centuries. But preachers should be cautious. The passage is less emotive than it may seem; it is undergirded by a complex theological pattern.

> [11]But Mary stood outside at the tomb, crying. As she was weeping, she stooped down into the tomb [12]and saw two angels in white sitting, one at the head and the other at the foot, where the body of Jesus had been laid. [13]They said to her, "Woman, why are you crying?" She answered them, "Because they have taken my Lord, and I don't know where they've put him."
> [14]Having thus spoken, she turned around and saw Jesus standing, but she did not know it was Jesus. [15]Jesus said to her, "Woman, why are you crying? Whom do you seek?" Thinking it was the gardener, she said to him, "Sir, if you carried him off, tell me where you put him, and I will take him away." [16]Jesus said to her, "Mary." Turning, she answered him, "Rabboni" [that is to say, "Teacher"]. [17]Jesus said to her, "Don't grip me, for I have not yet ascended to the Father, but go to my brothers and tell them, 'I am ascending to my Father and your Father, to my God and your God.'"
> [18]Mary came to the disciples declaring, "I have seen the Lord," and what he had told her.

In the first two verses of the chapter, Mary came to the tomb "while it was still dark" and found the stone removed. She raced back to inform the two disciples, saying, "They've taken our Lord from the tomb." The story then turns away from Mary to describe the two disciples. Now, once more, John's focus is on the figure of Mary.

She stands outside the grave crying. Then, like Peter and the other disciple, she bends down and looks into the tomb. To her surprise, she sees "two angels in white sitting, one at the head and the other at the foot, where the body of Jesus had been laid." As a few scholars suggest, the scene recalls the ark of the covenant, with cherubim at both ends of the mercy seat (Exod. 37:7-9).[55] If the position of the angels is an allusion to the Holy of Holies, then John supposes that the tomb is a place of new covenant where the power of God is present. Perhaps.

But Mary is preoccupied with the body of Jesus (vv. 2, 13, 15): "They have taken my Lord, and I don't know where they've put him." Whereupon, Mary turns and sees a man, but does not recognize him as Jesus. Jesus speaks: "Woman, why are you crying? Whom do you seek?"[56] Notice that the question is similar to the one Jesus addressed to disciples of John the Baptist in the first chapter of the Gospel (1:38). In v. 15, Mary supposes that Jesus is the gardener. The resurrection scene in a garden has prompted speculation: Is John suggesting a theme of new creation?[57] Again, Mary voices her question, "Sir, if you carried him off, tell me where you put him, and I will take him away."[58] Notice that Mary is still in the dark, obsessed with the bodily Jesus.

Suddenly Jesus addresses Mary by name, "Mary."[59] Probably John is underscoring an idea he ventured earlier in the sermon on the good shepherd: "He calls his own sheep by name. . . . Sheep will follow him because they know his voice" (10:3-4). Mary recognizes Christ's voice and replies, saying "Rabboni." Some scholars suppose that Rabboni is an intimate, almost playful term, but there is little to support the conjecture.[60] Instead we should notice the narrative parallels with 1:35-41,

---

[55] Smith, *Easter Gospels*, 161–62.

[56] On irony in the first question, see P. D. Duke, *Irony in the Fourth Gospel* (Atlanta: John Knox Press, 1985), 104–5.

[57] Most scholars do not suppose a symbolic allusion to Eden here, although see Smith, *Easter Gospels*, 163.

[58] Tertullian (c. 200), *On Spectacles*, 30, mentions a Jewish legend: Jesus was buried in a vegetable garden and the gardener removed the body because he did not want tomb visitors to trample his cabbages; cited by R. E. Brown, *The Virginal Conception and Bodily Resurrection of Jesus* (New York: Paulist Press, 1973), 122.

[59] Through the centuries, preachers have dramatized the moment of recognition; for example, see a stunning sermon by G. Taylor, "Two Names in the Morning," in *The Scarlet Thread: Nineteen Sermons* (Elgin, Ill: Progressive Baptist Publishing House, 1981).

[60] See Brown's discussion in *The Gospel according to John (xiii–xxi)*, 991–92.

a passage in which the disciples also acknowledge Jesus: "They said to him, 'Rabbi' (which translated means Teacher)." Mary is a disciple bound to a bodily master.

Jesus then tells Mary to let go: "Don't grip me." Mary must let go of the human Jesus if she is finally to confess a true faith, "I have seen the Lord" (v. 18). In John, Christ's death, resurrection, and ascension are one event; Christ is "being lifted up" to the Father. No wonder that Jesus declares, "Don't grip me, for I have not yet ascended to the Father." Instead, Jesus issues a commission, "Go to my brothers and tell them, 'I am ascending to my Father and your Father, to my God and your God.'" The use of the term *brothers* instead of *disciples* is deliberate and explained at once by the phrase "my Father and your Father." Jesus' oneness with the Father and with humanity has created a community of the Spirit in which we all are sisters and brothers and, emphatically, children of God.

Preachers should not psychologize the passage or romanticize the intimacy between Mary and Jesus, lest the theological agenda be lost.[61] Certainly Jesus, as a good shepherd, loves his sheep, and Mary is assuredly a member of the flock. But in the resurrection story, Mary begins in the dark and moves into light. Finally she accepts the evangelical commission in full faith; she leaves the "Rabboni" she has known, and says, "I have seen the Lord."

The Disciples in a Locked Room

Luke has told a story of Jesus appearing before disciples gathered in Jerusalem. John's story is highly stylized and very different indeed. In a few verses (20:19-23), John draws together the gift of peace, the commissioning of the community, and the breathing-in of the Spirit for ministry. John constitutes the community with a remarkably structured theology.

[19]Now on the evening of that day, the first day of the week, when the doors were locked by the disciples for fear of the Jews, Jesus came and stood among them, and said, "Peace to you." [20]When he had said this, he showed them both his hands and his side. The disciples, on seeing the Lord, rejoiced. [21]Then Jesus said to them again, "Peace to you. As the Father has sent me, I also send you." [22]When he had said this, he blew into them, saying, "Receive Holy Spirit. [23]Whose sins you forgive, they are forgiven. Whose you retain, they are retained."

---

[61] For a helpful study of the whole passage, see G. R. O'Day, *The Word Disclosed: John's Story and Narrative Preaching* (Saint Louis: CBP Press, 1987), 100–105.

In v. 19 we have the second of three references to "the first day of the week." Almost certainly, John is eager to relate resurrection to the usual time for Christian worship. The disciples are gathered in a locked room "for fear of the Jews."[62] Here John is portraying worldly opposition that the church must face. At the start of the story, the church responds in a typical way; it locks itself in! But the risen Christ appears and says, "Peace." "Peace" (*šālôm*) is a usual greeting, but here it functions as a revelatory word (Judges 6:23; Dan. 10:19) and as an assurance to the frightened disciples.

Jesus then proceeds to display "both his hands and his side" (19:34-37; Zech. 12:10). Here the purpose does not appear to be apologetic as it was in Luke, but a declaration that the wounded, crucified Christ has been raised. On seeing the risen Lord, the disciples rejoice as Jesus said they would — "I will see you again, and your hearts will rejoice" (16:16-24). The second "Peace to you" functions as a conferral; Jesus gives peace to the community as he promised (14:27). A formal commissioning follows: "As the Father has sent me, I also send you." Thus John links the community to Christ's own ministry, a theme that has been articulated in the so-called high-priestly prayer — "As you have sent me into the world, so I have sent them into the world" (17:18).

In v. 22, Jesus gives his disciples the Spirit. Notice that in John we do not have a separate, historicized Pentecost as Luke provides in Acts 2. Instead the conferral of the Spirit is connected with resurrection, perhaps reflecting a more primitive tradition. Jesus "blew into them, saying, 'Receive Holy Spirit.'" The odd verb "blew" obviously refers to the creation story (Gen. 2:7) in which God blows the breath of life into Earthling. Here Jesus gives a new living Spirit to the community.[63]

The final statement — "Whose sins you forgive, they are forgiven. Whose you retain, they are retained" — has occasioned controversy.[64] The saying is somewhat similar to Matthew 18:18, which offers a procedure for handling disputes among Christians. Here, however, the saying is connected to the commission of the church and the conferral of the Spirit. Thus, in the Spirit of Christ, the community can declare

---

[62] J. L. Martyn discusses estrangement from "the Jews" in the Gospel; see his *History & Theology in the Fourth Gospel*, 2d ed. (Nashville: Abingdon, 1979).

[63] On the conferring of the Spirit, see discussion in Schnackenburg, *The Gospel according to St. John*, 3:324-26, and in Brown, *The Gospel according to John (xiii-xxi)*, 1036-39, as well as Brown's study of "The Paraclete," in ibid., 1135-44. See also G. Johnston, "The Spirit-Paraclete in the Gospel of John," *Perspective* 9 (Pittsburgh Theological Seminary) (1968): 29-37.

[64] Brown, *The Gospel according to John (xiii-xxi)*, 1039-45.

the forgiveness of sins as a part of the gospel message. Such preaching can evoke both gratitude among liberated sinners who believe and a "hardening of heart" among self-righteous unbelievers.[65]

The passage is exceedingly difficult to preach because it has little narrative movement. Instead it hands out a theology of the church as constituted by the risen Christ. The church has received shalom, although it lives in a fearful world. The church continues the ministry of Christ — "As the Father has sent me, I also send you." Christ's ministry includes the forgiveness of sins. What animates the church in its ministry? Nothing less than the Spirit of Christ, which is God's Holy Spirit.

The Story of "Doubting Thomas"

Although the story has been a pulpit favorite,[66] it is surprisingly complex and almost brutal.

> [24]Thomas, one of the Twelve, called the twin [Didymus], was not with the disciples when Jesus came. [25]So, the other disciples kept telling him, "We have seen the Lord!" But Thomas said to them, "Unless I see the mark of the nails in his hands, put my finger into the nail holes, and my hand into his side, I'll never believe."
> [26]Eight days later, once again his disciples were inside, and Thomas was with them. Although doors were shut, Jesus came and stood among them and said, "Peace to you." [27]Then he said to Thomas, "Take your finger, here are my hands; take your fist, jam it in my side. Don't be faithless, but be faithful!" [28]Thomas answered him saying, "My Lord and my God." [29]Jesus said to him, "Because you've seen me, you believe. Blessed are those who haven't seen, but believe."

The original ending of the Gospel of John is explicit:

> [30]Now Jesus did many other signs in the presence of his disciples, which are not written in this book. [31]But these are written so that you may come to believe that Jesus is the Messiah, the Son of God, and that through believing you may have life in his name.

The Gospel tells a story so that, hearing of Jesus, we may believe. We can believe the word given us. But Thomas heard the testimony of the disciples and refused to believe; he demanded a sign: "Unless I see . . ." In the twentieth chapter, we are given examples of faith — Peter, the beloved disciple, Mary, and finally Thomas the doubter.

---

[65] Paul speaks of the same problem with respect to the gospel message: "To the one a fragrance from death to death, to the other a fragrance from life to life" (2 Cor. 2:15-16).

[66] I have previously studied the story of Thomas in "Homiletic Resources for the Easter Season," 71-75.

In v. 24, Thomas is tagged as "one of the Twelve." Matthew and Luke have been explicit, noting that with Judas absent, there are only eleven disciples (Matt. 28:16; Luke 24:33). John is using a title for the disciples that circulated in the early church, "the Twelve." Although the other disciples repeatedly tell Thomas, "We have seen the Lord!," he stubbornly voices his demand, "Unless I see the mark of the nails, . . . I'll never believe." Does mention of the wounds imply that Thomas wants to be sure that the risen one is actually the same Jesus who was crucified? Or does the verse stress seeing rather than merely hearing the good news?

The reference to eight days later (v. 26) may function in two ways: It reestablishes the "Lord's Day" that John has mentioned previously (vv. 1 and 19), and it may also have symbolic weight, for "the eighth day" was a term used of the new creation in Jewish/Christian lore.[67] Again, although the doors were shut, Jesus appears and says, "Peace." Then he turns to Thomas and is less than genial. The syntax of v. 27 is rough: "Take your finger, here are my hands; take your fist, jam it in my side. Don't be faithless, but be faithful!" All those sermons on how Jesus welcomes doubters may miss the mark. Perhaps, as Paul Tillich remarked, we are justified by doubt as well as faith, but not here. Here Thomas is sharply challenged by the risen Christ; he was supposed to believe the gospel message and did not. But the word of Christ backs Thomas down, down on his knees: "My Lord and my God," he exclaims. No doubt Thomas is reciting an early Christian liturgical/confessional formula.[68]

Then Jesus offers an extra beatitude:[69] "Blessed are those who haven't seen, but believe" (v. 29). All through the Gospel of John there have been "signs." Although people repeatedly believe by doing the word of Christ, their faith is confirmed and indeed enlarged by the signs they are given. The Gospel of John may regard the resurrection as the ultimate sign and, therefore, imply that there will be no more

---

[67] Brown, *The Gospel according to John (xiii–xxi)*, 1025, also cites the Epistle of Barnabas 15:9: "We celebrate with gladness the eighth day in which Jesus also rose from the dead and appeared and ascended into heaven."

[68] See, for example, Rev. 4:11, where twenty-four elders fall down before the throne of God, singing a doxology, "You are worthy, our Lord and God, to receive glory and honor and power." For discussion, see C. K. Barrett, *The Gospel according to St. John* (London: S.P.C.K., 1965), 476–77, and also M. H. Shepherd, Jr., *The Paschal Liturgy and the Apocalypse* (Richmond, Va.: John Knox Press, 1960).

[69] C. Westermann, *Blessing in the Bible and the Life of the Church*, trans. K. Crim (Philadelphia: Fortress Press, 1978).

signs. Now we are called upon to believe on the basis of the word alone, the word of the gospel message. The beatitude is scarcely a call to blind faith, which, of course, can harbor bigotry. No, properly, true faith seeks understanding. Now we are called to hear and, in hearing, to believe the good news without demanding that God produce dazzling signs.

An Appearing at the Sea of Tiberias

The last chapter of the Gospel of John, chapter 21, is an addendum. The Gospel was written and rewritten as the peripatetic community moved about the ancient world.[70] Then a chapter was added as an epilogue, no doubt by a final editor/writer.

[1] After these events, again Jesus disclosed himself to the disciples by the Sea of Tiberias; he disclosed himself in this way. [2] Simon Peter, Thomas called the Twin, Nathanael from Cana in Galilee, the sons of Zebedee, and two other disciples of his were all together. [3] Simon Peter said to them, "I'm going fishing." They said to him, "Come on, we'll go with you." They went out and got into the boat, but that night they caught nothing. [4] When morning came, Jesus stood on the shore, although the disciples did not know it was Jesus. [5] He said to them, "Boys, you haven't any food, have you?" They answered him, "No." [6] So he said to them, "Cast the net on the right side of the boat, and you'll find some." They cast and they were not able to haul it in because of the number of fish.

[7] Then the disciple whom Jesus loved said to Peter, "It is the Lord." When Simon heard that it was the Lord, he pulled on his shirt because he was naked, and threw himself into the sea. [8] The other disciples came along in a boat, dragging the net full of fish, for they were not far from land—about a hundred yards off.

[9] When they got up on land, they saw a charcoal fire prepared, with fish lying on it, and bread. [10] Jesus said to them, "Bring some of the fish you just caught." [11] So Simon Peter drew the net full of big fish to shore, a hundred and fifty-three of them. Although there were many, the net was not torn. [12] Then Jesus said to them, "Come and have breakfast." Now none of the disciples dared ask him, "Who are you?" They knew that it was the Lord. [13] Then Jesus came and took the bread and gave it to them, and the fish in the same way. [14] Now this was the third time that Jesus was disclosed to the disciples after he was raised from the dead.

The fish story that begins chapter 21 has puzzled scholars for centuries. Obviously the story matches up with Luke 5:1-11, where it is told as a call to discipleship: "From now on you will be catching people. . . . They left everything and followed him" (Luke 5:10-11).[71]

---

[70] See R. E. Brown, *The Community of the Beloved Disciple* (New York: Paulist Press, 1979), and also O. Cullmann, *The Johannine Circle,* trans. J. Bowden (Philadelphia: Westminster Press, 1976).

[71] See a remarkable study of the fishing metaphor in W. H. Wuellner, *The Meaning of "Fishers of Men"* (Philadelphia: Westminster Press, 1967).

But Luke does not have the added episode of the fish fry found in John 21:9-14. Was the story a resurrection appearance that Luke turned into a call? Or, conversely, was the story a call that John has transformed into a post-Easter appearance?[72] Could the story have been a "sign," in fact the third sign, in a sign collection available to John?[73] The problems may never be resolved. Meanwhile we have a splendid symbolic story to preach, a story that clearly connects resurrection and the church's missionary task.

Note that the story begins as if the resurrection has not yet happened, even though the editor has supplied the connective phrase "after these events." The fishing trip takes place on the Sea of Galilee, which was called the Sea of Tiberias in the second century. Earlier in the Gospel (6:16-21), Jesus had manifested himself (*egō eimi,* "I am") by striding the waves of the same sea. Seven disciples are involved, and some scholars read in the number a reference to the seven churches mentioned in Revelation, but such speculation is probably overdrawn.

"I'm going fishing," says Peter, and the others join him. Notice, the verse implies that after the crucifixion they return to their previous occupations. Of course, fishing is a familiar metaphor for the church's evangelical task; we are to fish for people with news of the gospel message. In the darkness, they catch nothing. Is the reference to "night" a symbol? Perhaps, for the story is told as if the light of Easter Day has not yet dawned. In v. 4, a contrast is established; with the dawn, Jesus appears, although "the disciples did not know it was Jesus." "Boys," says Jesus, using an affectionate term (*paidia*), "you haven't any food, have you?" Does the remark echo an earlier story of the loaves and fishes (6:1-15)? Clearly, as fishers of people, the disciples have failed; they have not even had a nibble.

In v. 6, Jesus issues a command, "Cast the net on the right side of the boat," and the disciples do the word of Jesus. Throughout the Gospel, John tends to regard the doing of Jesus' word as an act of faith. The disciples obey and their net is loaded with fish. Whereupon the beloved disciple announces, "It is the Lord."

At once the disciples head for shore, Peter, half-naked, leading the way. Just as in 20:1-10, the story of Peter and the other disciple at the

---

[72] For summaries of the discussion, see R. Brown, *The Gospel according to John (xiii–xxi),* 1077–85; Schnackenburg, *The Gospel according to St. John,* 3:341–51; and Smith, *Easter Gospels,* 171–76.

[73] So argues R. T. Fortna, *The Gospel of Signs: A Reconstruction of the Narrative Source Underlying the Fourth Gospel* (Cambridge: Cambridge University Press, 1970), 87–98.

tomb, we get a contrast drawn between the two disciples. The beloved disciple declares faith while Peter rushes toward shore. Again, we must caution against reading a rivalry into the story, particularly in chapter 21 where the relationship between the two disciples is treated with unusual sensitivity (vv. 15-25). Why do we have mention of Peter's putting on a shirt in order to leap into the water? We do not know, although the same verb (*diazōnnynai,* to tie on clothes) is used of Jesus in the footwashing scene (13:4).

On shore, the disciples spot fish on a fire with bread nearby. John now uses a different word for fish, *opsarion,* a word used previously in the story of the feeding of the crowd (chap. 6). Again, Jesus issues a command, "Bring some of the fish," he says. Peter obeys and drags in the net, untorn, full of big fish. Is reference to the untorn net a symbol of unity? Perhaps. Knowing that John is fond of using significant numbers, scholars have had a field day trying to figure out why the number of fish, 153, is mentioned.[74] Perhaps the large number functions as does mention of the many, many gallons of wine in the story of the marriage feast at Cana; or, perhaps, by mathematical ingenuity, it is a perfect number—in either case the number would be a symbol of fulfillment. Notice that in an expression of unity the catch of fish is added to those already caught.

In vv. 12-13, we have another meal in which Jesus takes bread and distributes it to disciples, and, as with the Emmaus Road story, the disciples know the Lord. Obviously we have still another eucharistic allusion, a breakfast Lord's Supper. Here the Lord sustains the community in its mission.

The passage addresses the contemporary church. Certainly our missionary impulse has not resulted in much of a catch lately. Yet the passage hands out a hope-filled image of fulfillment, the vision of a church united, gathered from different places, in a great, bright morning eucharist with the risen Lord. Meanwhile, what is our task? We must do the word of the Lord.

---

[74] For speculation on the number of fish, see Brown, *The Gospel according to John (xiii–xxi),* 1074–76; Smith, *Easter Gospels,* 180–81, provides still another solution.

PART TWO

*The Passion of Jesus Christ*_____

CHAPTER **5**

The Patterns
of Sin _____

TWO LARGE CATHOLIC parishes were located in roughly the same neighborhood in a midwestern city. Yet one congregation prospered while the other dwindled. Apparently the problem was not program or the quality of priesthood. Priests were changed around, and church programs were essentially the same. If anything, the dwindling parish seemed to have the better location with more convenient parking facilities. So what was the problem?

A survey seemed to indicate that the difference in the parishes was primarily architectural. In one church—the shrinking congregation—there was an old-fashioned crucifix with a quite realistic Christ nailed to a wooden cross. In the other church, there was an open-work, contemporary, decorative cross. When quizzed, young parents explained that they did not want their children to be troubled by the image of crucified Jesus Christ.

The figure of Christ crucified is troubling. His violent death confronts us all with the huge fact of sin. So let us begin by standing before the realism of Christ crucified and asking: What does the cross say about the shape of human sinfulness?

The Dark Mirror of the Cross

In every age preachers have painted a picture of the cross in their sermons; they have insisted that somehow, in some way we were "there when they crucified my Lord." Our sins stand out clearly reflected in the dark mirror of the cross. Although faces may change and costumes

95

alter — Roman robes are somewhat different from designer jeans —
pulpit strategy has been much the same; preachers hold up the cross
and say, "See, there is sin, our sin." The strategy is perennial but,
strange to say, the way in which sin is depicted changes in every sweeping cultural moment.

These days preachers tend to picture sin as an inner disposition. "We
all suffer from a heart disease — a spiritual heart disease," says Billy
Graham.[1] What crucified Christ? Why, our inner fears and guilts,
hostilities and anxieties; the cross happened because of a human pathol-
ogy. Nowadays, sin is primarily a psychological problem; it is a "heart
disease." Whether sin is labeled hubris or egocentricity or overreaching
desire, it is located within the self, in individual selves, and is expressed
in a range of unsavory symptoms, especially anxiety and hostility.
Reinhold Niebuhr described the mechanics of sin in some detail, linking sin with desire and anxiety.[2] Billy Graham summed it up in the
single word *heart.* But both Graham and Niebuhr put forth personal
generic models. Somehow, Jesus Christ threatened the sovereign selves
of people and, afraid, they lashed out in ungoverned hostility. Sinful
human beings crucified the Lord. For nearly fifty years, preachers have
described sin as an inner fault that seems to show up primarily in a
pattern of psychological symptoms.

When preachers push further to uncover the sources of sin they
usually draw on psychological explanation. Preachers will tell us that
guiltiness cannot bear to be exposed, particularly by a perfect purity
(i.e., Jesus) and therefore will seek to destroy whatever causes guilt — a
psychological analysis. Or they may argue that love is frightening,
especially to self-contained persons; we fear losing ourselves in love.
Therefore when Christ comes loving us and asking our love in return,
we respond first with a terrible fear and then with defensive hostility;
we cannot, indeed will not, risk love — again, a psychological explanation. Some ministers, particularly those with advanced training in
counseling, may even attempt to explain the mechanics of transference.
The hatreds we harbor from early childhood denials and subsequently
have turned toward ourselves must be drained cathartically for us to
become healthy. Just as an able psychoanalytically trained therapist

---

[1] Billy Graham, "In God Let Us Trust," in *And Our Defense Is Sure: Sermons and
Addresses from the Pentagon Protestant Pulpit,* eds. H. D. Moore, E. A. Ham, and C. E.
Hobgood (Nashville: Abingdon, 1964), 152.
[2] R. Niebuhr, *The Nature and Destiny of Man,* vol. 1 (New York: Charles Scribner's
Sons, 1949), esp. chap. 7.

will accept the transference of a patient, so Christ on the cross is a victim of human transference. We vent ourselves on Christ and, in so doing, become psychologically whole again. Ever since news of Dr. Freud floated across the Atlantic early in the century, psychological sermons have been on the rise.[3] The trend can be traced from Fosdick to Peale and beyond.[4] In the 1950s, psychology and existential personalism combined to produce a widespread "triumph of the therapeutic" in American pulpits. Sum it up and say that in most mainline pulpits, sin is a psychological condition.

Now we do not mean to suggest that psychological struggles are inconsequential; they are not. Our inner conflicts are real, painful, urgent, and often debilitating. What is more, our inner conflicts *are* tangled up with sinfulness; psychology and theology seldom can be neatly compartmentalized.[5] We all struggle for self-acceptance; trying to find some amiable way to reconcile the "me" and the "myself" within us. Further, most of us pass through times of profound depression, are freaked by fantasies, or suffer periodic bouts of fierce anxiety. Dwight L. Moody once admitted, "I've had more trouble with D. L. Moody than any other man I know."[6] Most of us could write our own names into the quote; we do have trouble with us. So obviously the pulpit must address the inward anguish of human beings, the frequently tragic dramas of the soul. Most of us need all the help we can get.

But, mark the truth, an inner one-to-one self is not the whole self. If Narcissus gazes too long into the mirrored pool, he can tumble down and drown in his own reflection. A wider world is also formed in human consciousness, a social world. Has Protestantism been too much influenced by Luther, who tended to describe the liberations of the gospel in rather personal terms? Justification is not an inner miracle alone; it

---

[3] Although Freud (1856–1939) did much significant work in the nineteenth century, his thought did not become widely available in America until around 1920. The novels of Ellen Glasgow, the dramas of Eugene O'Neill, and the homiletics of Fosdick are witness to an emerging awareness of the so-called new psychology.

[4] See my analysis, "Preaching in an *Un*brave New World," *The Spire* (Vanderbilt University Divinity School) 13, no. 1 (Summer/Fall 1988).

[5] E. Farley, "Psychopathology and Human Evil: Toward a Phenomenology and Theology of the Problematic of Human Being" (unpublished manuscript). The substance of his argument also appears in "Psychopathology and Human Evil: Toward a Theory of Differentiation," in *Crosscurrents in Phenomenology,* ed. R. Bruzina and B. Wilshire (The Hague: Nijhoff, 1978).

[6] Cited in *A Treasury of Sermon Illustrations,* ed. C. L. Wallis (Nashville: Abingdon-Cokesbury Press, 1950), 254.

has social concomitants.[7] We are more than privacies before God, a fact that the Great Commandment acknowledges. Personalist preaching has reduced the scope of the gospel, slicing off the social shape of sin and scaling down the high and holy God of Israel to a salve for inner problems.[8] But we do not stand one-to-one before God; there is a neighborhood in each of us that cannot be ignored.

Of course, in a way, psychological explanations of sin are inevitable. To be blunt: If we are going to preach personal salvation, then we are bound to describe sin in personal and inward terms. Many preachers suppose that, although ultimately heaven may be crowded, human beings are saved one-by-one via conversion and decision. Often salvation is presented as an inner miracle, a born-again self, distinguished by peace and joy and a fine, free sense of well-being. Come to Jesus and, in a personal relationship to Jesus, get saved. Jesus is an intimate savior who offers us inner adjustment now and some hope of heavenly bliss hereafter. Such a gospel will demand as its corollary an inward, psychological definition of sin; sin is conflict, unhappiness, and, above all, a lack of self-esteem. Psychology patched on to the gospel of nineteenth-century pietism has defined our pulpit message.[9]

A Look at the Passion Tradition

If we turn to scripture, we catch sight of a different picture. In scripture we do not bump into a bunch of unhappy people driven by inner, psychological hang-ups. No, the passion stories tell us of groups — chief priests, the Sanhedrin, swaggering Roman soldiers, Pilate's court, not to forget "patriots," Pharisees, scribes, Herodians, frightened disciples, and, of course, the festival crowd that filled Jerusalem. Groups. Whenever we do get mention of a particular person, the person is identified as a group member: Caiaphas is a high priest, Pilate is a Roman procurator, Barabbas is a robber (read: local insurrectionist). Although individuals are involved in the passion, they are seldom singled out for

---

[7] On the social meanings of justification, see A. Miller, *The Renewal of Man: A Twentieth Century Essay on Justification by Faith* (Garden City, N.Y.: Doubleday, 1955), esp. chaps. 4 and 5.

[8] See the argument in my article "Preaching in an *Un*brave New World." In therapeutic preaching, God is the one who solves our psychological hang-ups, a good carer who ministers to our bad feelings. But notice, in such preaching, God ceases to have any relationship to the wider sweep of human history or to social problems.

[9] See R. N. Bellah et al., *Habits of the Heart: Individualism and Commitment in American Life* (Berkeley: University of California Press, 1985), chap. 9.

psychological analysis. No, instead they function within groups and often out of group loyalty; they are motivated by their ideological commitments. So the Bible presents a very different picture: Yes, as an individual I may well struggle with inner dispositions, but in a group I become deadly.

At the time of Christ the guild of temple priests was powerful. In part, their power was conferred. When Israel stumbled back from exile, the rebuilding of the temple was a symbol of the people's new beginning.[10] But then, later, when the land was overrun by alien armies, all that Israel had left was their temple and the priesthood; the temple was Israel's identity. What is more, the temple was far and away the largest economic enterprise in Palestine.[11] Does the phrase "religious establishment" help? The temple was not merely a modest form of organized religion; it was power — proud, indigenous power. So, obviously, Jesus was a troubling figure. Those whom the temple excluded, he included — "free grace" will always threaten entrenched religion. Like Jeremiah before him, he accused the temple cult of lifeless institutionalism and did so, what is more, right in the midst of a hyped-up temple building program. Finally, he attacked where it hurt most; he directly disrupted the cash flow by chasing away moneychangers.[12] Why was Christ crucified? Easy: He was crucified in the name of God. Jesus was accused by the priestly temple guild of being antireligious, indeed anti-God; to them, he was an obvious blasphemer.

But, please note, religion was not merely lodged in the temple. Israel's religion was moral and its form was legal. Thus the religious establishment included not only priests but guardians of the law, the orthodox Sadducees and pietist Pharisees — both "conservatives" and "moderates," to borrow labels from the currently encamped Southern Baptist Convention.[13] In both cases Jesus was viewed with alarm because he seemed somewhat cavalier with regard to the law, God's holy law, in a law and order world. Now, all things considered, the

---

[10] See Haggai 1, in which the prophet urges the rebuilding of the temple.

[11] See R. A. Horsley and J. S. Hanson, *Bandits, Prophets, and Messiahs: Popular Movements at the Time of Jesus* (San Francisco: Harper & Row, 1985), 54–55; also G. Theissen, *Sociology of Early Palestinian Christians,* trans. J. Bowden (Philadelphia: Fortress Press, 1978), 42–45; and M. Hengel, *Judaism and Hellenism,* vol. 1 (Philadelphia: Fortress Press, 1974), 23–27.

[12] See E. P. Sanders, *Jesus and Judaism* (Philadelphia: Fortress Press, 1985), 61–76.

[13] On the Sadducees, see *The Interpreter's Dictionary of the Bible,* ed. G. A. Buttrick, vol. 4 (New York: Abingdon, 1962), 160–63. On Pharisees, see E. Rivkin, *A Hidden Revolution* (Nashville: Abingdon, 1978), and also W. D. Davies, *Introduction to Pharisaism* (Philadelphia: Fortress Press, 1967).

usual Lutheran portrait of Jesus as an early day Martin Luther who preached "justification by grace through faith" over against the law of the Hebrew scriptures is surely a distortion.[14] As a faithful Jew, Jesus endorsed God's law, but he was critical when the law legislated against outcasts, burdened the poor, or displaced God. Moreover, because Jesus preached news of God's new order, he may have promoted the notion of a new Torah.[15] Thus, all through his ministry, Jesus was in tension with the guardians of God's law. So, again, Jesus was labeled antireligious; he was a libertine antinomian as well as an obvious blasphemer.

When it came to politics, Jesus was also in trouble. He was crucified under Pontius Pilate. Crucifixion was a Roman cruelty reserved for rebel slaves, habitual criminals, and political insurrectionists.[16] So, embarrassingly, Jesus was sentenced as a political threat, in a word, as a subversive. The accusation "political subversive" was easy to establish. Jesus seemed to preach the insurrectionist slogan, "No king but God!" Further, Jesus announced the coming of a new sociopolitical order, a "kingdom of God," and, as a corollary, the moral bankruptcy of the current social order—Rome included. Perhaps he was harmless enough, a somewhat ludicrous hillbilly preacher with a small following, but he was from Galilee, a hotbed of insurrection, and, well, better safe than sorry.[17] The Pax Romana was stretched tight, and was kept in place by the removal of any even potential opposition. Although, generally, Roman law was impressive, the preservation of Roman power frequently superseded judicial due process.

Political patterns in Palestine were complex. In addition to Herod's supporters, Herodians, who backed a calculated policy of accommodation with the Roman occupation, there were patriotic, proto-zealot[18]

---

[14] Sanders, *Jesus and Judaism*, 245–69.

[15] See W. D. Davies, *Torah in the Messianic Age and/or the Age to Come* (Philadelphia: Society of Biblical Literature, 1952).

[16] See M. Hengel, *Crucifixion* (Philadelphia: Fortress Press, 1977), chaps. 7 and 8.

[17] Josephus describes Galileans as a turbulent and rebellious people, ready at the drop of a hat to rise up against the Romans; see *Antiquities of the Jews* 17.10.2; *History of the Jewish War* 2.10.6; 3.3.2.

[18] A recent study by R. A. Horsley and J. S. Hanson argues convincingly that "the old Zealot concept has been shown to be a historical fiction" because the Zealots did not come into being until 67–68 C.E. Instead, at the time of Christ there were local brigands and representatives of the Fourth Philosophy. Thus I use the term proto-zealot. See Horsley and Hanson, *Bandits*, xiii–xv.

resistance movements, a so-called Fourth Philosophy.[19] Their cause had considerable public support. Not only did they appeal to suppressed nationalism, but they could inflame the overtaxed poor in a land where around 10 percent of the population controlled nearly 90 percent of the wealth.[20] Jesus was suspect on two counts: his pacifism and the antipatriotic theme of a new, other "kingdom." Thus Jesus was regarded as neither a patriot nor a militant activist; his credentials were suspect. Some scholars suggest that the patriots whipped up the crowd in Jerusalem to pick Barabbas, a popular insurrectionist, in preference to Jesus.[21] Jesus' political position was precarious indeed; he was caught in the crossfire between Rome and the Fourth Philosophy, with Herodians off to the side sniping at him as well. His crime was political; he was considered a sure subversive. Pious Christians may have some difficulty in admitting Jesus' political influence, but there is no doubt that he was condemned as a political threat. Remember, crucifixion was a Roman punishment for political crime.

There is a famous joke about an older minister advising seminarians on how to make it in the ministry: "If you want to be successful in the pulpit," the old man pontificates, "steer clear of two subjects — politics and religion." Well, apparently someone failed to clue in Jesus. He was crucified as a subversive and a blasphemer — politics and religion. As a result, according to the biblical record, Jesus was sentenced to death by a concert of collective bodies that were both religious and political.[22] Oddly enough, the apostle Paul sees the picture clearly. Who crucified Christ? Not human being as a psychological isolate — the self, in fears and guilts and hates. No. Christ was crucified by human beings in their social patterns. How does Paul put it?: "None of the rulers of this age understood . . . for if they had, they would not have crucified the Lord of glory" (1 Cor. 2:8). What does he mean by "rulers of this age"? Paul is pointing to the social patterns of evil, the "principalities and powers,"

---

[19] The term Fourth Philosophy is from Josephus, who uses it in connection with a tax revolt led by "Judas, a Gaulonite" and Saddouk. By Fourth Philosophy, Josephus means a position added to that of Essenes, Sadducees, and Pharisees (*Antiquities of the Jews* 18.1).

[20] A statistic cited in a public address by R. Scroggs at United Theological Seminary in New Brighton, Minn.

[21] See discussion in G. Sloyan, *Jesus on Trial* (Philadelphia: Fortress Press, 1973), 61.

[22] L. Boff sees the religious/political condemnation of Christ quite clearly; see his *Passion of Christ, Passion of the World: The Facts, Their Interpretation, and Their Meaning Yesterday and Today* (Maryknoll, N.Y.: Orbis Books, 1987).

which hold human beings in captivity. Although we may preach personal sin and personal salvation, the Bible does not. The Bible sees the social shape of sin.

Sin and Social Identity

Maybe it is time for the pulpit to paint a more sophisticated picture of Golgotha. What do you see from the cross of Christ? You see human beings, yes, but specifically human beings defined within their social roles. Thus, you do not see Mr. A at the cross, a discrete human being with a name attached. No, you see Mr. A who is a Roman soldier and a true believer, sworn to uphold the Pax Romana; or Mr. A who is a pious champion of the law, a man who prays faithfully, and is a dedicated member of the Pharisaic party. To reduce us to single selves with nothing more than sin's psychological problems is to truncate human identity. Who is present at the cross? Why, you can see lawyers and priests, soldiers and zealous nationalists, religious conservatives and moderates. Such a picture is truer to the first-century world and, at the same time, truer to the social world of today. Incidentally, the social picture is psychologically truer. Our identities—who we are—are shaped by social patterning. If someone asks me who I am, will I not answer by citing my memberships? I am a Christian, a theological professor, a recalcitrant Presbyterian, an American, a Democrat, and so forth, right down to more singular groupings—I am an early riser, a book lover, a foreign car driver, and a long-time fan of the hapless Chicago Cubs. My memberships define me. More, they provide me with some degree of social self-justification. For within my social groups, I belong, I am accepted, indeed I am ratified. I cannot be reduced to an inward psychological arena without being deformed. From the cross of Christ, what do we see? We see human beings collectively patterned within a social world.

So, perhaps, we must broaden our definition of sin. Sin cannot be reduced to some inner fault within the self, for example, hubris; sin is a social captivity. Sin involves more than a psychological disposition; sin involves the preservation of social identities. If we are defined by the social affiliations in which "we live and move and have our being," then, above all, we must defend our social selves, namely our groups. If opponents attack our groups, they threaten us at the deepest level of our beings. When threatened, we rally to protect our groups and, yes, to destroy oppositions. According to scripture, God names us, and gives us our true identity. But, instead, we choose to secure ourselves in this world through the social groups in which we live. Thus, if we are American, it is easy to become "America-firsters" supporting a power-packed defense budget. If we work for a corporation, it is easy to be a company person eager to down all competitors. If we are church people, we can slide into an extreme denominationalism — rah-rah Presbyterians or rah-rah Methodists or rah-rah fundamentalists — even though intellectually we may suspect that our religious loyalties always turn demonic. Is sin defined by our social commitments? Perhaps, for we preserve who we are by protecting our social affiliations.

How do we preserve our social alignments? We seek to protect each group's time and space. So I will strive to enlarge my group's size, that is, its space, and to enhance its social power; in religious circles, I will chatter about "evangelism" — "a million more in '94!" Likewise, I will do all I can to ensure survival of my group, to keep it going for at least as long as I live. If my group is threatened, I will seek to defend it against all rivals. How do we humans sin? We sin in our corporate identities. We sin as Americans, as Republicans, Democrats, Socialists, liberals, conservatives, or what you will. Religiously, we sin either in competitive denominationalism — as Southern Baptists, Presbyterians, Catholics — or in theological identifications, as conservatives, liberals, Bible-thumping fundamentalists, and so forth. Our causes interlock and are many. They can be political, economic, racial, ethnic, regional, national, or connected with social class distinctions. Sin cannot be defined in terms of a personally motivated individual actor alone; we do most of our damage corporately. Thus, corporate power must be featured in any theological definition of sin. No wonder that when the Bible offers a diagnosis of sin, it depicts social groupings gathered at the cross.

The Return of the "Powers That Be"

Now let us turn around and acknowledge a change in the American public mind.[23] These days the people to whom we preach are beginning to sense their social captivities. Once more they have begun to catch sight of systemic evil, what the Bible calls the "powers that be."[24] Yes, back in the 1950s, Americans were much concerned with psychological

---

[23] Much of the argument that follows parallels material in my *Preaching Jesus Christ* (Philadelphia: Fortress Press, 1988), chap. 4.

[24] See n. 10, chap. 4, above.

structures that inhibited and prevented a full, free life. They saw themselves struggling with demonic inward forces — depression, obsessive-compulsive neuroses, schizophrenic patterns, somatized hysteria, and so on. So, if the pulpit offered inner peace, self-acceptance, personal happiness, and a positive self-image, people perked up and listened. They were eager to be born-again inside themselves. But now in the 1990s there seems to have been a subtle change of mind. Like dark-edged thunderheads that can disrupt the summer season, cloudy principalities and powers have suddenly massed in our awareness. We are beginning to realize that we live under the domination of collective forces. Yes, perhaps Jesus can tinker with our inner world or renovate our souls, but still we can be trapped in systems, gripped by ideologies, or coerced by our own corporate commitments. The terrible truth about America can be stated baldly: We have millions of born-again Jesus people who support the most appalling national policies. In our warmed hearts we are not killers, but we support an enlarged defense budget based on technological death; we crave stealth bombers. And in our religiously renovated souls we are not heartless, yet we endorse an economic policy that grinds out street people — now more than three million huddled in our urban doorways. What can we do about people who have accepted Jesus as their personal Savior but who appear to be trapped by demonic political enthusiasms? What good is a heart packed with Jesus if we are still captive to the powers that be? What we need is a new, born-again world!

Preachers cannot bypass the issue by simply deleting the social world from their sermons. Religion does not thrive in the province of the heart alone. So we can no longer stand in our pulpits and hand out personal salvation as a bundle of inner happiness as well as hope for a heavenly future full of bliss. Such a gospel is ultimately a cop-out. In many churches devoted to personal salvation, the social world is of no concern; it is either inconsequential stage scenery for dramas of personal redemption or is dismissed as hopelessly wicked. Long ago Gnostics offered their devotees inward release and peace; their Jesus was a mind Savior for people in the know. Of course the mundane social world was still around, so in some cases, prudently, they endorsed a second "savior" to stabilize the world.[25] Perhaps we have tumbled into the same heresy. Jesus is our heart Savior, but when it comes to politics or economics we eagerly embrace some other "savior"—

---

[25] So argues A. D. Galloway, *The Cosmic Christ* (London: James Nisbet, 1951).

communism or capitalism or free enterprise or fundamentalism or whatever. When people pick a second savior, its name is always spelled the same, I-S-M! Whenever we limit the realm of salvation we stumble into heresy. When the early church leaders repudiated Gnosticism they did so because they insisted that Jesus Christ was Savior of the whole wide world.

So we are called to preach a Christ who can deliver us by redeeming the social dominations that hold us captive. How can "new birth" be new if we are reborn into the same old power-dominated world? People nowadays dream of a wider liberation than inward renewal; they long for a new world in which to live, a liberated world.[26] For the only way we can truly be new people is within a transformed society. Rather clearly Jesus saw the issue. He did not preach inner renewal alone; he announced the coming of a new order — "The kingdom of God has come near." And early Christians, if the Epistles are any witness, preached a similar gospel. Does not Paul look forward to a time when the risen Christ will bring under subjection "every ruler and every authority and power" (1 Cor. 15:24)? Yes, in one way the powers that be are no-powers; they are social projections. But they still have sway over the minds of men and women and can coerce us mightily.[27] Jesus Christ is more than a heart Savior and, incidentally, more than an in-house church Savior. As a social symbol, the risen Christ has social potency; ultimately he will establish God's promised new order among us.

Individual or Social Gospel?

The American religious scene has been divided for years. In America, the gospel has been torn between social concern and individualism. Sometimes another dualism adds to the tension, namely, a subjective/objective split. Certainly such tensions were involved in the

---

[26] The theme shows up in contemporary novels; see, for example, recent works by W. Percy, as for example *Lancelot* (New York: Farrar, Straus & Giroux, 1977), 255–57; T. Rogers, *The Confession of a Child of the Century* (New York: Signet, 1973), 310–20; J. Cheever, *Oh What a Paradise It Seems* (New York: Alfred A. Knopf, 1982), 99–100, to cite only a few.

[27] P. L. Berger and T. Luckmann (*The Social Construction of Reality: A Treatise on the Sociology of Knowledge* [Garden City, N.Y.: Doubleday, 1967]) argue that (1) society is a human product; (2) society is an objective reality; and (3) human being is a social product. The sequence describes a kind of process: We project conventional wisdoms and behavioral patterns, give them objective status, and they in turn coerce us, shaping our thought and behavior. In a similar manner the "principalities and powers" are surely human, but are projected and sacralized; in turn they coerce us.

Old School/New School controversies that troubled the church in the eighteenth century. And we can see the same sort of split at the end of the nineteenth century with the social gospel emerging at the same time as revivalism.[28] But, arguably, in spite of tensions, the usual understanding of faith in America has been individualistic and subjective. Certainly Robert Bellah and his team of intrepid sociologists have recently documented American Christianity's individualistic bent in *Habits of the Heart*.[29] Through the years a social interpretation of Christianity has been voiced largely by a mainline minority or by leadership from the African American churches, for example, Walter Rauschenbusch or Martin Luther King, Jr. Recent church history has underscored the split. In the 1950s we witnessed a rise of pulpit personalism as pyschoanalytic and existentialist thought conjoined to produce a therapeutic pulpit. Yet, in the 1960s, social protest erupted in civil rights marches and over American military involvement in Vietnam. The protests of the period did generate some socially concerned preaching, although far less than many suppose. With the silent, somewhat romantic 1970s and the nostalgic 1980s, America reverted to a popular conservative personalism. In recent years, we have seen alternating currents of the individual/social split.

Of course, these days there is little social application of the gospel. Although common people are beginning to sense their social bondage, most mainline pulpits are still oriented personally and therapeutically, perhaps for safety's sake. Reactionary America—the America that gave Ronald Reagan a landslide victory and that largely populates Protestant parishes—does not readily welcome political criticism. If our sermons have social orientation, it is toward the church's mission as a socially compassionate institution. Edward Farley says it well:

> On the one side, the Christian message is preached, counseled, etc. as a biblically rooted message of therapeutic, a resource for assisting individuals to cope not so much with the effects and powers of sin as with the stressful situations of living. On the other side, all the activities of the church and ministry are thought to occur in a complex of institutional

---

[28] See the analysis of recurring conflicts in the paradigm of American Presbyterian history by R. Wuthnow, "The Restructuring of American Presbyterianism: Turmoil in One Denomination," in *The Presbyterian Predicament*, ed. M. Coalter, J. Mulder, and L. Weeks (Louisville, Ky.: Westminster/John Knox Press, 1990), 28–30.

[29] R. Bellah et al., *Habits of the Heart: Individualism and Commitment in American Life* (Berkeley: University of California Press, 1985).

systems which require managing. These two . . . become, then, the framework of contemporary clergy hermeneutics.[30]

But is a personalist gospel "biblically rooted"? No. According to scripture, our struggle is not against blood and flesh, "but against the rulers, against the authorities, against the cosmic powers of this present darkness" (Eph. 6:12). Somehow we who preach must reconsider the gospel message; Jesus Christ can save society as well as the human soul.

We are still entrapped in the split — self or society, subjectivity or objectivity. How hard it is to extricate ourselves from usual categories. Is it possible that we are dealing with distinctions that are far less distinct than we suppose? Perhaps objectivity/subjectivity are, after all, perspectives in human consciousness. Likewise, it is possible that self and society are not as separate as they may seem. Do not self-awareness and social awareness occur in the same consciousness? Do we not deal with a self-in-the-world and, oddly enough, a world-in-the-self as well? Perhaps the world we address is not "out there" at all, but is a world of images, attitudes, slogans, and so forth that is internalized and structured in shared consciousness:

> Each [person], therefore, inevitably lives in a world partly private, but — more importantly — [people] also share larger worlds, on which their private worlds are dependent. These larger worlds are made out of such elements as common physical endowments, the common earth, a common calendar, a common language, common needs, traditions, aspirations, and moral and political problems.[31]

The internalized world-in-consciousness, a world we actually live within, is the world that can be dominated by principalities and powers, those customs, attitudes, "isms," and images that with a kind of quasi-sacred power can rule our lives. But it is also a world that can be transformed into God's world by the preaching of the gospel. For fifty years, the American pulpit has pretty much addressed the self-within-the-self. Now, perhaps, preachers must speak to the "in-between," the interpersonal realm that may underlie both self and the social world. As we tumble into the twenty-first century, we must once more dare to preach to whole, *worldly* people.

---

[30] E. Farley, "Praxis and Piety: Hermeneutics beyond the New Dualism," in *Justice and the Holy: Essays in Honor of Walter Harrelson,* ed. D. Knight and P. Paris (Atlanta: Scholars Press, 1989), 239–55.

[31] R. R. Niebuhr, *Experiential Religion* (New York: Harper & Row, 1972), 27.

CHAPTER 6

The Crossed Man _____

SOME YEARS AGO the Spanish playwright Arrabal wrote a drama of the passion.[1] He pictured Jesus as a pleasant, if somewhat naive, jazz musician who loved to toot his trumpet for children. When asked why he made music, he would recite by rote a vacuous credo. Crucifixion catches up with him quite unexpectedly; he had not counted on crucifixion. In the last act of the play, he is hauled off and crucified across the handle bars of a bicycle. He dies with a look of complete surprise, quite unable to remember his carefully rehearsed credo. The drama caused a scandal when first performed, but, to be truthful, it may be wiser than many sermons. For sometimes, listening to sermons, you get the impression that Jesus is in full command of his destiny. Instead of having the cross thrust on him, he seems to embrace the crossbeams with deliberate forethought. You can almost imagine Jesus saying to himself, "Let's see now, I'm supposed to die for the sins of the world. What shall I do? Aha, I know. I'll arrange to have a cross set up on Golgotha, outside Jerusalem." So, let us ask questions: What was Jesus' role in the crucifixion? What did he know and how did he die?

Knowing or Unknowing

At the outset, can we admit a conflict, a conflict between scripture and our creedal tradition? Scriptural testimony and our christological creeds seem to be at odds. At times, the biblical documents depict

---

[1] Arrabal, *The Automobile Graveyard and the Two Executioners,* trans. R. Howard (New York: Grove Press, 1960).

Jesus moving toward the cross with a terrible foreknowledge: "He began to teach them that the Son of Man must undergo great suffering, and be rejected by the elders, the chief priests, and the scribes, and be killed, and after three days rise again" (Mark 8:31). By contrast, according to the creeds Christ is "fully human," which obviously means that he died without a clue, as we all must die, not foreseeing the outcome of his death. If scripture is certain, the creeds are wrong; but if the creeds are right, then what do we make of the scriptural record? We face a quandary, a puzzlement that has troubled the church for centuries. Did Jesus have a fortune-teller's crystal ball for a brain, or did he die uncertain of his dying and assuredly unsure of his destiny?

The issue hinges on the character of the Gospels' records. The Gospels — Matthew, Mark, Luke, and John — are more homiletic than historical.[2] They are narrative *preaching*. Obviously they were all written after the fact of resurrection, probably sometime between 65 and 115 C.E. What is more, they were produced by early Christian communities that had discovered in their common life signs of a redemptive new order; good heavens, they were being saved! If Christ was risen and they were being saved, how could they explain to themselves and others his trial, his rejection, and his fearful death? They searched the Hebrew scriptures for precedents, perusing passages such as Psalm 22 and Isaiah 53 as well as the melodramatic tales of brave martyrdom in 2 Maccabees. As they told the story of the cross they put explanations on Jesus' lips, theological understandings of his own death. In the Gospels, the figure of Christ interprets his death to first-century Christian assemblies.

Are the Gospels true? Yes, of course they are true because they open the deep saving significance of Christ's death for believers, indeed for believers who have been surprised by grace in their common life. To ask if the Gospels are factual history is to ask a wrong-headed, twentieth-century question. They are Gospels, a forceful form of preaching, and were not intended to be textbooks in first-century, objective history. We crave facts, "nothing but the facts"; we Americans are a tediously literal people. The Gospels do include a sketchy story of Jesus' life and death and resurrection. But primarily the Gospels are

---

[2] On the genre of Gospels, see M. A. Tolbert, *Sowing the Gospel: Mark's World in Literary-historical Perspective* (Minneapolis: Fortress Press, 1989), 55–79; for further discussion, see H. C. Kee, *Community of the New Age: Studies in Mark's Gospel* (Philadelphia: Westminster Press, 1977), 17–49.

not concerned with the category of historical facticity. The Gospels are for faith; they are words to use as "faith seeks understanding."

Being honest about the scriptures, however, does not solve our quandary. Let us restate the problem as bluntly as possible. The ancient creeds say that Jesus, although assuredly God-with-us, was fully human.[3] He was one with us, sharing our ways of living and of dying. Yet, if Jesus knew in advance the outcome of his death, then the whole awful agony of the passion is undercut. He may have suffered, yes, but did he suffer *as we suffer* if he knew in advance there would be a payoff, namely, resurrection glory? If he had advance inside information, then his pain was not like our pain and his death was less human than our dying. For most mortals, even true believers, the terror of dying is dying without a guarantee.[4] No matter how trusting, brave, or full of faith, ultimately we do not know. After all, there is a wide difference between a cry of faith, "I die: God, receive me," and a cocksure, timetable printout, "Now I die, but in three days I am scheduled to rise again." If Christ did have a complete advance knowledge of God's plans, then although his death on the cross was painful and humiliating, it was not the same as our terminal uncertainty. He was merely role playing a prewritten script, emoting a tearful, tragic death scene while anticipating a triumphant resurrection curtain call. So here we sit, theology in one hand and the biblical record in the other, puzzling over a problem — a problem much argued but still unresolved.

Who Do You Think You Are?

The quandary drives us toward a deeper question, the question of Jesus' self-understanding. Who on earth did Jesus think he was? Did Jesus know for sure he was a Savior, anointed by God for the saving of a wayward humanity? According to the Bible, when brash Peter exclaimed, "You are the Messiah," Jesus acknowledged the confession (Mark 8:29). Of course, as a corrective, Jesus immediately followed up

---

[3] On the early christological creeds, see a brief but helpful chapter in A. Richardson, *Creeds in the Making* (London: SCM Press, 1953), chap. 4. For a more detailed introduction, see the standard work by J. N. D. Kelly, *Early Christian Doctrines* (New York: Harper & Row, 1959), chaps. 6 and 12.

[4] On biblical understandings of death, see L. R. Bailey, Sr., *Biblical Perspectives on Death* (Philadelphia: Fortress Press, 1979); also O. Kaiser and E. Lohse, *Death and Life*, trans. J. R. Steely (Nashville: Abingdon, 1981). On more recent attitudes toward death, see a remarkable book by P. Ariès, *Western Attitudes toward Death from the Middle Ages to the Present*, trans. P. M. Ranum (Baltimore: Johns Hopkins University Press, 1974).

with a passion prediction that threw Peter into a tizzy of sorts; but notice, according to the scriptural testimony, Jesus did accept the title.[5] Who did Jesus suppose he was?

To tell the truth, it is difficult to describe Jewish messianic expectations at the time of Christ with any certainty. Although the Christian scriptures pick up many messianic images—a prophet like Moses, Elijah redivivus, the Suffering Servant, an apocalyptic Son of Man, a priest-king after the order of Melchizedek, a royal son of David—there is no evidence that these images were actually in the popular mind during the period. There was no general expectation of the Messiah at the time of Christ; people were not all agog with hope.[6] In fact the word *Messiah* does not appear often in the literature of the time. Yes, there may have been a kind of *mañana* dream of a king like David who could restore Israel's fortunes, fulfilling the prophecy in 2 Samuel 7:16: "Your house and your kingdom shall be made sure forever before me; your throne shall be established forever."[7] And there was the peculiar double expectation of the Essene community for a priestly Aaronic Messiah as well as a royal Messiah, both preceded by a prophetic herald, fulfilling Malachi 4:5.[8] But the Essenes were scarcely representative of the common mind of the age. We can say that there were dreams of liberation and that, here and there, such dreams may have drawn on either prophetic or apocalyptic texts. But the messianic images gathered by the writers of the Gospels probably do not reflect widespread Jewish expectation at the time of Christ. About all we can say is that Jesus may have seen himself playing a special role with respect to the coming new order of God. Mark sums up his message: "The time is fulfilled, and the kingdom of God has come near; repent, and believe in the good news" (Mark 1:15). So, at minimum, Jesus saw himself as an announcer

---

[5] The story of Peter's confession in Mark 8:27-33 is similar in effect to the Transfiguration story in 9:2-13 and the reply to the Sons of Zebedee in 10:32-45. In each case a triumphalist understanding of messiahship is put down and a passion prediction is presented instead. It would appear that Mark is attempting to straighten out some errant theological thinking in his community. See a summary position in T. J. Weeden, Sr., "The Cross as Power in Weakness," in *The Passion in Mark: Studies on Mark 14–16*, ed. W. H. Kelber (Philadelphia: Fortress Press, 1976), 116–21.

[6] See J. Neusner, *Messiah in Context: Israel's History and Destiny in Formative Judaism* (Philadelphia: Fortress Press, 1984).

[7] R. A. Horsley and J. S. Hanson, *Bandits, Prophets, and Messiahs: Popular Movements at the Time of Jesus* (San Francisco: Harper & Row, 1985), chap. 3.

[8] G. A. Riggan, *Messianic Theology and Christian Faith* (Philadelphia: Westminster Press, 1967), chap. 4.

of the kingdom, a new order due to arrive by God's design almost immediately.

What of the so-called messianic secret that is featured in the Gospel of Mark and, subsequently, is picked up by other Gospels? Although Jesus did not publicly announce his messianic credentials, according to scripture, privately he knew who he was. But if we read Mark with care, the whole idea of a messianic secret collapses. Mary Ann Tolbert sums up the matter tersely:

> [The] argument that secrecy in Mark is related to Jesus' messianic iden-
> tity has long been rejected on basically two grounds. First, Jesus'
> commands to secrecy and the narrator's comments on Jesus' attempts to
> stay hidden often occur in contexts that have nothing to do with claims
> about Messiahship (e.g., 1:44-45; 7:24; 9:30). Second, it is hard to locate
> any for whom Jesus' claim of messianic identity is a secret: the audience
> learns of it in the first line (1:1), Peter confesses it (8:29), the demons all
> know, and the scribes and the Jerusalem leaders know (12:12; 14:61-62).[9]

Instead, we may regard Jesus' pleas for secrecy as a modest reluctance to court fame, widespread crowd support, or public attention. Jesus' reluctance may contrast with triumphalist impulses in the Markan community. But did Jesus actually believe himself to be Messiah? Probably not. Messianic claims in the Gospels are most likely the product of the faith of first-century Christian communities.[10]

Tomorrow We Die

What about his death? Would he have expected to die violently? Surely he would have sensed a growing opposition to his preaching, and, as surely, he must have realized that his death was possible: "Jerusalem, Jerusalem, the city that kills the prophets and stones those who are sent to it" shows up on the lips of Jesus in the "Q" tradition (Luke 13:34). Likewise the passion predictions in Mark may reflect a growing apprehension in Jesus' own mind. He lived in a bloody age,

---

[9] Tolbert, *Sowing,* 227; see her subsequent discussion on 227–30. For another perspective, see Kee, *Community,* 165–75.

[10] J. Knox (*The Death of Christ: The Cross in New Testament History and Faith* [Nashville:
Abingdon, 1958], chaps. 4 and 5) has provided what is still a remarkably lucid discussion of the issue. He concludes that, on the basis of scripture, it is impossible to claim
that Jesus knew he was Messiah in any traditional sense of the word. For an alternative
viewpoint, see R. H. Fuller, *The Mission and Achievement of Jesus: An Examination of the
Presuppositions of New Testament Theology* (London: SCM Press, 1954).

an age of indiscriminate and repressive violence, when powers that be were defensive and given to sudden cruelty. So, yes, we can assume that Jesus must have speculated the possibility of his own terrible death. But would he have anticipated an immediate, miraculous resurrection? Not likely. Although many pious Pharisees looked for resurrection as a form of acquittal for good behavior, the notion of an immediate, singular resurrection simply did not figure in the first-century mind.[11] So what can we assume? We can assume that Jesus, like a wary storm watcher, spotted a mounting darkness and, realistically, may have expected a violent death.

How would Jesus respond to the prospect of dying, perhaps cruel, painful dying? He would not welcome death; he was no depressed masochist beset by "sickness unto death." No, the scriptures picture him in Gethsemane recoiling from the prospect of pain and dying: "Take this cup from me," he is said to have shouted. He did not want to die. And certainly he was not dumb. Yes, some scholars suppose that Jesus' last lone cry ("My God, my God, why have you forsaken me?" [Mark 15:34]) was prompted by disillusionment. They suggest that, all along, Jesus expected some sudden divine intervention, a last act *deus ex machina,* when God would wave magic-wand power and rescue him from the cross. Thus the cry from the cross, they argue, was a terrifying expression of disappointed faith. But to so portray Christ would be to imply that he was truly stupid and profoundly lacking in practical discernment, not to mention theological acumen. Surely as a child of the Hebrew scriptures Jesus knew that the sinful human world would again and again reject the overtures of God in rebellious disobedience. More, how could he not help but know that anyone caught in between God's purposes and human sin could be slaughtered.[12] Perhaps he saw himself in the prophetic tradition as a speaker for God. If so, then surely he knew how the prophets had been greeted and mistreated in days of old. Jesus must have anticipated his death. How did Jesus react to the threat of dying? The Gospels picture him in the garden praying, "Not what I want, but what you want" (Mark 14:36).

---

[11] See the famous little essay by O. Cullmann, *Immortality of the Soul or Resurrection of the Dead: The Witness of the New Testament* (New York: Macmillan, 1958). See also essays in *Immortality and Resurrection,* ed. P. Benoit and R. Murphy (New York: Herder and Herder, 1970).

[12] See M. A. Tolbert's analysis of the parable of the wicked tenants in *Sowing,* 233–39.

Patterns of Temptation

Let us now venture *the* question: What was Jesus' own role in the crucifixion? The Gospels provide some framework for an answer. The key word is *temptation*. Earlier in the Gospels, immediately after his baptismal "ordination" to ministry, Jesus is tempted (Luke 4:1-13). Several temptations seem to circle around popular messianic expectations: He can be a Moses providing bread in the wilderness, or a political ruler commanding the kingdoms of earth, or a dazzling miracle doer casting himself down on safety-net angels while a crowd cheers with delight.[13] But Jesus refuses to play out popular fantasies and, instead, vows to do God's will—whatever God's will may be. Oddly enough, as he faces the cross, the temptations return, all of them. He thirsts—like Israel in the wilderness. He is ironically labeled King of the Jews. And the crowd dares him to establish credentials by "casting himself down." Once again he chooses to cling to God's mysterious purpose alone as a true servant-child of God. The Gospels show Jesus as he faces the cross to be tempted yet faithful to God—"Not my will but yours be done." Throughout his ministry, according to the Gospels, Jesus is tempted by popular expectations; he is tempted to fulfill some sort of socially defined messianic role.

Look more closely at the theme of temptation. Present-day clergy types should be sympathetic experts on the problem. In any parish anywhere, ministers confront expectations of what a minister ought to be and do. If such expectations are not apparent in a parish, they are certainly bouncing around in the general social mind. Will we be success-story evangelists for bus 'em in church triumphalism? Will we be sage counselors, wise as Freud and as perceptive as both Menningers combined, miraculously able to unshackle the troubled mind? Will we be activist pastors taking on every hot-potato political issue from American foreign policy to Supreme Court decisions on abortion? How easy it is to be trapped in social expectations. To turn the equation around, how difficult it is to ignore all expectations and allow God to define our ministry in every new situation; we are bound to crave social approvals. No wonder ministry is so desperately exhausting these days. Inauthenticity is a singularly ministerial temptation and, one way or another, most of us clerics succumb.

Ministerial temptation is more agonizing than we know. Long ago

---

[13] For a survey of scholarship on the temptation stories, see J. A. Fitzmyer, *The Gospel according to St. Luke I–IX* (Garden City, N.Y.: Doubleday, 1981), 506-13.

George Herbert Mead, a wise man, described our human condition. In everyone, he argued, there is a split self, a "me" and a "myself." The "me" is a living, acting, speaking, venturing self, whereas the "myself" is the self we view, a self-image created by the ways in which others speak and act toward us.[14] So the problem is obvious: How can a human being live in any kind of harmony? The popular answer is equally obvious: We can win social approval and, therefore, be socially justified. If enough people speak and act favorably toward us, maybe we will be able to enjoy our own company and even manage a modicum of self-esteem. If we are ministers, we can try to fulfill social expectations, earn approval, and thus have some basis for self-approval. So what is *the* great temptation? We are tempted, every one of us, to seek social self-justification rather than justification by grace alone. Social justifications are available and can be earned, whereas justification by grace alone is a matter of hard, relentless, trusting faith in God.

Now perhaps we can see why again and again the Gospels show Jesus tempted to give in to social expectations. The passion stories play on the theme. As Jesus marches into Jerusalem, the crowds cheer, "Hosanna! Blessed is the one who comes in the name of the Lord!" (Mark 11:9). But then, almost immediately, Jesus passes up praise and condemns the temple for its prejudice and greed. Again, when a woman pours out more than ten thousand dollars worth of perfume in an epic gesture of love, Jesus counters the popular reaction, "This ointment could have been sold . . . and the money given to the poor" (Mark 14:5). Hauled before Pontius Pilate where he is asked point blank, "Are you the King of the Jews?," he shrugs off the question with a diffident reply, "You say so" (Mark 15:2). He never justifies himself. And, on the cross, amid catcalls and cursing, when the crowd taunts him, saying, "Let the Messiah, the King of Israel, come down from the cross now, so that we may see and believe," he answers nothing (Mark 15:32). Bread for the poor, political power, and miracles — repeatedly he is tempted to cater to social expectations, but always he bends his will to the will of God.

Temptation Doubled

The struggle within Christ is more intense than we may suppose. Think again of how frail our own ministerial egos are. When we are

---

[14] G. H. Mead, *Mind, Self and Society from the Standpoint of a Social Behaviorist* (Chicago: University of Chicago Press, 1934).

criticized, we bridle; when we are attacked, we burn with embarrassed resentment; when we are rejected, we usually reject. Oh, because we are trained clergy, we can restrain ourselves to a degree. We seldom risk public outbursts. But then, our passive/aggressive strategies often may be more deadly. Who can bear being rejected? The agonizing split between the inner "me" and the "myself" is aggravated by rejection. So we justify ourselves, or we bracket our critics and appeal to others in a congregation for approval, or we start playing politics to secure ourselves. Rejection, even minor rejection, can be devastating, particularly by groups we respect. If we are honest, we can begin to sense the awful interpersonal temptations Christ faced, for he was totally rejected. The leadership of the temple, his temple, turned against him. The crowds rejected him. Soldiers abused him. Even his own disciples deserted him, denying his name. And finally, as he is strung up on a cross, everyone seems to join in a mounting crescendo of abuse designed to ridicule his helplessness. What can he do? How can he answer?

There is a great Negro spiritual with a sad refrain: "He never said a mumblin' word."[15] The spiritual is right up to a point. Again and again, when attacked, Christ stands mute. His silence is not caused by shock, for he sees quite clearly what is taking place. "One of you will betray me," he says at supper; "You will all become deserters," he adds, matter-of-factly (Mark 14:18, 27). Later, when he is arrested in the garden, he is ironically objective: "Have you come out with swords and clubs to arrest me?" (Mark 14:48). Jesus sees exactly what is going on; he is unsurprised. But when tempted to answer rejection with rejection or abuse with anger, Jesus "never said a mumblin' word." In the Markan tradition, Christ is silent. In Luke, when he does speak, he speaks mercy: "Father, forgive them; for they know not what they are doing" (Luke 23:34). And when a brigand on the cross nearby calls to him, he promises nothing less than divine absolution, "Today you will be with me in Paradise" (Luke 23:43). The writers of the Gospels assume that we can understand Christ's temptation — rancor, retaliation, self-justification — but they portray his absolute restraint. On the cross, Jesus Christ loved his neighbors, so "he never said a mumblin' word."

What is Christ's role on the cross? He resists temptation. Although tempted to turn from God, to turn against neighbors, and to reject rejection, he stands firm: "Yet, not what I want, but what you want"

---

[15] Spiritual: "He Nevuh Said a Mumbalin' Word," in *Songs of Zion* (Nashville: Abingdon, 1981).

(Mark 14:36). Could Jesus see in advance the outcome of his dying? Probably not. Could he guess the glory of an Easter Day? No, such foreknowledge is unlikely. He suffered rejection on top of rejection. His religion rejected him. The people he came to save turned against him. His own disciples dumped him unceremoniously. And finally it seemed he was all alone: "My God, my God, why have *you* forsaken me?" (Mark 15:34). Nevertheless, he was faithful and still obedient. "Your will be done," he said in his terrible unknowing.

A Tracing of God's Purpose

We come to a crucial question: What did Jesus know of God's purpose? Could Christ even guess what his death might mean? As a good Jew, Jesus would have grown up within a theological model. He had heard the old stories of God and Israel, stories that, when set within the myths of creation and eschaton, became a prototypical story of God and humanity. Had not God picked Israel out in free, covenantal love? And had God not led the children of Israel out of Egypt to freedom, sustained them in the wilderness, and given them the good law on Mount Sinai? Surely God loved recalcitrant Israel and chose Israel as a witness to all the other peoples of earth. But Jesus knew not only a theological model, God and Israel, and a story that plotted God's purposes through Israel, but he had also heard the words of the prophets. In days gone by, God's prophets had repeatedly called Israel to repent and turn toward justice. God was astonishingly patient considering the people's chronic religious promiscuity, for God never stopped speaking to chosen Israel. Jesus may not have grasped the full, final meaning of the cross, but he could understand Golgotha within his theological framework as a rejection of the word of God by God's own sinful, chosen people. Although Israel was in covenant with God, did not the prophets testify to Israel's propensity for violent rebellion? With certainty, we can assume that Jesus had profound theological understanding.

The prophets were covenant moralists, yes, but visionaries as well. At the time of Christ, the prophetic tradition had turned toward apocalyptic envisioning; people looked for "a new heaven and a new earth." Concern for God's future was almost inevitable in an economically diminished land overrun by a foreign conqueror and undercut by both religious and political corruptions. Jesus grew up in a turbulent and yet expectant age: Someday the lion would bed down with the lamb; someday weapons of war would be beaten into farm implements; someday there would be justice for the poor. Things were so bad that God would surely intervene to make divine promises come true. Now we must be cautious; Jesus was not a triumphalist, dreaming up a success-story Israel — no early-day Zionist was he.[16] Israel would never become a towering cedar of Lebanon but, instead, would be a mustard weed at best.[17] Yet Jesus did look toward God's new order and, with apocalyptic urgency, declared its imminent arrival. He envisioned a new aeon filled with the Spirit of God, a second creation with a new temple and a written-on-the-heart law. Now, cried Jesus, "the kingdom of God has come near; repent, and believe in the good news." So Jesus saw his ministry as related to the future of God. His life was lived in God's unfolding purpose for humanity. Presumably, in dying, he still affirmed the future of God.

Can we push Jesus' prescience much past his theological discernment? Not really. We must never preach Jesus as if he possessed a vest-pocket schedule of coming events: "Let's see now, on Friday I'm scheduled to die for the sins of the world. Then, if I've got the timetable straight, on Easter Day, I'll rise and ascend to a heavenly throne." Such preaching simply will not do. On the one hand, Jesus' humanity is destroyed; on the other hand, his fidelity is reduced to outright puppetry with God pulling his strings on schedule. True faithfulness is possible only in a mix of freedom and destiny. Courage is only courage in the midst of unknowing. So whenever we bump into particular biblical texts that seem to propose a peculiar omniscience, we must dare to revise them in light of Christ's full, true humanity. For unless Jesus was truly human, his divinity becomes unbearable. We must affirm that in dying he did not know the outcome of his death; he could not guess a resurrection day. Yes, his theological model was sure and surely informed him. As surely, he trusted the promises of God, a God who was ever faithful. But could Jesus spell out the significance of his death or see the saving power of the cross? Not likely. "My God, my God, why have *you* forsaken me?" he cried out, and he died.

But regard his faithfulness. Forsaken, he still speaks to God. Even

---

[16] See J. Riches, *Jesus and the Transformation of Judaism* (New York: Seabury Press, 1982), chap. 5.

[17] R. W. Funk understands the parable of the mustard seed to be a burlesque on triumphant cedar of Lebanon passages (e.g., Ezek. 31:2-9). Instead of a towering tree to which the "birds of the air" (pagan nations?) must turn for shelter, Jesus hands out a fragile and despised mustard weed to which, surprisingly, the birds come. See R. W. Funk, "The Looking-glass Tree Is for the Birds," *Interpretation* 27 (1973): 3–9; reprinted in *Jesus as Precursor* (Philadelphia: Fortress Press, 1975), 19–28.

in dying, he holds to God's will. Throughout his life he resists every temptation to play up to the crowds, to curry social favor, to get in good with the in-groups. Instead, he embraces God's will, which he may not fully understand, and, prophetically, speaks God's word. Although rebuffed, he never rejects his neighbors, fellow human beings with whom he is in baptized covenant. He identifies with poor sinners, yet is ever loyal to God. See the faithfulness of Jesus Christ.

Through the centuries, Christian theology has affirmed the so-called sinlessness of Jesus. The notion has been difficult for many Christians to grasp. Sinlessness can never be an alabaster purity without scratch or nick or defect. Such a definition would turn Christ into a put-up paragon without humanity. We must assume that Jesus was tempted as we are. Therefore, did Jesus have sexual fantasies, greeds, and furies as we do? Of course he did. But his sinlessness can be defined; he is one in whom temptation was continually being overcome. Although Christ was in every way tempted as we are, again and again, he resisted temptation. In him, temptation is continually broken in the power of God's love. Even in dying, he keeps faith. In the Book of Hebrews, Christ is likened to a high priest who, please note, offers an obedient *life* to God.[18] He is human and in his humanity shares our suffering and our dying. But, in all, he offers not so much his death as the lifeblood of his obedience. To the end, he resists all other justifications and clings to God's will alone. To the end, he forgoes vengeance and, in utter irrational weakness, affirms common humanity. No wonder that Paul can insist that we are justified by his faithfulness.

God, who has called him into being, accepts him in his dying life, and we are wondrously saved.

---

[18] On Heb. 9:23-28, see F. F. Bruce, *The Epistle to the Hebrews* (Grand Rapids, Mich.: William B. Eerdmans, 1964), 217-24.

CHAPTER 7

The Mystery
of God _____

SOME YEARS AGO there was an exhibit of religious sculpture. The exhibit included an astonishing statue of the crucified Christ done in copper and what looked like onyx. The single sculpture contained two crosses. One cross was small, a stick figure Christ, done in weathered coppery metal. The other cross was of dark onyx. It stood behind the little crucifix but was six times larger. Perhaps the artist was trying to picture God's involvement at Golgotha — a larger cross behind the cross. Jesus of Nazareth was crucified outside Jerusalem around 28 C.E., but somehow God was there in the cruel event as well. Was God a stand-offish spectator, merely on hand to receive the self-offering of Christ or, to borrow Moltmann's radical phrase, was God a "crucified God"?[1] We who preach hand out the same sort of image. In our sermons, we say that, on the cross, God forgives us, saves us, suffers and dies for us. But how can God die in Christ's death? How can God be said to suffer? We preach through images — a cross behind the cross — but what exactly are we trying to say about God?

Can God Suffer?

Begin with an affirmation: For centuries Christian preachers have pointed to the figure of Christ and said in effect, "There is God." We believe that a first-century human being, Jesus of Nazareth, has some-how opened the mystery of God to us. How did William Lyon Phelps

---

[1] J. Moltmann, *The Crucified God: The Cross of Christ as the Foundation and Criticism of Christian Theology* (New York; Harper & Row, 1974).

describe Jesus Christ? Somewhat glibly, he wrote, "He is the only man I ever heard of who looks like God, who talks like God, and who acts like God."[2] Although Phelps is extravagant (you want to ask him, How can you tell?), he does have warrant for his claim in the Gospel of John: "If you knew me, you would know my Father also" (John 8:19); "Whoever has seen me has seen the Father" (John 14:9). At times we modify our preaching by using metaphor, as when we say that Jesus in his humanity was Son of God, a person who obeyed God's will and spoke God's word. But, at other times, we baldly declare that Jesus Christ was God-with-us, or that in some mysterious way, "God was in Christ."[3] We speak of identity, underscoring the living unity of human and divine, implying that somehow Jesus Christ and God are *one*. The language of our preaching prompts some startling questions: Is God on trial in the trial of Christ? Does God suffer in the sufferings of Christ? And (dare we venture the idea?) does God somehow die in the dying of Christ? We are shocked by our own implied logic. How can God suffer or die, and still be God?

No wonder that for centuries the church has fended off the inexorable logic of its own christology. Patripassianism, the idea that in Christ's passion God suffers pain, has always been condemned as heresy. Certainly the extravagant notion that in Christ's death God dies is quite unthinkable; by definition, God is above and beyond mortality.[4] God is exempt from pains of terminal suffering simply because God is eternal; God is "from everlasting to everlasting." Moreover, God is omnipotent and therefore unassailable. As for pangs of mental anguish, if God is perfect, how can God feel any lack or loneliness or hurt? Bluntly, to say that God suffers seems to imply that God, by definition, is less than God. There is an astonishing episode in a Graham Greene novel when an agnostic doctor, who is counting up patients in an African leper colony, complains to a priest: "Your God must feel a bit disappointed, when he looks at this world." The priest answers, "When you were a boy, they can't have taught you theology very well. God cannot feel disappointment or pain." "Perhaps," the doctor replies, "that's why I

---

[2] Cited in Paul L. McKay, "Christmas and Meaning," in *Pulpit* 26, no. 12 (December 1955), 8.

[3] See D. M. Baillie, *God Was In Christ: An Essay on Incarnation and Atonement* (New York: Charles Scribner's Sons, 1948).

[4] Although see the "Death of God" in the devout theology of T. J. J. Altizer, *The Gospel of Christian Atheism* (Philadelphia: Westminster Press, 1966), and also essays in *The Theology of Altizer: Critique and Response,* ed. J. B. Cobb (Philadelphia: Westminster Press, 1970).

don't care to believe."[5] God cannot feel — Christian theology has long insisted. So how can God be said to suffer?

But, hold on, we must reckon with biblical tradition. When we flip through the pages of scripture, we do run across any number of passages in which God seems to feel. In the Bible, an anthropomorphic God becomes angry, yearns, is jealous, is heartbroken. God may well be high and holy, an alien mystery, lost in lofty clouds of majesty, a transcendent otherness; yet God is also a God-with-us and, emphatically, a God-with-Israel. We can read texts in which God speaks love for Israel and, therefore, is distressed by Israel's rejection of love: "O Israel, if you would but listen to me!" (Ps. 81:8). Other texts testify to God's empathy for suffering humanity: "I know their sufferings," says God of the Israelites in Egypt (Exod. 3:7). Finally, the Hebrew Bible has texts that seem to picture God actually in the process of suffering over Israel, "I will cry out like a woman in labor, I will gasp and pant" (Isa. 42:14). Notice that all these texts relate to God's self-giving love. In other words, if God did not love Israel, there would be no talk of suffering. But because God loves creation, because God longs for human partnership, God is said to have compassion and in some way to suffer with the suffering of Israel.[6] Christian writings, singularly the Book of Hebrews (4:14 — 5:10), contain the odd suggestion that God learns suffering by suffering with Christ:

> So also Christ did not glorify himself in becoming a high priest, but was appointed by the one who said to him, "You are my Son, / today I have begotten you." . . . In the days of his flesh, Jesus offered up prayers and supplications, with loud cries and tears, to the one who was able to save him from death, and he was heard because of his reverent submission. Although he was a Son, he learned obedience through what he suffered; and having been made perfect, he became the source of eternal salvation for all who obey him. (Heb. 5:5-9)

Although such texts in Hebrew and Christian scriptures do seem to explain God's involvement in the passion of the cross as a love that suffers *with,* we are still stuck with a tension, a logical tension built into the very nature of God: Love suffers with; God is love; yet God to be God cannot be said to suffer.

---

[5] Graham Greene, *A Burnt-out Case* (New York: Viking Press, 1961), 248.

[6] On the Hebrew scripture references to God's suffering, see a splendid study by T. E. Fretheim, *The Suffering of God* (Philadelphia: Fortress Press, 1984).

A Puzzle of God-talk

Let us slow down and be cautious. We cannot dismiss the tension by labeling two different traditions—one Greek/philosophical and the other Hebrew/biblical—as we were wont to do during the heyday of the Biblical Theology movement.[7] Categorical labels are always untrue and seldom helpful. No, we are not dealing with two different traditions of thought, Greek versus Hebrew; we are dealing with a contrast in our own minds, and, indeed, in our own preaching.

How do we speak of God? Do we not appeal to the whole wide created world when we conceive of God? Arguments from creation are not simply Christian summer-camp ploys. In our sermons, all of us depict the complex, mysterious beauty of the world—breathtaking sunsets, still silver lakes, the precise geometry of snowflakes, or the miracle of a butterfly emerging from a dry cocoon—and then sum up the wonders of creation and say, "God." We argue God's greatness, ingenuity, and power from the fact of the universe, its spaciousness and intricacy. In spite of Karl Barth's chronic grouch about the dangers of Natural Theology, we dare to argue from creation in our sermons, and, oddly enough, so does the Bible.[8] How can the mighty God of creation suffer as a creature? If God is the God of creation, then in the words of that painfully pompous hymn, "How Great Thou Art!"[9]

In our sermons, of course, we also speak of God's providence. God is provident as a "ground of being" who gives life to growing things and who meets our need for food, drink, clothing, and shelter. At least once a year, late in November, we celebrate the harvest of God's goodness. But do we not speak of God's providence in another way? We tell of God's supervision of human history. Thus, we preach God as a sovereign over history or as an actor in history. God is a doer and a dominator, always in control of human affairs. Yes, we humans may have freedom, but our freedom is by permission within God's sovereign, destining power. To be God, God must ultimately control the happenings of history, moving all things toward a final purpose.

---

[7] See J. Barr, *Old and New in Interpretation: A Study of the Two Testaments* (London: SCM Press, 1966), 34–64.

[8] James Barr's soon to be published Gifford Lectures will argue a case for the Bible's "natural theology." Certainly, Psalm 8 seems to engage in a primitive natural theology.

[9] "How Great Thou Art" was written in 1885 by C. G. Boberg. The English version is by S. K. Hine, 1953. Copyright assigned to Manna Music in 1955, renewed in 1981 by Manna Music, Inc.

Notice, in our sermons we never depict God as being acted upon. Certainly God is never a victim. How could a sovereign God possibly suffer?

We speak of God in still another way; we argue from our own obvious finitude. Do we not describe God in terms of what we are *not?* We are small-time bundles of breath; we are born, live briefly, and die. We have but limited wisdom; about the past we are absent-minded, and of the future, speechless — we live in a cloud of unknowing. There was a recluse who, isolated from a normal childhood, read virtually all the books in a library where his mother worked as a custodian. During a TV interview, he hung his head and confessed what we all confess, "There is so much I do not know." As for our much ballyhooed power (laser, missile, and nuclear bomb), in the cosmic sweep of things, we are a galaxy about as significant as a grain of sand. In view of our obvious limitations, how do we speak of God in sermons? We tell of One who is unlimited — all-knowing, all-powerful, eternal, and free. We attribute to God everything we are not. So do the Hebrew scriptures. They speak of the creator who is greater than creation, of the almighty whose might is unlimited. The God of the Bible is an absolute God. And an absolute God is the God we preach. But the question remains: How can such a God be said to suffer?

What has been our usual solution? We have proffered a kind of bipolar God. God in God's own self cannot suffer because God is not needy and does not die. By definition, God is passionless and quite removed from human agony. Nevertheless, when God forgoes impassivity to reach out in love, then God has compassion; God cares and can even be divinely discomfited. So although God as God cannot suffer, God's heart can be broken, God's will can be thwarted, God's eyes can be shocked, God's love can be rebuffed. Traditional Christian theology ends up with a split in the character of God. There is God in God's self-sufficient self and then there is God-toward-humanity; the one is transcendent and quite beyond pain; the other is with us and full of compassion. One half of God's face can weep while the other half is frozen in divine impassivity. We preachers have created a split between the nature of God and the activity of God that is unresolved; we bow before a divine schizophrenia. These days God is a problem for preachers.

What Is at Stake?

Martin Luther may have been somewhat disorganized, but he was a theological genius. One of his insights was to distinguish between what he called a *theologia crucis* and a *theologia gloriae.* [10] The *theologia crucis* discerns God's omnipotent presence not in triumphant power, but in the weakness and foolishness of the cross. Thus, the theology of the cross finds God where God seems most absent, in failure, suffering, weakness, and rejection. Luther goes so far as to speak of *Deus crucifixus,* the crucified God. Faith in such a God is the opposite of self-esteem, confidence, and triumphant expectation. No, a theology of the cross knows that human life is inexorably tragic and that human progress is sham; our lives are cruciform. Yet God's grace is known at the cross and in the dark. [11]

Of course, it is probably true to say that a *theologia crucis* will not be readily accepted. It is all very well to have slogans printed on our coffee mugs, "Life's a bitch, and then you die," as long as we can giggle together when we read them. But if we must begin faith by affirming life's tragic character and, in fact, find God in the tragic, such a faith will scarcely sell in America. Americans are into self-fulfillment, success, the necessity of self-esteem, and the uses of power. We admire mastery. We applaud people who have "got themselves together." In a land where denominations compete for the American soul, a religion that admits that life is inevitably tragic and "then we die" will lose out. No, instead, most Americans will prefer a pew in the Crystal Cathedral under sunny California skies.

Luther knew that a theology of glory was intimately connected with the pretensions of the church. To say it simply: The church cannot let go of the absolute God, the God of power and glory, the triumphant God. For if God is anything less than unlimited power and wisdom, then the church, God's church, is diminished. We can see Luther's insight all around. We can see it in authority fights. Why do we crave a Bible that is an inerrant word of God? Because the Bible is the church's book. [12] Why must we hyper-evangelize without much concern for our "victims"? Because God's chosen church should be a winner in the world. And why should we legislate the morals of a moral majority? Because God's law is possessed by the church for everyone's social good.

---

[10] Luther first used the terms in a series of theses, the Heidelberg Disputation, in 1518. See *Martin Luther: Selections from His Writings,* ed. J. Dillenberger (Garden City, N.Y.: Doubleday, 1961), 500–503.

[11] See D. J. Hall, *Lighten Our Darkness: Toward an Indigenous Theology of the Cross* (Philadelphia: Westminster Press, 1976), esp. chap. 4.

[12] For a discussion of the authority issue, see my *Homiletic* (Philadelphia: Fortress Press, 1987), chap. 15; for a more discerning study, see E. Farley, *Ecclesial Reflection: An Anatomy of Theological Method* (Philadelphia: Fortress Press, 1982), pt. 1.

In declaring a God of absolute power and truth, the church can bask in God's reflected glory.

But what about that little man, the crucified Jesus? What about the Jesus who was tossed in a Jerusalem drunk tank, who was baptized in soldier spit, who bawled for a drink when dying, who cried "My God, my God, why have you forsaken me?" No wonder that so many of our "free churches" skip Holy Week. To step from Palm Sunday immediately to Easter Day retains the note of triumph we crave.[13] The truth is that we are embarrassed by the crucified Christ. For if Jesus on the cross is the revealing of God, then the church may be called to a very different social role, namely, to suffer and die for the world. But these days, when the churches are caught up in a competitive drive for self-preservation, how can we even open our minds to the possibility that denominations, particularly our denomination, may be called to die out? Instead, we are eager to preserve the tradition of a God who is a dominating mightiness—omnipotent, omniscient, perfect in truth, and, of course, eternal. Thus we preach an absolute God and then regard the witness of the cross as a divine concession, an unexpected gesture from God's heart.

But consider a big "what if": What if we were to take our Christian faith seriously? What if we were to stand before the cross of Christ and confess that there, there on Calvary, we see the full revelation of God's essential character? What then? We can begin to see what happens when we read the daring beginning of Paul's First Letter to the Corinthians. The cross, Paul insists, *is* the power and wisdom of God. He holds up broken Jesus and says in effect: There is your God! Such a claim is an offense to Greeks, he notes, because the Greeks hanker for absolute wisdom and, to their surprise, get a foolish Christ who died not knowing—"My God, my God, why . . .?" But the cross is also an offense to Jews, says Paul, because the Jews chase power, whereas in weakness Jesus is nailed down and impotent. Paul dares to redefine all those Latinate words—omnipotent, omniscient, immortal, impassive— in terms of Christ's dying in foolish weakness. Then, in an even more astonishing move, he scales down the church to a huddle of weak and foolish people. Not many V.I.P.s, he observes, not many smart or rich or well-born; the church is by definition a "nothing," a broken, blundering body of Christ. Ernst Käsemann expresses Paul's position well:

---

[13] The trend is noticeable. For the most part, even in ethnic areas of the North, the three-hour Good Friday vigil has disappeared, not so much eroded by Easter commercialism as by the church's will to social self-preservation and incipient triumphalism.

Does this mean that we must not speak of the glory of a Christian or of the church? . . . For [Paul] Jesus' glory consists in the fact that he makes his earthly disciples willing and able to take up the cross after him; and the glory of the church and of the Christian life is that they are thought worthy to praise the one who was crucified as the power and the wisdom of God, to seek salvation in him alone and to turn their existence into the service of God under the token of Golgotha. Here the theology of the resurrection is a chapter in the theology of the cross, not the excelling of it. Since Paul, all theological controversy has radiated ultimately from one central point and can hence only be decided at that point: *Crux sola nostra theologia.*[14]

Well maybe, just maybe, we are called to preach Paul's gospel. The cross is not merely a heart flutter from an otherwise impassive God, or an exceptional concession of the divine sovereignty; no, through the cross we see into the mystery of God's own self-giving self.

On Beginning in the Middle

Do you sense what has been happening? We are turning around a usual sequence. Normally we begin at a beginning; we start with creation. God the all-powerful fashions the universe in a flurry of divine creativity. But because creation tumbles into sin, God shows up with tablets of law to be tossed down from Mount Sinai. Usually we begin by presuming a God of unlimited power, a law-and-order God whose control is absolute. Hollywood producer Samuel Goldwyn reportedly wrote a stage direction for one of his religious films: "Begin with an earthquake and work up to a climax." Normally we do theology by introducing a big-bang God almighty from the start.

Then we flip to the Christian scriptures and start chattering about redemption. God almighty, a holy terror, relents. God unclenches the divine fist and lets a little heart show through at the cross; as a result, we are "saved by the blood," as they say. Because we are properly committed to substitutionary atonement, we end up with God's love sacrificing Jesus, who is God-with-us, to God's justice in order to redeem a fouled-up creation. Our usual sequence is to begin with creation, an enterprise that demonstrates the absolute power of God, and then to introduce redemption as a moderating of God's power with something we tend to label "love."

But suppose we start with the cross and work ourselves back to creation. What then? Suppose we begin, as does Paul, with the foolish

---

[14] E. Käsemann, *Perspectives on Paul* (Philadelphia: Fortress Press, 1971), 59.

weakness of the cross. Yes, obviously the universe is an awesome display of power; a big-bang God has been at work. But what *kind* of power is God's power? Perhaps God's power is the modest power of a God willing to shatter divine perfections in order to give life. Perhaps creation is not so much an act of masculine domination as of self-giving, something like the agony of childbirth. And suppose the founding of the law on Sinai is not so much strong-armed police action or judicial regulation as a motherly kindness that seeks to offer freedom within protective guidance.[15] Maybe all along, all through Israel's childhood and rebellious adolescence, indeed ever since humanity emerged from primordial sludge, God has been aching for the human world to be both grown-up and loving.

Do you see now how the cross redefines our doctrines of God? The embarrassing pulpit split between God the creator and God the redeemer is overcome. God's attributes — omnipotence, omniscience, omnipresence, perfection — are all redefined by the broken body of the crucified Christ. God's self-abnegating love, a willing-to-die love, is written across all time and space. So the cross is not a desperate concession, something almighty God is forced to do because nothing else seems to work; no, the cross is consistent with God's faithfulness from the beginning. Here is a God who all along has been willing to be impotent, to not know, to suffer with, to die for a people, a dearly loved people. Here is a God whose real name, long hidden from our minds, is Compassion (*com pati* = to suffer with).[16] In a way, we can even say that on the cross God is crucified and dies. But the God who dies is the God of our self-aggrandizing projections, a God of dominance. On the cross we can see the true God, the God whose name is Compassion and who, all along, has been suffering with poor, befuddled, sin-struck humanity. With the resurrection, the crucified Christ is taken up into the nature of God. God's glory is nothing less than the glory of self-giving love — "Love so amazing, so divine . . . ."

But we must still deal with the issue: How can an eternal, perfect God be compassionate? In Anselm's words: "How art thou compassionate, and, at the same time, passionless?"[17] Wendy Farley makes a

---

[15] See a helpful article by E. Farley, "God as Dominator and Image-giver: Divine Sovereignty and the New Anthropology," *Journal of Ecumenical Studies* 6, no. 3 (1969): 354-75.

[16] W. Farley, *Tragic Visions and Divine Compassion: A Contemporary Theodicy* (Louisville, Ky.: Westminster/John Knox Press, 1990), chap. 3.

[17] From Anselm's *Proslogium*, 8; see *Saint Anselm: Basic Writings*, trans. S. W. Deane (LaSalle, Ill.: Open Court, 1962), 13.

careful set of distinctions. She rejects the notion that we cannot understand the sufferings of others without ourselves suffering. Instead she
speaks of "sympathetic knowledge" that is not primal experience. Compassion is an enduring disposition, grounded in love, that through
"sympathetic knowledge" understands the sufferings of others and seeks
their liberation.[18] Thus we can argue that while God cannot feel as we
feel, nevertheless God's essential character is compassion. God understands human agonies, indeed is with us in our agonies ever seeking to
enable us to resist, overcome, withstand, and be free.

Are we ready to take a final step? What about the church? In particular, what about our several churches? We have clung to a triumphant, masculine God, an almighty God of authority and power. And
we have bowed in reverence before a triumphant, risen Christ with
every wound smoothed over. Like brash Peter on the Mount of Transfiguration we have cheered, "It's great to be here! Let's build!" But what
are we to do with a God who, like a mother, constantly self-sacrifices
for the sake of human children, whose only force is the impotence of
love, who accepts our rejection, inflicted pain, and outright disobedience in order to be faithful? Does such an image call the church to live
quite differently in the world? Will we have to yield our bigger and
better power games — masculine competitiveness and the lust for domination? Of course we must. "You must be holy as I am holy," sings out
the voice of God. God's holiness is the strange modesty of faithful, self-
giving love. So perhaps we are called to be a church of compassion, not
triumph; a church ever willing to die so that the world may truly live.

A few years ago a novel was written about an old evangelist. He has
his problems; he never seems to be able to manage his sex life, his
finances, or his faith. Yet he is faithful in his own strange way. Late
in life, he and his daughter Sharon converse. She says: "What is it
makes people want to dump on you, Bip? Your whole life they've been
dumping on you." The old evangelist speaks: "Jesus never let on it was
going to be any different. It goes with the territory."[19] The church's
territory is the world, a world God loves, and our way of living in the
world must be God's way. We are not called to be big-steeple success
stories. People will dump on us. So, again and again, we must set ourselves aside and be willing to die if need be for the sake of the world.
We have no power but the power of word, and no glory but the foolish
glory of love. If we boast, as Paul insists, we will boast nothing but

---

[18] See W. Farley, *Tragic Visions,* 69–94.
[19] F. Buechner, *Love Feast* (New York: Atheneum, 1974), 229–30.

Christ crucified—he who is foolish and weak, yet the presence of the living God-with-us.

In another land there is a church with a painted ceiling. On the ceiling is a picture of the creation—the great God Jehovah with a sweeping arm flinging out the stars. Way down below in the nave there is a small cross on a table. The church is an image of our pulpit practice. Yes, we preach the cross; we have done so for centuries. But we preach the cross beneath the awesome image of Jehovah, a God of unlimited power—our Judge, our Author, our King. In our age, the ceiling is whitewashed; the picture has faded. Most people have no sense of the presence of God; they sense absence. So perhaps we must repaint the heavens, projecting from the little cross a larger cross. We can preach the astonishing crossed shape of God's encompassing love.

CHAPTER 8

The Gospel Traditions _____

PREACHERS HAVE PREACHED on the passion since the earliest moments of the Christian faith; the church remembers Jesus Christ. The formation of a passion tradition, which probably was assembled prior to the writing of the Gospels, is impossible to trace. Instead we have the Markan passion, which apparently was picked up and revised by Matthew and Luke; separate materials added by Matthew and Luke — some from the elusive "Q" source; and the Johannine account, which is somewhat singular.

A number of scholars have analyzed the Markan passion drama. In addition, there have been comparative studies of the different Synoptic passion stories.[1] Because I am concerned with the major texts that preachers preach, I will analyze the Markan tradition as a primary source. But I will also draw in those pericopes from Matthew and Luke that are not found in Mark. In effect I will be presenting a harmony of Synoptic passion texts. In presenting these passages, for the most part I will follow the sequence and the numbering system provided by Huck's *Synopsis,* which is employed in *Gospel Parallels.*[2] Then, I will add

---

[1] On the Markan passion drama see the extensive bibliography in W. H. Kelber, ed., *The Passion in Mark: Studies on Mark 14–16* (Philadelphia: Fortress Press, 1976), 181–89; for comparative studies of the Synoptic passion stories see the bibliography in F. J. Matera, *Passion Narratives and Gospel Theologies: Interpreting the Synoptics through Their Passion Stories* (New York: Paulist Press, 1986), 245–53.

[2] *Gospel Parallels,* ed. B. H. Throckmorton (New York: Thomas Nelson & Sons, 1949). The symbol § followed by a number refers to the numbering system in *Gospel Parallels.*

a separate section studying those Johannine materials that are so inter-
related as to suggest that they must be looked at as an isolated whole.

Readers will want to consult different kinds of commentaries. The
exegetical/expositional sections I provide are brief. My aim is to get at
the theological substance of texts, that is, the gospel to be preached. I
will not provide lengthy historical excursuses, for we are not trying to
establish historical veracity. The texts we are studying are already a
form of preaching, and, therefore, we are looking at them as preaching.

Again, I must mention my translations, which may well trouble
some readers. Although I have tried to follow the vocabulary and syntax of the texts with care, I have also tried to bring out their narrative/
colloquial character and their metaphorical power. I have made two
substitutions that may seem unfortunate: I have replaced the phrase
"Son of Man" with "Humanity's Child," and frequently I have sub-
stituted "God's new order" for "kingdom of God"; in both cases, I am
seeking a more inclusive language. Preachers should consult the
original Greek text or fine contemporary translations, such as the New
Revised Standard Version, the New International Version, or the careful translations by Richmond Lattimore.[3]

Although I discuss homiletic procedures at times, I do so from a particular perspective. Readers may wish to consult an earlier work of
mine, *Homiletic*.[4]

THE SYNOPTIC GOSPELS

The passion narratives appear to be carefully designed stories.[5] They
take up a sizeable chunk of each Gospel.[6] Why were the passion narratives written? Certainly, they were written to tell the story of Jesus
Christ to second-generation Christians. But were there more specific
reasons? If Jesus had been raised on Easter Day, then, truly, he was
Messiah, God's anointed one. Yet, if he was Messiah, the Christ, then

---

[3] R. A. Lattimore, trans., *The Four Gospels and the Revelation* (New York: Farrar,
Straus & Giroux, 1979), and idem, trans., *Acts and Letters of the Apostles* (New York:
Farrar, Straus & Giroux, 1982).

[4] D. G. Buttrick, *Homiletic* (Philadelphia: Fortress Press, 1987).

[5] For summary histories of passion tradition scholarship, see J. R. Donahue, "Introduction: From Passion Traditions to Passion Narrative," in *The Passion in Mark*, ed.
Kelber, 1–20; see also B. L. Mack, *A Myth of Innocence: Mark and Christian Origins* (Philadelphia: Fortress Press, 1988), 249–312.

[6] In 1892, Martin Kähler argued that the Gospels are merely passion narratives with
extended introductions; see his *The So-called Historical Jesus and the Historic, Biblical Christ*,
trans. C. E. Braaten (Philadelphia: Fortress Press, 1964), 11.

(1) Why did he suffer and die? And, more, (2) Why was he rejected by his own people? Early Christians had to answer questions not only for themselves but also for others to whom they delivered the gospel message. Bluntly, they had to make sense out of the scandalous cross. Whatever their popular style, ultimately the Gospels are theological documents.

In our century, Martin Dibelius, an early-day form critic, argued that the passion accounts were assembled prior to the Gospels. They were designed apologetically to demonstrate that Jesus' death was "according to the scriptures." As a result the passion stories cited particular Hebrew Bible texts that seemed to have been fulfilled in Christ's death, for example Psalm 22. The passion accounts were also shaped so as to line up with such texts.[7] Subsequently, C. H. Dodd proposed that early Christians not only linked the passion with particular Hebrew Bible verses, such as Psalm 22, but drew on the same passages, specifically Isaiah 52 and 53, for theology to interpret Christ's dreadful death.[8] Barnabas Lindars has continued such research brilliantly in our own time.[9] More recently, there have been studies of the Righteous Sufferer in wisdom literature as well as in Qumran texts.[10] All such scholarship demonstrates that early Christian communities were busy trying to make sense of the passion in view of the resurrection. They wanted not only to understand the death of Christ but also to explain the event to skeptical Jews and Gentiles.

Another form critic, Rudolf Bultmann, traced a process of assembly that he supposed gathered independent traditions into one pre-Markan passion story.[11] But in the 1970s a number of scholars attempted reconstruction of a pre-Markan tradition. Perhaps the most important of these was by Eta Linnemann, for she established (1) a theological purpose for every pericope—all pericopes depict Jesus as a righteous sufferer; and (2) the likelihood that the overall narrative structure was Markan in design. Since Linnemann's work, most scholars have

---

[7] M. Dibelius, *From Tradition to Gospel*, trans. B. L. Woolf (New York: Charles Scribner's Sons, 1935).

[8] C. H. Dodd, *According to the Scriptures* (New York: Charles Scribner's Sons, 1953). J. Jeremias argued that the "servant" in Isaiah 53 was the crucial precedent for interpreting the death of Christ; see J. Jeremias and W. Zimmerli, *The Servant of God* (London: SCM Press, 1965).

[9] B. Lindars, *Christian Apologetics: The Doctrinal Significance of the Old Testament Quotations* (London: SCM Press, 1961).

[10] On the work of L. Ruppert, see Donahue, "Introduction," 4–5.

[11] R. Bultmann, *The History of the Synoptic Tradition*, trans. J. Marsh (New York: Harper & Row, 1968), 262–84.

regarded Mark as a theological/literary genius rather than as merely a compiler of source materials. The most massive analysis of materials in the passion tradition is by D. Dormeyer.[12]

The work of Norman Perrin has also been tremendously important.[13] Perrin regards Mark as an "apocalyptic drama" and urges a literary approach to the study of the Gospel.[14] His call for a literary analysis has been taken up by Werner Kelber and Theodore Weeden.[15] Most recently, Mary Ann Tolbert has provided a thoroughgoing literary/rhetorical analysis of Mark with particular attention to the passion materials.[16]

Another purpose for the passion story was liturgical.[17] Christian communities celebrated a Good Friday/Easter sequence quite early, a sequence that was soon extended into a primitive Holy Week.[18] Liturgical need may well have assembled the passion pericopes into a dramatic sequence for use in connection with Good Friday/Easter baptismal ritual.

But whatever the source of the passion story, it was always interpreted in the light of Christian experience. The early Christians were surprised by structures of redemptive life happening in community; they were indeed alive together in a new way. Redeemed life seemed to have emerged from the passion; the death of Christ had given them life. Thus the passion accounts were not unrelieved tragic dramas. No, the narrative of the passion is ultimately a story of salvation.

---

[12] E. Linnemann, *Studien zur Passionsgeschichte* (Göttingen: Vandenhoeck & Ruprecht, 1970); D. Dormeyer, *Die Passion Jesu als Verhaltensmodell* (Münster: Aschendorff, 1974).

[13] See N. Perrin, *A Modern Pilgrimage in New Testament Christology* (Philadelphia: Fortress Press, 1974), chaps. 3 and 5, and D. Allison, Jr., *The End of the Ages Has Come: An Early Interpretation of the Passion and Resurrection of Jesus* (Philadelphia: Fortress Press, 1985); for a somewhat similar conclusion, see H. C. Kee, *Community of the New Age: Studies in Mark's Gospel* (Philadelphia: Westminster Press, 1977).

[14] See N. Perrin, *The New Testament: An Introduction* (New York: Harcourt, Brace, Jovanovich, 1974), 143–67.

[15] W. Kelber, *The Kingdom in Mark: A New Place and a New Time* (Philadelphia: Fortress Press, 1974); idem, *The Oral and the Written Gospel: The Hermeneutics of Speaking and Writing in the Synoptic Tradition, Mark, Paul, and Q* (Philadelphia: Fortress Press, 1982); also T. J. Weeden, *Mark: Traditions in Conflict* (Philadelphia: Fortress Press, 1971).

[16] M. A. Tolbert, *Sowing the Gospel: Mark's World in Literary-historical Perspective* (Minneapolis: Fortress Press, 1989).

[17] Donahue, "Introduction," 6–7.

[18] See T. J. Talley, *The Origins of the Liturgical Year* (New York: Pueblo, 1986), pt. 1.

The Story Begins (§231; Mark 14:1-2)

At the beginning of the passion narrative, we learn that the chief priests and the scribes were plotting to kill Jesus. They were cautious, afraid of public reaction:

> [1]Now in two days it would be the Passover and the Unleavened Bread. The chief priests and scribes were looking for a way to nab him surreptitiously so as to kill him. [2]But they said: "Not at the feast, lest there be rioting among the people."

Thereafter, the passion story unfolds in a series of episodes.

The Anointing at Bethany (§232; Mark 14:3-9)

At once, the Gospels draw a contrast between the conniving priests and scribes and the lavish devotion of a woman at Bethany.[19] Therefore, ministers may want to read 14:1-2 as a prologue to the story of the anointing, as well as vv. 10-11 as an epilogue.

> [3]When he was in Bethany in the house of Simon the leper, while he relaxed at table, a woman came with an alabaster jar of perfume, pure expensive nard. Smashing the alabaster jar, she poured [the perfume] over his head. [4]Some of the people grumbled among themselves, "Why was there this waste of perfume? [5]The perfume could have been sold for more than ten thousand dollars to give to the poor!" They were furious with her.
> [6]But Jesus said, "Let her be. Why are you giving her a hard time? She has done a good thing for me. [7]For you will always have the poor with you, and whenever you want you can be good to them, but you will not always have me. [8]What she could, she did; she anointed my body ahead of time for burial. [9]Truly, I'm telling you, wherever the gospel is preached through all the world, what she did will be told in her memory."

The story of the anointing at Bethany appears in Mark, Matthew, and John. Of course, there is an extensive anointing narrative in Luke (7:36-50), but in a very different context.[20] Although Mark's account

---

[19] Other versions: Matt. 26:6-13; Luke 7:36-50; John 12:1-8. In Matthew those who complain are disciples. No monetary value is put on the nard; instead it "could have been sold for much." In Matthew and in John the phrase "whenever you want you can be good to them" is dropped. In John it is Judas Iscariot who complains and who is said to steal from the disciples' purse. John also identifies the woman as Mary, Martha's sister. Their brother, Lazarus, is said to be present, but Simon the leper has disappeared. In John, as in Luke's account, the woman anoints Jesus' feet rather than his head, wiping his feet with her hair — perhaps to parallel the footwashing story. John also skips Mark's "What she could, she did; she anointed my body ahead of time for burial." He relocates the event "six days before the Passover," prior to the entry into Jerusalem.

[20] P. Tillich has a brilliant sermon on Luke's version of the anointing; see "To Whom Much Is Forgiven . . . ," *The New Being* (New York: Charles Scribner's Sons, 1955), 3–14.

ends with "wherever the gospel is preached . . . what she did will be told in her memory," he neglects to give us her name. He does, however, introduce Jesus' host as Simon the leper. Inasmuch as Hansen's disease, what we call leprosy, was not known in first-century Palestine, the word *leper* refers to some sort of cured skin eruption. The woman anoints Jesus with costly nard, a base for most perfumes, which according to Mark was worth "more than three hundred denarii." We do not know exactly what a denarius was worth, but according to the parable of the workers and hours (Matt. 20:9) it matched a field worker's daily pay, nowadays about thirty-five dollars. Thus I have translated "more than three hundred denarii" as "more than ten thousand dollars."[21] A tidy sum indeed!

Bystanders were incensed: "They were furious with her" (*embrimaomai* = to lash out at). "The perfume could have been sold . . . to give to the poor!" they explain. Care for the poor was, of course, a requisite of Jewish piety, as it should be with us. In answering, Jesus seems to be paraphasing Deuteronomy 15:11, "Since there will never cease to be some in need on the earth, I therefore command you, 'Open your hand to the poor and needy neighbor in your land'" (NRSV). Certainly, "you will always have the poor with you" cannot be understood as a counsel of neglect, particularly as Mark adds "whenever you want you can be good to them." Often the verse has been used to justify lavish spending on church decor or for church programs, rather than benevolences; that is to say, we must honor Jesus now, for the poor will always be hanging around. No, the verse refers to the woman at Bethany; it is not ecclesial law. After Christ's death and resurrection, when "he is not here," we can lavish ourselves on the poor, as we should. Likewise, the King James Version's translation of v. 6, "she has done a beautiful thing," does not endorse aesthetic celebrations of Christ as being more desirable than charity. Verses 6-7 have been tragically mispreached for centuries.

Please notice: In Mark, the woman anoints Jesus' head, a ritual used to designate kings. Thus, although chief priests and scribes may plot to murder Jesus, a faithful woman acknowledges his royal status. Notice that the passage may relate to the resurrection story in Mark 16:1, where faithful women come to the tomb to anoint Christ's body.[22]

---

[21] When reading scripture publicly, it seems useful for preachers to translate biblical monetary figures into contemporary equivalents.

[22] See Tolbert, *Sowing,* 273-74; see also the discussion on 274 n. 3.

The passage is filled with subtle contrasts: (1) between the cautious plotters in vv. 1-2 and the woman's extravagant love; (2) between the woman's spontaneous tribute and the calculating, price-tag reading moralism of "the perfume could have been sold . . ."; (3) between the woman's royal anointing and Christ's prophecy, "she anointed my body . . . for burial"; and (4) between the murderous intent of the officially religious and the fidelity of a low-status woman. Is there an even more subtle parallel being drawn between the outpouring of the woman's devotion and the soon to come outpouring of Christ's love on the cross? Of course the statement in v. 9 has come true; the passage is still being preached — by us.

There follows another contrast (§233): a two-verse entr'acte telling of how Judas sold out Christ for cash. Thus, the anointing at Bethany is bracketed by cruel oppositions.

> 10And Judas Iscariot, one of the twelve, went to the chief priests so as to betray him to them. 11When they heard him, they were delighted and promised to give him money. And he looked for an opportunity to betray him.

Preparation for the Passover (§234; Mark 14:12-16)

The detailed story of how disciples prepared for the Last Supper is seldom preached, perhaps because it does not seem to contain much of a message.[23] But the passage is packed with meaning:

> 12On the first day of the Unleavened Bread, when they used to sacrifice the Passover lambs, his disciples said to him: "Where do you want us to go and prepare for you to eat the Passover?" 13And he sent two of his disciples, telling them, "Go into the city, and a man carrying a jug of water will meet you. Follow him and, 14wherever he goes in, say to the homeowner, 'The Teacher asks, Where is my guest room where I will eat the Passover with my disciples?' 15He will show you a spacious upper room, furnished and ready. You prepare for us there." 16So the disciples went off and came into the city, and found everything as he had told them. They prepared the Passover.

Begin by noticing some similarities: Read 1 Samuel 10:1-9 and also Mark 11:1-10. Twice Mark tells stories of two disciples entering the city on Jesus' orders and, in each case, finding the orders they have

---

23 Other versions: Matt. 26:17-19; Luke 22:7-13. Matthew reduces the story. He omits reference to the sacrifice of Passover lambs, possibly because he knows Mark's time schedule is incorrect. He drops "two disciples" as well as mention of the jug of water. He also skips description of the upper room. He adds, however, the phrase, "My time is at hand." Luke introduces his familiar notion of the necessity of Christ's death by mentioning "the day . . . on which the Passover lamb *had* to be sacrificed." He specifies the two disciples: "Jesus sent Peter and John."

been given amazingly confirmed. After the first story, Jesus enters the city and pronounces an end to the temple, and after the second story he goes, step by step, to his death on the cross.[24] In 1 Samuel, young *anointed* King Saul is sent on a journey with instructions that also come true; he goes and finds out about a donkey and then, later, meets men carrying three kids, three loaves of bread, and a skin of wine. So in Mark 11, two disciples go out and collect a colt for Jesus' entry into Jerusalem and here, in chapter 14, again two disciples go to meet a man who is toting a jug. Once more, by alluding to 1 Samuel, Mark introduces the theme of kingship.

The story of the two disciples going to set up the Last Supper is strangely anonymous: Names are not mentioned. "Two disciples," who are they? "A man with a jug," who is he? Who is the "homeowner"? Where is the "upper room"? Details seem deliberately suppressed and, thus, mysterious. The mysterious character of the story may serve to convey certain ideas: (1) Jesus' prescience is a witness to his prophetic insight, thus certifying the truth of his apocalyptic predictions in chapter 13. (2) Anonymous details heighten the sense of a drama unfolding: The faithless have organized; chief priests and scribes, along with Judas, are in place. And the faithful have acted; Christ has been anointed. Now, the inevitable drama will continue in its inevitable course. (3) The reduction of historical details heightens a huge sense of divine destining.

The first verse of the passage is very significant: "On the first day of the Unleavened Bread, when they used to sacrifice the Passover lambs." Here we have themes of liberation and of sacrifice signaled at the outset. Vernon K. Robbins has called attention to the heaped allusions to bread in Mark, chapters 6–8.[25] In these earlier chapters, bread is something that Christ, like Moses, provides for all; whereas bread is restricted by the Pharisees (7:1–21), and the multiplication of the loaves is incomprehensible to the disciples (6:52). Now, through the death of Christ, the world is to be given the bread of life.

So can the passage be preached? Its strange, anonymous character

---

[24] W. H. Kelber, *Mark's Story of Jesus* (Philadelphia: Fortress Press, 1979), 73; also Tolbert, *Sowing,* 257–59.

[25] V. K. Robbins, "Last Meal: Preparation, Betrayal, and Absence," in *The Passion in Mark,* ed. Kelber, 21–40. In 6:8, the disciples are sent out two by two with "no bread"; a first feeding of the crowd with bread occurs in 6:34-44; in 7:1-23, there is a discussion of "clean" foods; in 8:1-11, a second crowd is fed with bread; a discourse on bread follows in 8:14-21; in 8:15 the disciples are warned to beware of the leaven of the Pharisees and of Herod.

befits our Christian lives. Martyrs may blaze, but often all we have to do is handle prosaic arrangements anonymously. Nevertheless in all we do there may be conflict between the way of the worldly world and ways of charity that obey Christ. And, through all things, even through what may appear to be minor matters, the purposes of God are moving. The purposes of God lead toward an image of a great, world-sized messianic banquet.

The Traitor (§235; Mark 14:17-21)

The story of the Last Supper[26] begins with Christ's dramatic prophecy of the betrayal:

> [17]When it was evening, he arrived with the twelve. [18]As they were relaxed, eating, Jesus said, "Truly, I'm telling you, one of you will betray me, one who is eating with me." [19]And they were deeply hurt and began to say to him, one by one, "Surely, not I?" [20]He said to them, "One of the twelve; one who is dipping in the same dish with me. [21]Yes, Humanity's Child must go as it is written, but woe to the person through whom Humanity's Child is betrayed; better for him, if he had not been born."

Although readers already know who will betray Jesus, Mark pictures the disciples as being in the dark; they know nothing of the plot. So when Jesus announces point-blank, "one of you will betray me, one who is eating with me," they ask, each one, "Surely, not I?" The dialogue is stunning. Jesus tells the matter-of-fact truth, and instead of being aghast, the disciples become vaguely defensive. In other words, they admit that almost any one of us human beings is capable of treachery; we are known sinners. The questioning, "Surely, not I?" is scarcely an emphatic denial full of bravado, "Not I, *no way!*" They are forced to stare with widened eyes into their own souls. Yet Jesus is quite certain: "One of the twelve; one who is dipping in the same dish with me."

Notice that the announcement of the betrayal occurs at table where food is shared family style at a sacred meal. So in the midst of holy

---

[26] Other versions: Matt. 26:20-29; Luke 22:14, 21-23; John 13:21-30. Matthew follows the Markan version rather closely, omitting Mark 14:18b, "one who is eating with me," which is a quote from Ps. 41:9. He adds, however, a final word from Judas (Matt. 26:25) not found in Mark. Luke has altered the sequence of the passage. Luke alone has 22:15-16 at the start of the meal. Luke also saves discussion of the betrayal until the conclusion of the supper. Notice that whereas Mark and Matthew begin the account with mention of "the twelve," Luke substitutes the word *apostles* instead, perhaps anticipating their subsequent role in Acts. John has created a much more elaborate story involving the beloved disciple, Peter, and Judas.

unity, treachery is announced. See the movement of God toward communion and the tug of sin tearing at unity. More, although the twelve have been chosen to be a new people, they are stuck with the same old-Adam sinfulness. Fortunately, for all of us, the Savior presides.

The final verse is a strong theological statement. The scene displays two wills at work, the self-giving of God and the human will to refuse God's gift: "Humanity's Child must go as it is written, but woe to the person through whom Humanity's Child is betrayed." Here is the paradox of divine purpose and fierce, yet responsible, human freedom.

The Institution of the Lord's Supper
(§236; Mark 14:22-25)

22As they were eating, he took a loaf and blessed it and broke it and gave it to them, saying, "Take, this is my body." 23And, taking a cup, he offered thanks and gave it to them; and they all drank from it. 24He said to them, "This is my blood of the covenant, poured out for many. 25Truly, I'm telling you, I will not drink anymore from the fruit of the vine until I drink it new in God's new order."

As many scholars have noted, although Mark refers to celebrating a Passover, the supper he portrays is emphatically *not* a Passover meal.[27] To mention only two matters, there is no reference to the Exodus event and no lamb being eaten.[28] Historians may worry and anxiously try to

----

[27] Other versions: Matt. 26:26-29; Luke 22:15-20; also 1 Cor. 11:23-25. Scholars have chased the different forms of the Lord's Supper tradition for years. Although some argue for the primacy of Mark's eucharistic words, most scholars accept the tradition reported in 1 Corinthians as the earliest record we possess. In Paul's version, the bread and cup bracket the meal, and the words "This cup is the new covenant in my blood" do not establish a body/blood parallel as in Mark. Paul also adds, "Do this . . . for the remembering of me." Matthew follows Mark, but adds "eat" to the imperative "take," and turns Mark's "and they all drank of it" into a parallel imperative, "Drink of it, all of you." Also note, "my Father's kingdom" instead of "the kingdom of God." Luke has a very different tradition that some scholars argue predates other traditions, although such a claim is difficult to support. In Luke we have two references to the coming kingdom of God (v. 16 and v. 18), specific reference to "eating the Passover" (v. 15), and a radical reversing of the cup and the bread. The phrase over the cup is unique: "Take this and divide it among yourselves." In Luke the covenant theme disappears, and the saying regarding the bread seems to dangle at the conclusion of the ritual. The various traditions no doubt reflect different liturgical practices in different early Christian communities.

[28] The complicated question of what exactly the Last Supper was has intrigued scholars. For discussion, see G. Dix, *The Shape of the Liturgy* (London: Dacre Press, 1945), chap. 4; A. J. B. Higgins, *The Lord's Supper in the New Testament* (London: SCM Press, 1952), chap. 2; and, more recently, I. H. Marshall, *Last Supper and Lord's Supper* (Grand Rapids, Mich.: William B. Eerdmans, 1980), pt. 3, chap. 3. For a fairly

establish that the supper was a Passover because, after all, the Bible says so; but Mark's purpose is less historical than theological. All the accounts of the Last Supper present not so much a Passover meal as a prototypical Christian Lord's Supper. What is more, all accounts reflect different theological and literary purposes. Werner H. Kelber is helpful:

> This last meal is as little a traditional Passover as the Kingdom of God is like the kingdom of father David, or the anointment at Bethany was like the expected royal investiture. Whatever they are eating, their meal is not centered around the paschal lamb, and Jesus' words do not commemorate the Exodus events. Instead Jesus drastically recasts the traditional Passover in view of his death.[29]

The supper is bracketed by dire passion predictions, v. 21 and vv. 27-28; Jesus speaks of betrayal and of desertion. The passion predictions echo a series of previous predictions, all of which were delivered in conjunction with overconfident, triumphalist exclamations by the disciples (see 8:29, 31; 9:5, 12; 10:33, 37). Yet here Christ breaks bread and shares a cup, making covenant with a broken, treacherous humanity.

What do the eucharistic words mean in Mark's context?[30] They point in two directions at once: to the coming death of Christ and, at the same time, to Christian communities yet to come that will continue to break bread and share one cup using the same formulaic words. Whereas people will plot to take Christ's life, here he willingly gives himself: "This is my body [*sōma*]."[31] Likewise, the word connected with the cup, "This is my blood of the covenant,"[32] which harkens back to Exodus 24,

---

popular presentation of the Passover tradition, see T. H. Gaster, *Passover: Its History and Traditions* (Boston: Beacon Press, 1949).

[29] Kelber, *Mark's Story*, 74.

[30] For discussion see J. Jeremias, *The Eucharistic Words of Jesus,* trans. N. Perrin, 3d German ed. (New York: Charles Scribner's Sons, 1960; Philadelphia: Fortress Press, 1978); and W. Marxsen, *The Lord's Supper as a Christological Problem,* trans. L. Nieting (Philadelphia: Fortress Press, 1970); see also E. Schweizer, *The Lord's Supper according to the New Testament,* trans. J. M. Davis (Philadelphia: Fortress Press, 1967), and, more recently, X. Léon-Dufour, *Sharing the Eucharistic Bread: The Witness of the New Testament,* trans. M. J. O'Connell (New York: Paulist Press, 1982).

[31] As Andreas Carlstadt and, more recently, William Orr have noted, a neuter "this" (*touto*) scarcely can modify the masculine "bread" (*ton arton*); see W. F. Orr and J. A. Walther, *I Corinthians* (Garden City, N.Y.: Doubleday, 1976), 268–75. Instead, the word *this* may refer to the gathering that will die with Christ's death and, subsequently, be redeemed by his death.

[32] Some manuscripts add the word "new" before "covenant," but the NRSV does not accept the addition.

refers not only to Christ's sacrificial death that will give life to a new humanity, but also to Christ's covenantal love pledged to a most unreliable discipleship. Recall a previous use of "cup" (10:35-45). When the sons of Zebedee engaged in a power grab, Jesus asked, "Can you drink the cup I drink?," a reference to his coming death. The disciples, as obtuse as ever, answer glibly, "Sure we can!" Here they literally drink Christ's cup, although soon they will "fall away." Mark's irony is subtle.

To bring out the full meaning of the supper in Mark, ministers will wish to read an extended passage so that the meal is hedged by the themes of betrayal and denial. In the midst of treachery and timid desertion, here is a self-giving Christ celebrating covenantal unity with his chosen, if sinful, people. Yet, at the same time, he looks toward God's future new order, which will be populated with forgiven sinners (v. 25).

Last Words (§237; Luke 22:24-38)

Luke has rearranged the story of the supper, the announcement of the betrayal, and the prediction of Peter's denial.[33] As the supper draws to a close, he has Jesus speak a few words. The speech poses many, many problems:[34]

[24]There was an argument among them over who was considered the greatest. [25]So he said to them, "The kings of the pagans lord it over them, and those in authority call themselves 'Benefactors.' [26]Not so with you! No, the greatest among you must be like the youngest; and those in authority, like servants. [27]For who is greater? One at table or the server? Isn't it the one at table? Yet I am among you as one who serves.

[28]"You are those who have stuck with me during my trials. [29]As the Father has conferred on me, I confer kingship on you, [30]so you may eat and drink at my table in my new order and sit on thrones, judging the twelve tribes of Israel.

[31]"Simon, Simon, look! Satan has begged to sift you all like wheat, [32]but I have asked that your faith will not fail you; and that, when you have turned around, you will strengthen your brothers [and sisters]." [33]He said to him, "Lord, I'm ready to go along with you to prison and to death!" [34]But he replied, "I'm telling you, Peter, the rooster will not crow today until you have denied you know me three times."

---

[33] Other versions: Only Luke locates the material as a Last Supper discourse. Mark attaches the teaching about servanthood to the story of the sons of Zebedee who ask for positions of power in the kingdom (Mark 10:42-45). Matthew also has such sayings in 20:25-28. Matthew speaks of thrones to judge the tribes in Matt. 19:28. John concludes the footwashing with similar teachings on servanthood. Luke alone has the material in vv. 35-38.

[34] For a detailed treatment of the passage, see the careful analysis by M. L. Soards, *The Passion in Luke: The Special Material of Luke 22,* Journal for the Study of the New Testament, Supplement Series 14 (Sheffield, Eng.: JSOT Press, 1987).

[35]He said to them, "When I sent you out without a purse, or baggage, or sandals, did you want for anything?" "Nothing," they said. [36]Then he said to them, "Now, whoever has a purse, hold on to it; likewise baggage. Whoever is unarmed, sell your clothes and buy a sword! [37]For I tell you, what has been written will be fulfilled in me: 'He was numbered among the outlaws.' Indeed, everything about me is coming to a conclusion." [38]They said, "Look, Lord, here are two swords!" He said to them, "That's enough."

The discourse begins with a contrast. Among the pagans (*ethnōn*), kings "lord it over" people and have themselves called "Benefactor." The title "Benefactor" was given to rulers in Syria and Egypt, as well as to Roman emperors, for example, Caesar Augustus and Nero. Jesus addresses his disciples who, evidently, hanker for status; they want to be "great." But, says Jesus, among Christians "greatness" is defined by service to others. Jesus is not urging humility or a democratic leveling of all distinctions. But he is calling for self-giving as a way of true leadership. He adds a rhetorical question: Who is greater in our eyes, he asks, the person at table or the waiter (*diakonōn*)? Obviously, we regard the one at table as more important. Yet, says Jesus, "I am among you as one who serves [*diakonōn*]."[35] The passage as a whole reflects the Christian community toward the end of the first century. So Luke has Jesus addressing leaders of the early church.

The discourse shifts somewhat: "You are those who have stuck with me during my trials," says Jesus. Presumably, Jesus is referring to conflicts with established religion. But, more likely, Luke may have in mind the trials of early Christian communities. Christian servant-leadership may anticipate a place at the great messianic banquet (Luke 13:29), and will share like "judges" of ancient Israel in Christ's magisterial office. Again, Luke may be looking toward the authoritative role of apostles in the early church. Psalm 122:3-4 may lie behind his words:

> Jerusalem — built as a city
>   that is bound firmly together.
> To it the tribes go up,
>   the tribes of the Lord,
> as was decreed for Israel,
>   to give thanks to the name of the Lord.
> For there the thrones for judgment were set up,
>   the thrones of the house of David.

---

[35] For an interpretation of the passage, see P. S. Minear, *To Heal and to Reveal: The Prophetic Vocation according to Luke* (New York: Seabury Press, 1976), 3-30.

Luke then inserts the tradition with regard to Peter. Because Peter will play a positive role in Acts, Luke has softened the finality of Peter's denial: "When you have turned around, you will strengthen your brothers [and sisters]." Peter will be preserved in faith.

The last part of Jesus' table talk is found only in Luke. Earlier in the Gospel Jesus has dispatched the "seventy," as "lambs among wolves," to "every town and place." At that time he specified "no purse, no bag, no sandals." They were to accept the welcome of townspeople or, when unwelcome, leave. Suddenly, here, there is a distinct change of mood — the crisis of the cross has begun. Soon, Christ will be "numbered among the outlaws" (Isa. 53:12) and so will his followers (Acts 4:1-3). The disciples, who lack insight into the future, take Jesus literally: "Look, Lord, here are two swords!" Are they offering one of the swords to Jesus? Jesus' reply has occasioned some debate. Is he saying, ironically, "Well, if the answer were force, two swords ought to be enough"? Or, as some suggest, is he simply saying, "Enough of that"?

The specificity of the verse, "*two* swords," has led some interpreters — usually those who are as literal-minded as the disciples — to read all sorts of extra meaning into the text. But Jesus is not predicting super-power conflicts or endorsing big budget defense spending. "No more of this!" he says later in the Garden of Gethsemane when one of his disciples wields a sword. Christian apostles are armed with no force except the word of the gospel and the power of the Spirit.

The discourse is strange and strangely expressed. If preachers try to set it into the setting of the supper, prior to the cross, the passage may be difficult to interpret. Instead, we must view Jesus' speech as addressed to us who are church people today. Christian leadership is servant-leadership, and Christian power is the swordless power of the Spirit of love. Certainly we cannot expect public welcome in a time of crisis. But in every trial we can try to stick with the Lord Jesus Christ.

Peter's Denial Prophesied
(§238; Mark 14:26-31)

26Having sung a hymn, they went out to the Mount of Olives. 27And Jesus said to them, "You will all fall away, because it is written, 'I will strike the shepherd and the sheep will be scattered,' 28but, after I am raised, I will go on ahead of you into Galilee."

29Then Peter said to him, "Even if everyone fails you, I won't!" 30And Jesus answered him, "Truly, I'm telling you, today, during this night, before a rooster crows twice, you will disown me three times." 31But he replied hotly, "Even if I have to die with you, no way will I deny you!" And they all said the same thing.

The little passage[36] works in two ways: it concludes the supper narrative with a prediction of desertion, and it prepares for the story of Peter's denial. The citation from Zechariah 13:7 matches no known version of the text but serves admirably to pick up a significant term, "fall away" (*skandalisthēsontai*). As Mary Ann Tolbert notes, the word has appeared earlier in the extended explanation of the parable of the sower (4:16-17): "And these are the ones sown on rocky ground: when they hear the word, they immediately receive it with joy. But they have no root, and endure only for a while; then, when trouble or persecution arises on account of the word, immediately they fall away [*skandalizontai*]."[37]

Peter is, of course, pathetically wrong; he does not appear to have much insight into his own soul. He becomes vehement: "Even if I have to die with you, no way will I deny you!" But he will deny Jesus. None of the disciples will answer the call to suffering and death. And none of them even notices the odd resurrection prophecy that will be echoed at the empty tomb, "After I am raised, I will go on ahead of you into Galilee." Success story dreams can deceive us all.

The little passage will probably not be preached as a separate pericope. Verses 26-28 may attach to the supper narrative, and vv. 29-31 to the story of Peter's denial. The passage also underscores Jesus' prophetic reliability; what he says will be, will be.

Jesus in Gethsemane (§239; Mark 14:32-42)

Earlier in the Gospel, in chapter 13, Jesus has delivered an extended apocalyptic prophecy that concludes: "Therefore, keep awake — for you do not know when the master of the house will come, in the evening, or at midnight, or at cockcrow, or at dawn, or else he may find you asleep when he comes suddenly. And what I say to you I say to all:

---

[36] Other versions: Matt. 26:30-35; Luke 22:31-34; John 13:36-38. Matthew follows Mark with only minor changes. He adds "because of me this night" and alters the citation from Zech. 13:7, adding "of the flock." He also drops Mark's "twice." Luke, who has rearranged the material radically so as to include a final discourse at table, has told of Peter's denial previously in 22:31-34, following the discussion of true greatness and Christ's appointing of the twelve. Luke has Jesus say, "Satan has demanded to sift you like wheat, but I have prayed for you that your own faith may not fail; and you, when once you have turned back, strengthen your brothers." After all, Luke will picture Peter heroically in Acts. John abbreviates Jesus' prediction, but creates a dialogue (13:36-37) to preface the prophecy.

[37] Tolbert, *Sowing,* 212.

Keep awake" (Mark 13:35-37).[38] In the garden,[39] however, the disciples sleep:[40]

> [32]They came into a place named Gethsemane, and he said to his disciples, "Sit down here while I pray." [33]He took with him Peter and James and John, and he began to shake all over and to be agitated; [34]and he said to them, "Now my soul is in anguish to the point of death; stay here and keep watch." [35]And going forward a little, he threw himself down on the ground and prayed that, if possible, the hour might pass him by; [36]"Abba, Father," he said, "all things are possible for you—take this cup from me; nevertheless, not what I want, but what you want." [37]Then he came back and found them sleeping, and he said to Peter, "Simon, are you sleeping? Couldn't you keep watch for a single hour? [38]Watch and pray, lest you be put to the test. The spirit is willing, yes, but the flesh is weak." [39]Going away again, he prayed saying the same words. [40]He returned and found them sleeping again, for their eyes had become heavy. They did not know what to say to him. [41]A third time he came back, and he said to them, "Do you still sleep and rest? Enough! Look, the hour has come for Humanity's Child to be betrayed into the hands of sinners. [42]Get up, let's go; see, my betrayer has drawn near."

In the Gospel of Mark there are references to geography; the names of places are important. Jesus was anointed in Bethany while priests and scribes plotted in Jerusalem. Now we enter the Garden of Gethsemane, which, significantly, is between Bethany and Jerusalem. The name Gethsemane means "olive press." Here Christ, the anointed one, will be pressured and in agony.

The story begins with Jesus telling the disciples, "Sit down here while I pray," a command that may recall Abraham's words in Genesis 22:5 as he prepares to go up to the place of sacrifice with his unsuspecting son, Isaac. Jesus takes with him Peter, James, and John, all future leaders of the church. The same three disciples were on hand for the raising of Jairus's daughter (5:37-43) and were also with Jesus on the Mount of Transfiguration (9:2). The description of Jesus' agony is extreme, particularly given Mark's usual restraint, but this moment is

---

[38] The injunction to "keep awake" is stressed throughout chapter 13: v. 23, "be alert"; v. 33, "beware, keep alert."

[39] Other versions: Matt. 26:36-46; Luke 22:40-46. Matthew follows Mark's version with only minor changes. He offers a slightly different reading of Jesus' prayer and he mentions Jesus' leaving the disciples for a third time, which Mark does not report. Luke greatly abbreviates the account, adding an angel to strengthen Christ and the description of sweat like "great drops of blood falling down on the ground," an addition that is found in most reliable manuscripts of the Gospel. The last two prayers disappear as well as repeated visits to the sleeping disciples; in effect, Mark 14:38b-42 is skipped.

[40] On the Gethsemane story, see W. H. Kelber, "The Hour of the Son of Man and the Temptation of the Disciples," in *The Passion in Mark,* ed. Kelber, 41-60; Tolbert, *Sowing,* 214-18; also D. M. Stanley, *Jesus in Gethsemane: The Early Church Reflects on the Suffering of Jesus* (New York: Paulist Press, 1980).

the time of crisis: "Now my soul is in anguish to the point of death."[41] Jesus tells the three disciples to stay and keep watch.

The prayer in the garden is Christ's moment of decision. He prays that "the hour might pass him by." "The hour" is a phrase that Jesus used earlier on the Mount of Olives when he delivered his apocalyptic "sermon" (chap. 13); it is the hour of great tribulation "when they bring you to trial and hand you over" (13:11), and, ultimately, the hour when Humanity's Child will come: "About that day or hour no one knows. . . . Beware, keep alert, for you do not know when the time will come" (13:32-33). What is at stake in the Garden of Gethsemane? Nothing less than the coming of God's new order—through suffering!

The prayer begins with the Aramaic "Abba," an intimate word for father, not unlike our word "daddy."[42] The prayer itself unfolds in three clauses: "all things are possible for you"; "take this cup from me"; and "nevertheless, not what I want, but what you want." The first clause affirms the sovereign freedom of God and, at the same time, our freedom within God's freedom. The second clause uses the cup metaphor that has been used with the sons of Zebedee ("Can you drink the cup I drink?") and also at the supper ("This is my blood of the covenant poured out for many"); it is the cup of suffering and death.[43] The last clause is, of course, a word of wrenching faithfulness—"not what I want, but what you want." Jesus is not a helpless puppet, tugged by fixed destiny toward the cross; nor is he a self-pitying martyr "half in love with easeful death": He does not want to suffer and die. Nevertheless, in freedom, Christ bends his will to the will of his "Abba."

Abruptly, the story turns to the dozing disciples. Jesus speaks to Peter, using the name Simon, which was the name he was known by before his call to discipleship (3:16): "Simon, are you sleeping? Couldn't you keep watch for a single hour?" Then he addresses the group: "Watch and pray, lest you be put to the test," words that recall the conclusion to Christ's apocalyptic discourse (13:32-37). Jesus himself has been tested and has bowed to the will of God. Now the disciples are tested and fail—terribly. Three times Jesus finds the disciples asleep, "for their eyes had become heavy." They can neither

---

[41] The words may echo Ps. 42:11, "Why are you cast down, O my soul, and why are you disquieted within me?" (NRSV).

[42] For discussion of "Abba," see J. Jeremias, *The Prayers of Jesus* (London: SCM Press, 1967), 11-65.

[43] See Lam. 4:21; also Jer. 25:15-28 and Isa. 51:17, where the cup is the cup of God's wrath.

watch nor pray, and cannot answer their Lord. "Do you still sleep and rest?"[44] Jesus asks; and then with an awful finality he says, "Enough!" (*apechei*). Scholars explain that the word we have translated as "enough" was a frequently used commercial term; on a receipted bill it meant "paid in full."[45] Thus, although the disciples have been given three opportunities for faithfulness, they have failed; their account is closed. Now the "hour" has come: "See, my betrayer has drawn near."

The scene in the Garden of Gethsemane should not be split in two by preachers. We are meant to see our own terrifying weakness at the same time as we see Christ, shaken and in anguish, bending his will to the will of God. The passage includes *all* disciples, although only the three leaders are named. Only as the church faces up to its chronic apostasy can it be fit to follow the risen Christ Jesus.

Jesus Taken Captive (§240; Mark 14:43-52)

Following Jesus' abrupt "Enough!" the action intensifies; he is betrayed, arrested, and deserted.[46] The passage begins, breathlessly, "all at once."

[43]As he was still speaking, all at once, Judas, one of the twelve, came up; and with him was a mob with swords and clubs from the chief priests, scribes, and elders. [44]Now his betrayer had arranged a signal for them, saying, "The one I kiss, he's it! Grab him, and take him away under guard." [45]Immediately, he came up to him and said: "Rabbi," and kissed him. [46]And they took hold of him and arrested him. [47]But someone who was standing by drew a sword and struck the high priest's slave, cutting off his ear. [48]Then Jesus said, "Have you come with swords and clubs to

---

[44] The sentence has troubled translators for centuries. Does it read, "Sleep on now and take your rest," as in the King James Version? If so, Jesus urges sleep in one sentence and then, almost immediately, says, "Get up." Along with some other versions, we have translated the sentence into an ironic question, "Do you still sleep and rest?"

[45] Tolbert, *Sowing*, 216–17. For a summary of options, see C. E. B. Cranfield, *The Gospel according to Saint Mark* (Cambridge: Cambridge University Press, 1972), 435–36.

[46] Other versions: Matt. 26:47-56; Luke 22:47-53; John 18:2-12. Matthew follows Mark, making only a few changes. He has Jesus respond to Judas by saying, "Friend, do what you are here to do." Matthew also adds an extended comment with regard to the person who sliced off the ear of the high priest's slave: "Put your sword back. . . ." (Matt. 26:52-54). Luke abbreviates Mark's account, dropping reference to the armed mob, as well as information about the prearranged signal. In Luke, Judas comes to kiss Jesus and, apparently, Jesus stops him: "Judas, would you betray the Son of Man with a kiss?" When someone cuts off the slave's ear, Jesus says, "No more of this!" and promptly heals the man's ear. Luke also adds "This is your hour, and the power of darkness" to Jesus' remark about teaching in the temple. Both Luke and Matthew drop mention of the shirtless young man. John has a very different treatment of the account, which we will discuss in our review of his passion narrative.

arrest me as if I were a crook? [49]Every day I was among you in the temple teaching, and you didn't arrest me. But—let the scriptures be fulfilled." [50]Then, deserting him, they all ran away. [51]A certain man was following him, wearing nothing but a shirt over his bare body. [52]They grabbed him but, dropping his shirt, he ran away naked.

Earlier in the Gospel, Jesus had told the parable of the vineyard owner's son (12:1-12), which tells of how the tenant farmworkers seized and killed the owner's son. Those who heard the parable "wanted to arrest him." Here Jesus is seized.

The scene begins with Judas's arrival; he is apparently leading a gang of hired "muscle." "Every *day* I was among you in the temple teaching, and you didn't arrest me," Jesus says, pointing out the surreptitious character of his arrest at night. Notice that the chief priests, scribes, and elders do not appear; they have sent others "with swords and clubs" to do their dirty work. Judas has arranged a signal for the mob ("The one I kiss, he's it!); they do not even know the man they will grab. So Judas, one of the twelve, comes to kiss his "Rabbi." The sign of love has become a signal for betrayal.

Notice that the disciples, who earlier had echoed Peter's rash pledge ("Even if I have to die with you, no way will I deny you!"), run for their lives. And although Peter will follow at a safe distance (14:54), ultimately he too will save his own skin. Only two people seem to stand out in the episode: the swordsman and the naked young man. An unnamed bystander pulls out his sword and, of all things, chops an ear off the high priest's slave. The other unnamed figure is much more interesting. He wears a linen "cloth" (*sindona*) and drops his cloth to race from the garden. Later, we will learn that Jesus' body is wrapped in a linen cloth (*sindoni*) (15:46), and we will be greeted on Easter Day by a "young man" in a white robe announcing the risen Christ (16:5). Is the young man a symbolic figure who is stripped naked by the passion of Christ, buried with him, and raised in a white baptismal robe to proclaim the gospel message? Perhaps.

Jesus' last words almost seem to reiterate his garden prayer, "Not what I want, but what you want." Jesus says, "Let the scriptures be fulfilled."

The passage is dramatic. Jesus is betrayed with a sign of love by "one of the twelve," and is deserted by all the other disciples. We followers of Christ can scarcely boast of faithfulness. For cash, we betray our Lord, and when the chips are down, we desert him posthaste. How should we stand? Not with a sword! The death of Christ strips us of all pretense. Only the mercy of God, the God who has raised up Jesus, can deliver us.

Jesus before the Sanhedrin
(§241 Part 1; Mark 14:53-65)

Mark deliberately conjoins the Sanhedrin meeting with the story of Peter's denial so as to display the contrast between Christ's confessional bravery and Peter's cowardice.[47] The whole idea of a nighttime Sanhedrin meeting is highly irregular and somewhat doubtful. Moreover, to our knowledge, the assembly had no power to impose a sentence of death.[48] Nevertheless, here is Mark's story:

> [53]They led Jesus off to the high priest's, where all the chief priests and elders and scribes were assembled. [54]Peter had followed at a distance right into the courtyard of the high priest, and was sitting with attendants warming himself by a fire. [55]Now the chief priests and the whole Sanhedrin were looking for evidence against Jesus so as to put him to death, but they could find none; [56]for although there were many perjured witnesses against him, their testimony did not agree. [57]Then some stood up and testified falsely against him, saying, [58]"We heard him say, 'I will tear down this handmade temple and, after three days, I will build up a new one, not made with hands.'" [59]But even their testimony did not agree. [60]Then, standing up among them, the high priest questioned Jesus, saying, "Aren't you going to answer what these men have said against you?" [61]But he was silent and did not answer. Again, the high priest questioned him, "Are you the Christ, the Son of the Blessed One?" [62]And Jesus said, "I am, and you will see Humanity's Child sitting at the right hand of power and coming on clouds of the sky." [63]And the high priest tore his clothes, saying, "Do we need any more witnesses? [64]You've heard the blasphemy. What does it look like to you?" They all condemned him as deserving the death penalty. [65]Then some of them began to spit on him. [They] blindfolded him and began to slug him, saying to him, "Prophesy!" Then the guards took over and beat him up.

Earlier, in his apocalyptic "sermon," Jesus had announced: "They will hand you over to councils. . . . When they bring you to trial and hand you over, do not worry beforehand about what you are to say; but

---

[47] Other versions: Matt. 26:57-68; Luke 22:54, 67-70; John 18:12-14, 19-24. Matthew follows Mark's version with only minor changes. He removes the phrases "handmade" and "not made with hands" from the description of the temple. He adds, "I put you under oath before the living God, tell us," before the high priest's final question. Luke, on the other hand, recasts the section, placing Peter's denial prior to a daytime meeting of the assembly. Luke skips the witnesses who misquote Jesus' temple prophecy (Mark 14:55-59). When finally Jesus is asked if he is the Christ, he does not answer baldly, "I am" (*egō eimi*), as in Mark, but somewhat equivocally, "If I tell you, you will not believe; and if I question, you will not answer." Luke then has the question repeated, "All of them asked, 'Are you, then, the Son of God?'" to which Jesus replies, "You say that I am."

[48] Many scholars have examined the narrative of the Sanhedrin meeting in the light of proper legal procedures; for discussion see J. Donahue, *Are You the Christ? The Trial Narrative in the Gospel of Mark* (Missoula, Mont.: University of Montana Press, 1973); G. S. Sloyan, *Jesus on Trial* (Philadelphia: Fortress Press, 1973); and, in particular, D. Juel, *The Trial of Jesus in the Gospel of Mark* (Missoula, Mont.: Scholars Press, 1977).

say whatever is given you at that time, for it is not you who speak, but the Holy Spirit" (13:9b, 11). Here Jesus appears before a council and is given words to speak. The story of Jesus' trial before the Sanhedrin is well crafted and full of irony. We know at the outset what the chief priests, elders, and scribes are after; they want evidence so as to put Jesus to death (v. 55). But even in an irregular hearing, there are problems. There are plenty of false witnesses but they do not agree, and two corroborative witnesses are required (Deut. 19:15). Then some witnesses stand up and testify, "We heard him say, 'I will tear down this handmade temple and, after three days, I will build up a new one, not made with hands.'" But readers of Mark's story know that the testimony is false. Yes, Jesus has deliberately condemned the temple cult. Three times he entered Jerusalem and, each time, went directly to the temple (11:11, 15, 27). He likened the temple to a barren fig tree and, in a prophetic demonstration, tipped over the money changers' tables. And, finally, he did announce the end of the temple (13:1-2): "As he came out of the temple, one of his disciples said to him, 'Look, Teacher, what large stones and what large buildings!' Then Jesus asked him, 'Do you see these great buildings? Not one stone will be left here upon another; all will be thrown down.'"

But notice how the testimony tinkers with Christ's prophecy. First, the witnesses imply that Christ himself will bring down the temple ("I will tear down . . ."). Second, the offensive term *handmade* is introduced to counter Jewish conviction that the sanctuary of the temple (*naon*) was of divine origin. Third, the phrase "after three days" is added, drawn from Jesus' passion predictions: "Then he began to teach them that [Humanity's Child] must undergo great suffering, and be rejected by the elders, the chief priests, and the scribes, and be killed, and after three days rise again. He said all this quite openly" (8:31-32a). Clearly, the accusation is a lie, so Christ stands mute. The distorted testimony, of course, fulfills Psalm 27:12: "for false witnesses have risen against me" (also Ps. 35:12). Yet the reported prophecy against the temple, occurring in the midst of fund raising and an elaborate temple renovation program, was bound to raise pious anger.

Climactically, Mark has the high priest himself take over interrogation: "Are you the Christ, the Son of the Blessed One?"[49] The phrase "Son of the Blessed One" is unique and may reflect some sort of liturgical affirmation from within early Christian communities, but it also ties

---

[49] In my discussion, I draw on N. Perrin, "The High Priest's Question and Jesus' Answer," in *The Passion in Mark,* ed. Kelber, 80–95.

in with Mark's previous "Son of God" sayings (1:1; 3:11). Jesus' answer is astonishing: "I am, and you will see Humanity's Child sitting at the right hand of power and coming on clouds of the sky." The first clause, "I am" (*egō eimi*), is a messianic claim that, heretofore, Mark has suppressed as a secret (see 1:34; 3:12; 8:30; 9:9; 9:30-31) lest Jesus be misunderstood. To Mark, the Messiah-King must suffer and Jesus' "I am" is an open acceptance of such a vocation. The second clause draws on apocalyptic expectation, as, for example, in Daniel 7:13-14:

> I saw one like a [Child of Humanity]
>   coming with the clouds of heaven.
> And he came to the Ancient One
>   and was presented before him.
> To him was given dominion
>   and glory and kingship,
> that all peoples, nations, and languages
>   should serve him.
> His dominion is an everlasting dominion
>   that shall not pass away,
> and his kingship is one
>   that shall never be destroyed.

Mark has previously spoken of the future coming of Humanity's Child in Christ's apocalyptic discourse: "Then they will see [Humanity's Child] coming in clouds with great power and glory" (13:26). So in Christ's reply we have the acknowledgment of his messianic suffering and death, and a prophecy of his future coming. The high priest has heard enough; he tears his clothing (2 Kings 18:37−19:1), saying: "You've heard the blasphemy. What does it look like to you?" The question may be addressed to us who hear the story.

Then, having concurred with the death penalty, some of the council begin to abuse Jesus, spitting on him, and taunting him: "Prophesy!" they cry. The cry is ironic because, previously, Jesus has prophetically predicted just such abuse (8:31; 9:12; and, particularly, 10:33-34).

The trial before the Sanhedrin is a difficult passage to preach. Again and again, Mark's narrative technique brings out irony; we are in on a secret that the members of the Sanhedrin simply do not grasp. Yet in view of v. 64 ("What does it look like to you?") the passage is meant to be preached in a decisive fashion. Maybe we hear the accusations and, from the standpoint of the Sanhedrin, agree with their severity; after all, we too defend organized religion. We then can be appalled at the seeming bravado of Christ's prediction—"you will see Humanity's Child sitting at the right hand of power." We can then be terrified by the Jesus who is condemned and beaten up; his role as Messiah is to suffer faithfully. Finally, we can face up to our own decision with regard to the Christ.

Peter's Denial
(§241 Part 2; Mark 14:66-72)

[66]While Peter was down in the courtyard, one of the high priest's serving girls came by. [67]Seeing Peter warming himself, she looked at him and said, "You were there with the Nazarene, this Jesus?" [68]But he denied it, saying, "I don't know or care about what you're saying." He went out to the foyer. [69]Catching sight of him again, the same serving girl began saying to those who were standing around, "This man is one of them." [70]Again, he denied it. After a while, those who were standing by again said to Peter, "You are one of them for sure, because you're Galilean." [71]Peter cursed and began to swear up and down, "I don't know the man you're talking about!" [72]Immediately a rooster crowed for the second time. And Peter remembered the words Jesus had spoken to him, "Before a rooster crows twice, you will disown me three times." He broke down and wept.

Although the story of Peter's denial[50] is often preached as a separate episode, it is designed as a contrast to the three accusations against Jesus by the Sanhedrin, and Jesus' brave confession, "I am." Peter's denial also matches the prophecy in Jesus' apocalyptic discourse: "Keep awake—for you do not know when the master of the house will come, in the evening, or at midnight, or at cockcrow, or at dawn" (13:35). We have seen the disciples sleeping in the evening, attended a trial of Jesus at midnight, and now Peter faces temptation at cockcrow.

The story is simple and needs little explication.[51] Peter has been a key figure in Mark's Gospel. Again and again, he has witnessed Christ's power. Peter was the first disciple called by Jesus (1:16) and the first

[50] Other versions: Matt. 26:69-75; Luke 22:56-62; John 18:15-18, 25-27. Matthew smooths out the story but essentially follows Mark closely. He inserts the name Jesus of Nazareth, and he explains the Galilean accent. And he makes sure that Peter's reply is voiced three times. Luke reduces the narrative somewhat, but varies Peter's replies, and adds, "And the Lord turned and looked at Peter."

[51] See the interpretation by K. E. Dewey, "Peter's Curse and Cursed Peter," in *The Passion in Mark,* ed. Kelber, 96–114; and also R. E. Brown, K. P. Donfried, and J. Reumann, eds., *Peter in the New Testament* (Minneapolis: Augsburg, 1973), chap. 5.

sent out to preach (3:16). His own mother-in-law has been healed (1:30), and he has watched the raising of Jairus's daughter (5:35-43). Peter has left everything to follow Jesus and, in turn, has received promise of eternal life (10:28-30). And yet, repeatedly, Peter fails. He confesses enthusiastically, "You are the Christ," only to be scandalized by Jesus' passion prediction (8:29-33). As a result, an angry Jesus turns on him, saying, "Get behind me, Satan." Then, later, on the Mount of Transfiguration, Peter cries out, "It's great to be here; let's build . . . ," only to be scolded by an ominous cloud: "This is my Son . . . listen to him!" (9:5-7). What was Peter to hear? Obviously a call to faithfulness ("let them deny themselves and take up their cross and follow me") as well as a warning ("those who are ashamed of me . . . of them [Humanity's Child] will be ashamed") (8:34, 38). Peter imagines a Messiah who is triumphant. He chases dreams of victory but, in the end, saves his own neck.

Peter's downfall is the passion. Although he boasts his own loyalty ("no way will I deny you!"), in fact he sleeps during Christ's garden agony and, finally at cockcrow, denies his Lord emphatically: "I don't know the man," swears Peter. There is some debate over the clause I have translated "Peter cursed and began to swear up and down" (*ērxato anathematizein kai omnynai*, literally, "he began to curse and swear"). Is Peter cursing himself; saying in effect, may I be cursed if I'm lying? Or is Peter cursing Jesus? The verse may be deliberately ambiguous. In any event, when the rooster crows, Peter remembers and breaks down, weeping. The story ends with a terrible finality.

The passage is often preached as a story of individual failure and subsequent redemption: Peter, subject to temptation, denies the Lord but is ultimately forgiven. But Peter is more than an individual Christian in the Gospel of Mark. Peter clearly stands for a certain impulse in the church, which is characterized by both triumphalism and self-preservation. Such an impulse is obviously with us still, particularly in our all-American, competitive denominationalism; we want to make it big with Jesus! And if faced with a choice between following the Lord and denominational preservation, why, we will pick the denomination hands down. Mark's story, sensing the severity of Peter's denial, offers no quick-fix forgiveness. Peter is never mentioned again during the account of the passion. Only later at the empty tomb does the white-robed young man say, "Go tell his disciples and Peter that he is going on ahead of you into Galilee." Ultimately, the message of the resurrection is Peter's good news.

The Death of Judas
(§§242-43; Matthew 27:1-10)

Briefly, let us turn to the Gospel of Matthew[52] for an account of Judas's suicide.[53]

> [1]Early in the morning, all the chief priests and elders met together against Jesus so as to put him to death. [2]Having tied him up, they led him away and turned him over to Pilate the governor.
> [3]When Judas, who had betrayed him, saw that [Jesus] was doomed, he repented and returned the thirty silver coins to the chief priests and elders, [4]saying, "I have sinned by betraying innocent blood." But they answered, "What's that to us? Look out for yourself!" [5]Throwing down the silver coins in the temple, he left and went out and hanged himself. [6]The chief priests took the silver, saying, "It's not lawful to put them in the treasury, since it's blood money." [7]So, together, they decided to buy a potter's field as a place to bury aliens. [8]That is why the field has been called the Field of Blood to this day. [9]Thus was fulfilled the word of the prophet Jeremiah, saying: "They took thirty silver coins, the price set on the priced one by the children of Israel, [10]and gave them for the potter's field, as the Lord commanded me."

Although many scholars dismiss the story of Judas's suicide as legendary, which is probable, nonetheless it is a subtle story and useful in preaching. The story seems to have been wedged somewhat awkwardly into the transfer of Jesus from the Sanhedrin to the court of Pilate.

Earlier, at supper, Jesus had announced his betrayal: "Woe to the person through whom Humanity's Child is betrayed; better for him, if he had not been born." The word *betrayed* (*paradidotai*) is echoed here in v. 2: "they . . . turned him over [*paredōkan*] to Pilate." Is Matthew linking Judas and the chief priests in common guilt? Perhaps.

In any event, Judas repents and tries to return the cash he has received. Significantly, he throws the money down in the temple sanctuary (*naon*) and then goes out and hangs himself. The chief priests have tried to disassociate themselves from the betrayal by implying that Judas must deal with his own complicity ("What's that to us? Look out for yourself!"), but now, embarrassingly enough, they are stuck with the bribe. Like good religious people, they attempt to use it in some appropriate way. They cannot put it in their religious treasury because

---

[52] Another version: Acts 1:18-20a. In Acts, Luke tells a very different legend. The only connection between the two stories is the name Field of Blood. But Luke also appeals to prophecy, citing Pss. 69:25 and 109:8 from the LXX.

[53] A. H. M'Neile offers useful background information on Matt. 27:3-10 in *The Gospel according to St. Matthew* (1915; reprint, London: Macmillan, 1961), 408-9. D. Patte, *The Gospel according to Matthew: A Structural Commentary on Matthew's Faith* (Philadelphia: Fortress Press, 1987), 376-77, is especially helpful.

it is "blood money," even though it originally came from them. So they buy a potter's field in which to bury foreigners. The story is filled with irony.

Jerusalem probably had a cemetery for foreigners: "The field has been called the Field of Blood to this day." But Matthew is not tracing the origin of some local place name; he is interested in prophecy— "Thus was fulfilled the word of the prophet Jeremiah." Unfortunately, the quotation Matthew supplies is garbled so that it matches no known passage in Jeremiah or Zechariah. Instead it appears to be an odd conflation of texts from Jeremiah 18:2 ("go down to the potter's house") and 32:9 ("I bought the field") as well as Zechariah 11:12b-13: "So they weighed out as my wages thirty shekels of silver. Then the Lord said to me, 'Throw it into the treasury'—this lordly price at which I was valued by them. So I took the thirty shekels of silver and threw them into the treasury in the house of the Lord."

The issue for preachers is, of course, the attempt on the part of religious people to distance themselves from social guilt. Often the strategy is to label *a* guilty individual, as if sin is individual and human guilt is not interconnected. There is no way that churches can be innocent, particularly when cash is involved. But notice: Judas does repent, and from his terrible death provision is made—albeit by a circuitous route—for the alien dead. The story is strange, and strangely subtle.

The Trial before Pilate
(§242; §§244-45; Mark 15:1-5; Luke 23:1-16)

Mark 15:1-5 provides only a skimpy account of Jesus in Pilate's court and emphasizes Jesus' reticence:

> [1]As soon as it was daylight, the chief priests with the elders and scribes reached an agreement in full assembly. Having bound Jesus, [they] led him away and handed him over to Pilate. [2]Pilate questioned him: "You are king of the Jews?" Answering him, [Jesus] said, "Whatever you say." [3]Then chief priests accused him of many things. [4]But Pilate again questioned him: "Aren't you going to answer? See how many things they accuse you of." [5]Jesus answered nothing more, so Pilate wondered.

Because Mark conveys the impression that there was a second meeting of the Sanhedrin, Matthew rewrites vv. 1-2 and supplies a brief sentence prior to Pilate's otherwise abrupt question. But Luke rearranges the material radically and adds the account of an additional trial before Herod. We shall study Luke's story:

¹The whole assembly got up and took him before Pilate. ²They began to accuse him, saying, "This man we found subverting the nation, opposing the payment of taxes to Caesar, and claiming he was Christ, a king." ³And Pilate questioned him saying, "You are king of the Jews?" Jesus answered, "Whatever you say." ⁴And Pilate spoke to the chief priests and the mob: "No, I find no guilt in this man." ⁵But they persisted, saying, "He agitates the people with his teaching all over Judea, from Galilee to here." ⁶Listening, Pilate asked if the man was a Galilean. ⁷Realizing that he was under the jurisdiction of Herod, he sent him off to Herod, who happened to be in Jerusalem at the time.

⁸Herod was greatly pleased to see Jesus; he had wanted to see him for a long time, because he had heard about him and hoped to see him do a miracle. ⁹He questioned him extensively, but [Jesus] answered nothing. ¹⁰The chief priests and the scribes stood by accusing him even more stridently. ¹¹So Herod and his troops contemptuously made fun of him and, in mockery, threw elegant garments on him and sent him back to Pilate. ¹²The same day, Herod and Pilate, who had previously been mutual enemies, became friends.

¹³Calling together the chief priests, the leaders, and the people, Pilate ¹⁴said to them, "You brought me this man as one who was subverting the people. Look, I have examined him in your presence and I find none of the crimes of which you have accused him. ¹⁵Neither did Herod, for he sent him back to us. Look, he has done nothing to deserve death. ¹⁶So, I'll whip him and let him go."

Obviously Luke is writing for a Gentile audience, for he all but exonerates Pilate: "I find no guilt in this man," Pilate observes. The same tendency can be seen throughout Acts; Roman officials are remarkably fair, whereas Jewish leaders are shown in a bad light. Thus, although Luke has made the gospel acceptable to a Gentile world, he has left us with a legacy of unfortunate anti-Semitism.[54] More, he may convey the impression that Jesus was condemned largely for religious reasons, which could not be the case. Although the charge of blasphemy was evidently leveled against Jesus, he was surely put to death by political powers as an insurrectionist.[55] Yet Luke wishes to portray Jesus as an innocent martyr and to show that political charges against him were blatantly false.

Did another trial before King Herod actually happen? Scholars are divided:[56] (1) Some suppose that Luke has a separate source and that

---

[54] The problem of anti-Semitism in the Christian scriptures should be of serious concern to preachers. See a general discussion by S. Sandmel in the *Interpreter's Dictionary of the Bible,* supplementary volume (Nashville: Abingdon, 1976), 477–78; see also R. Ruether, *Faith and Fratricide: The Theological Roots of Antisemitism* (New York: Seabury Press, 1974), with an introductory essay by G. Baum.

[55] The discussion by L. Boff, *Passion of Christ, Passion of the World: The Facts, Their Interpretation, and Their Meaning Yesterday and Today,* trans. R. R. Barr (Maryknoll, N.Y.: Orbis Books, 1987) is particularly helpful in viewing the social and political meanings of Christ's death.

[56] For a survey of positions, see J. A. Fitzmyer, *The Gospel according to Luke (X–XXIV)* (Garden City, N.Y.: Doubleday, 1985), 1478–80.

the account is essentially true. (2) Others claim that the story is prompted by Psalm 2:2, "The kings of the earth set themselves, / and the rulers take counsel together, / against the Lord and his anointed." (3) Still others argue that the story of Herod is a Lukan creation, formed for apologetic reasons, that is, to exonerate Pilate and establish Jesus' innocence. Does Jesus' appearance before two rulers satisfy the requirement for two witnesses stated in Deuteronomy 19:15? The discussion cannot be resolved, and need not be; the passage is eminently preachable.

Presumably, the Sanhedrin ships Jesus off to Pilate because it is not empowered to order capital punishment; Pilate is. The accusations against Jesus are designed to provoke Pilate: "This man we found subverting the nation, opposing the payment of taxes to Caesar, and claiming he was Christ, a king." Readers of Luke's Gospel are well aware that these accusations are blatantly false (19:41-44; 20:21-25; 22:67-70). So Pilate asks, "Are you king of the Jews?" Jesus' answer is oddly evasive. Literally, he says, "You said it." Probably the statement tosses the decision in Pilate's direction. In effect, Jesus answers: "Whatever you say." Then Pilate emphatically pronounces Jesus' innocence.

The chief priests persist: "He agitates the people with his teaching all over Judea, from Galilee to here." The word *Galilee* is supposed to get to Pilate — Galilee was a hotbed of local insurrection — but instead it offers him an out; he bundles Jesus off to Herod, who "happened to be in Jerusalem at the time."

The depiction of Herod is most peculiar. Herod hoped to see Jesus "do a miracle." Perhaps Luke is picking up an earlier allusion: "This generation is an evil generation; it asks for a sign, but no sign will be given to it except the sign of Jonah" (Luke 11:29). Herod persists, questioning Jesus "extensively." But Jesus stands mute (see Sir. 20:5-8). A third time the chief priests accuse Jesus — "even more stridently." As a result, Herod and his guards abuse Jesus, mocking him and dressing him up in royal robes as a pretender-king. The final verse is no doubt ironic: "The same day, Herod and Pilate . . . became friends."

Subsequently, Pilate once more declares Jesus innocent: "Look, he has done nothing to deserve death." But, of course, ultimately Pilate will yield to public opinion.

Luke's theology of the cross is somewhat thin; he has no developed understanding of atonement. Instead, he pictures Jesus as an exemplary martyr whose death parallels the brave deaths of prophets (Luke 13:33) and is a model for Christian faithfulness. Like Maccabean martyrs of old, Jesus endures in silence. No wonder that Luke views the martyrdom of Stephen in Acts as a replication of Jesus' trial and death (Acts 7:54-60).

In terms of preaching, v. 12 of the passage suggests a perspective. Both Herod and Pilate are concerned with protecting a socio-political status quo, and so acquiesce to Christ's death. And, in spite of Luke's exoneration of Pilate, the two rulers agree. They are surely right. While Jesus does not stir insurrection, he preached God's new order, which rather clearly supposes the displacement of our social order. Moreover, in his preaching, Christ announces the true sovereignty of God over all earthly powers. Herod and Pilate are both concerned with the maintenance of power. W. H. Auden catches the mood when he imagines Herod, alarmed by news of God-in-Christ, exclaiming, "One needn't be much of a psychologist to realise that if this rumor is not stamped out now, in a few years it is capable of diseasing the whole Empire, and one doesn't have to be a prophet to predict the consequences if it should."[57]

In preaching, we can use the very verses Luke supposes will exonerate Christ — he preaches peace, he sets God over every Caesar, and he is indeed a "king," although of a different order. Jesus is tried, but obviously Herod and Pilate are found wanting.

The Sentence of Death
(§246; Mark 15:6-15)

The story of the release of Barabbas and Jesus' sentence of death is filled with strange irony.[58] Look at Mark's portrayal of the scene:

6Now during the festival, he customarily set one prisoner free whom the [people] chose. 7There was one named Barabbas, jailed with the revolutionaries, who had commited murder during the uprising. 8The crowd came up and began to demand that he do for them what he usually did. 9But Pilate answered them saying, "Do you want me to set free the King of the Jews for you?" 10He knew that the chief priests had handed him over out of spite. 11But the chief priests stirred up the crowd to

---

[57] W. H. Auden, "For the Time Being: A Christmas Oratorio," *The Collected Poetry of W. H. Auden* (New York: Random House, 1945), 458.

[58] Other versions: Matt. 27:15-26; Luke 23:18-25; John 18:38 – 19:16. Matthew follows Mark with only minor changes (Matt. 27:16-17, 26) except for two additions: the story of Pilate's wife's dream and the account of Pilate's handwashing. Luke, on the other hand, has made drastic changes. He skips Mark 15:6-10 so that he has no reference to the custom of amnesty. Instead Pilate wishes to release Jesus because he finds him not guilty as charged. Although the NRSV drops v. 17 from Luke, there is fairly good manuscript support for its inclusion.

demand he free Barabbas instead. ¹²So, answering, Pilate said to them again, "What shall I do with the one you call King of the Jews?" ¹³But again they shouted, "Crucify him!" ¹⁴But Pilate said to them, "Why? What harm has he done?" All the more, they shouted, "Crucify him!" ¹⁵Determined to satisfy the crowd, he set Barabbas free for them and, having lashed Jesus, he handed him over to be crucified.

Once again we can sense that the evangelists, rejected by synagogues and now engaged in a mission to the Gentiles, are eager to portray Pilate in a reasonably good light. In turn, they tend to lay blame on not only Jewish leaders but even on the Jewish populace. No wonder that Matthew adds a cry from the crowd: "May his blood be on us and on our children!" Preachers must be on guard lest, in preaching, we fan hot flames of anti-Semitism. Theologically, as sinners, we were all there when they crucified the Lord. As for the picture of Pilate, extrabiblical documents testify to Pilate's well-deserved reputation for both corruption and cruelty.⁵⁹

There are some interesting questions about the peculiar name Barabbas. If its roots are "bar" and "abba," it would mean "son of the father"; if its roots are "bar" and "sabba," it would mean "son of the old man." Although the name is odd, it is not impossible; two rabbis mentioned in the Talmud were named Barabbas. The problem: There ought to be a proper name. Some manuscripts of Matthew supply the name Jesus Barabbas, which would not be unusual — Jesus was a common name then as it is today in many Spanish-speaking lands. But most manuscripts simply offer the name Barabbas.

Apparently Barabbas was an insurrectionist and, therefore, would have had popular support. When the crowd demands release of a prisoner,⁶⁰ Pilate's answer is contemptuous: "Do you want me to set free the King of the Jews?" Yet the remark is ironic. All through the Gospel, Mark has been drawing parallels between David and Jesus, particularly drawing on 2 Samuel, chapters 15 and 16. King David is accompanied by three chosen followers (2 Sam. 15:19-24) when in a time of trial he climbs the Mount of Olives (2 Sam. 15:30). David is

---

⁵⁹ In a letter from Agrippa I to Caligula, Pilate is described as "inflexible, merciless, and obstinate." The letter details Pilate's violence. Josephus also remarks Pilate's political machinations and cruelty. For sources, see V. Taylor, *The Gospel according to St. Mark* (New York: St. Martin's Press, 1966), 578–79; see also R. A. Horsley and J. S. Hanson, *Bandits, Prophets, and Messiahs: Popular Movements at the Time of Jesus* (San Francisco: Harper & Row, 1985), 38–39.

⁶⁰ We have no record of a customary release of a prisoner during the Passover season. In particular cases, a local governor did have power to grant amnesty; see A. Deissmann, *Light from the Ancient Past* (New York: G. H. Doran, 1927), 269.

betrayed by a trusted member of his immediate circle, Ahithophel (2 Sam. 15:31). When David is attacked, one of his followers wants to wield a sword (2 Sam. 16:9-11).[61] Of course, to Mark, Jesus' kingship is of a very different order and his enthronement is a future promise. Nevertheless, as hearers of Mark's Gospel we are meant to grasp the irony of Pilate's derision; although Pilate may speak with contempt when he says, "King of the Jews," inadvertently he is quite correct.

Are we meant to contrast the two figures, Barabbas and Jesus? Probably. If Barabbas was an insurrectionist, then he was seeking to establish a political kingdom by force. Clearly, Jesus announced the coming of God's new order and called for a quite different response. In preaching, however, we should not contrast a visible, political realm with something inward and "faithy." God's new order is not ephemeral; it is a social order, but distinguished by love, mutual service, and exchanges of mercy. Political bravado will always seem more heroic; thus, Barabbas types are usually popular figures.

The crowd, perhaps angered by Pilate's contempt, howls for blood: "Crucify him!" Pilate decides to play politics. Long before the pollsters tapped public opinion, Pilate knew how to gauge the public will. So, although he asks, "What harm has he done?," finally he releases Barabbas and hands over (*paredōken*) Jesus to be crucified.

How do we preach the dramatic scene? We must be willing to portray the rather "natural" (read: sinful) way in which political realities conspired to crucify Christ. The temple priests, like most ministers, did not welcome sectarian movements within their congregation; they wanted to protect the sacred temple cult. And politicians are bound to worry if the people become restless. Compromise is political wisdom. As for the crowd—"democracy in action"—their vote was no doubt patriotic. If, picking up mention of the priests' conspiracy (vv. 10-11), we picture Jesus as crucified by plotting villains, we will misunderstand the passage.

Of course, the question in v. 12 may well be addressed to all those who hear the story: "What shall I do with the one you call King of the Jews?"

---

[61] See J. R. Donahue, "Temple, Trial, and Royal Christology," in *The Passion in Mark*, ed. Kelber, 61–79.

Jesus Is Mocked and Goes to the Cross
(§§247–48; Mark 15:16-21)

For a third time (see 14:65; 15:15), Mark mentions the mockery of Jesus by armed guards:[62]

16Then the soldiers led him away to the courtyard, that is, the praetorium, and they called together the whole battalion. 17And they put purple on him, and twisted a thorny crown around him, 18and they began to salute him: "Hail, King of the Jews!" 19They struck him on the head with a stick, and spit on him, and bending down on their knees, worshiped him. 20When they had mocked him, they took the purple off him and put his own clothes back on him. And they led him out to crucify him.

21A certain Simon, a Cyrenian, the father of Alexander and Rufus, was coming in from the country, and they forced him to carry the cross.

Did the mockery occur? Almost certainly.[63] Prisoners scheduled for crucifixion were usually whipped, often nearly skinned by whips with bits of stone or metal attached. The fact that Simon of Cyrene was co-opted to carry the crossbar of the cross may indicate that Jesus was badly beaten up. Although the scourging almost certainly occurred, we should note a fulfillment of prophecy, particularly of two verses from Isaiah:

> I gave my back to those who struck me,
>   and my cheeks to those who pulled out the beard;
> I did not hide my face
>   from insult and spitting. (Isa. 50:6)

> But he was wounded for our transgressions,
>   crushed for our iniquities;
> upon him was the punishment that made us whole,
>   and by his bruises we are healed. (Isa. 53:5)

What of the royal robe and crown of thorns? Were criminals, particularly messianic pretenders, so mocked? Again, the story is likely,[64]

---

62 Other versions: Matt. 27:27-32; Luke 23:11, 26; John 19:1-3. Matthew changes a few details in Mark's story: Mark's "purple" becomes a scarlet robe, a "reed in his right hand" is added. Luke deletes the section because he has already told of a scourging by Herod's guard, and because he does not wish to portray Roman abuse. Both Matthew and Luke remove the names of Simon of Cyrene's sons. Luke has Simon carry the cross behind Jesus. In addition Luke adds a substantial passage about Jesus' words to the crowd that watches (Luke 23:27-32). John seems to abbreviate Mark's account of the mockery, locating it in the midst of Pilate's dialogue with the crowd. Simon of Cyrene disappears: "carrying the cross by himself, he went out . . ." (John 19:17).

63 See M. Hengel, *Crucifixion* (Philadelphia: Fortress Press, 1977), chap. 4.

64 The ancient world had customs involving "mock" kings, many of which have been noted by J. Frazer in *The Golden Bough* (New York: Macmillan, 1948), 264–89. There was a mock king involved in the Roman Saturnalia and also in the Babylonian feast

although given Mark's interest in "royal theology," it also fits a literary purpose. In any event, according to Mark's account, Jesus was led into a courtyard,[65] and beaten by a cadre of soldiers.[66] Although Mark says, "they called together the whole battalion," the group of soldiers was more likely some local mercenaries employed by Pilate as a guard.

More important for Mark's theology is the mocking of Jesus, dressed in purple with a crown of thorns, as a king: "Hail, King of the Jews!" While some scholars claim that "purple" (*porphyran*) refers to the color of a soldier's faded red cloak, Mark is rather clearly concerned with royal trappings. Jesus, beaten up now, will come in the new order as God's appointed ruler. The description is clearly ironic.

Previously Mark has had disciples yearn for a regal Messiah. When Peter confesses, "You are the Messiah" (8:29), he seems to have a triumphant figure in mind. Later when the sons of Zebedee, consumed by ambition, come begging enthroned power, they may have a similar conception: "Grant us to sit, one at your right hand and one at your left, in your glory." Jesus instructs them:

> You know that among the Gentiles those whom they recognize as their rulers lord it over them, and their great ones are tyrants over them. But it is not so among you; but whoever wishes to become great among you must be your servant, and whoever wishes to be first among you must be slave of all. For [Humanity's Child] came not to be served but to serve, and to give his life a ransom for many. (10:42b-45)

Instead of receiving royal homage, Christ is beaten, mocked, and ultimately crucified. Nevertheless, Mark is sure he will come enthroned in God's promised new order.

Then, abruptly, Mark shows us a Christian, Simon of Cyrene, whose sons are evidently known to the Markan community, forced to

---

of the Sacaea. Philo (*In Flaccum* 6) reports how citizens of Alexandria in order to poke fun at King Agrippa I got hold of an imbecile Jew, whose name was Carabas (note the similarity to Barabbas), put a paper hat on his head for a crown, used a floor mat for a robe, placed a reed in his hand for a scepter, and then, with cruel laughter, beat him to death.

[65] There is debate over the place of the scourging. Does the term *praetorium* refer to Herod's palace or the fortress of Antonia? See Taylor, *The Gospel according to St. Mark,* 585.

[66] H. Daniel-Rops has an ingenious theory. He claims that excavations at the fortress of Antonia seem to show marks of what looks like a hopscotch court in which the final circle was a "royal place," a king's court. He theorizes that Jesus' appearance interrupted a game soldiers were playing and that, cruelly, they mocked him in their "royal" game circle. The theory is fanciful, at best; see H. Daniel-Rops, *Jesus and His Times,* vol. 2 (Garden City, N.Y.: Image Books, 1958), 186–92.

shoulder the cross. The royal king we craved has been mocked, and instead of triumph, we are handed a cross. Said Jesus: "If any want to become my followers, let them deny themselves and take up their cross and follow me" (8:34). Christ must be rejected, ridiculed, and crucified. Those who follow him, the church, must expect no less.

"Daughters of Jerusalem"
(§248; Luke 23:27-31)

Luke adds a special section to Christ's climb to the cross that rings like a prophetic oracle:

> [26]As they led him away, they grabbed Simon, a certain Cyrenian, who was coming in from the country; and they laid the cross on him, to carry it following Jesus. [27]And a large crowd of people followed him, and women who mourned and wailed for him. [28]Turning to them, Jesus said, "Daughters of Jerusalem, do not cry over me; but cry for yourselves and your children. [29]Because, look, days are coming when they will say: 'Blessed are the barren, the wombs that do not bear, and the breasts that do not feed.' [30]Then, they will begin to say to the mountains, 'fall on us'; and to the hills, 'Cover us.' [31]Because if they do these things when wood is moist, what will they do when it's dry?"

The passage is peculiar to Luke and has puzzled scholars for years.[67] Earlier in Luke's story, a woman in the crowd around Jesus "raised her voice and said to him, 'Blessed is the womb that bore you and the breasts that nursed you!'" (Luke 11:27-28). Jesus replied, bluntly, "Blessed rather are those who hear the word of God and obey it!" Whereupon Jesus launches into a sharp attack that begins, "This generation is an evil generation. . . ." Later, after his march into Jerusalem, he weeps over the city, saying:

> If you, even you, had only recognized on this day the things that make for peace! But now they are hidden from your eyes. Indeed, the days will come upon you, when your enemies will set up ramparts around you and surround you, and hem you in on every side. They will crush you to the ground, you and your children within you, and they will not leave within you one stone upon another; because you did not recognize the time of your visitation from God. (Luke 19:42-44)

The passage in Luke 23 echoes language from these earlier texts and, indeed, some of the ideas.

All through Luke's Gospel, women are supportive of Jesus; here they

---

[67] For a fine, detailed study of the passage, see M. L. Soards, "Tradition, Composition, and Theology in Jesus' Speech to the 'Daughters of Jerusalem,'" *Biblica* 68, fasc. 2 (1987): 221-44.

follow along weeping for him. Jesus addresses them as "Daughters of Jerusalem," a prophetic phrase in the LXX that is also used in the Song of Songs. Although no scriptural source has been identified, evidently Jesus is quoting when he says: "Blessed are the barren, the wombs that do not bear, and the breasts that do not feed." He is quoting scripture, however, when he adds slightly misarranged words from Hosea 10:8b, which reads: "They shall say to the mountains, Cover us, and to the hills, Fall on us." In v. 31 there is probably still another quote, perhaps loosely based on some text in the wisdom writings: "If they do these things when wood is moist, what will they do when it's dry?"

What is the speech about? Is Jesus merely pointing toward the fall of Jerusalem, as some scholars suppose? No, the words have a wider reference. Surely the "moist wood" is the time of God's visitation in Christ Jesus. But Jesus has repeatedly warned of eschatological trials yet to come (e.g., 17:22-37; 21:7-36) — some of which are realized in the martyrdoms reported in Acts. The quotation that begins "Blessed are the barren . . ." deliberately contrasts with the earlier exclamation from the woman in the crowd (11:27-28), again suggesting that although the womb that bore Christ is blessed, in the future child-bearing may be under threat.

Certainly the passage underscores Christian realism. Yes, the world has rejected Christ and crucified him, but followers of Christ will, like Simon of Cyrene, have to shoulder future rejection and possible martyrdom. The passage stands as a corrective for glib, success story Christianity that, in premature euphoria, imagines all will be well in the world.

The Crucifixion (§249; Mark 15:22-32)

[22]They took him to the place Golgotha, which, translated, means the Place of the Skull. [23]And they tried to give him wine mixed with myrrh, which he would not take. [24]Then they crucified him, dividing up his clothes, casting lots for them to see who would get what.

[25]Now it was nine o'clock, and they crucified him. [26]An inscription of the charge against him read: "THE KING OF THE JEWS." [27]They crucified two robbers with him, one on his right and one on his left. [[28]The scripture was fulfilled that says, "He was counted among the lawbreakers."] [29]And those who passed by insulted him, shaking their heads and saying, "Ha! You were going to tear down the temple and build it up in three days; [30]come down from the cross, and save yourself!" [31]In the same way, the chief priests and the scribes, joking among themselves, said, "Others he saved, but he can't save himself! [32]The Christ, the King of Israel! Come down from the cross, so we may see and believe." And the others crucified with him taunted him.

A word about crucifixion:[68] Crucifixion was the ultimate Roman punishment (*summa supplicia*), although used mostly for slaves (*servile supplicium*).[69] Basically, crucifixion was an X-rated public spectacle, a blood sport in which those being punished were beaten, nailed to crossbeams — sometimes in grotesque positions — and then subject to public ridicule, often including jibes about their naked genitals. Sometimes Christian art pictures the dying Christ posed on the cross rather gracefully. Not a chance.

The passage in Mark is complex and very difficult.[70] There are allusions to scripture — the offer of wine, the casting of lots for Christ's clothing, and the mention of robbers are meant to recall Psalms 69 and 22 as well as Isaiah 53. Cumulatively, they introduce a sense of God's predestining purpose into the account. All the phrases used in taunting have figured in earlier episodes as accusations: the Sanhedrin brought up the temple prophecy (14:58); Pilate asked, "You are King of the

---

[68] Other versions: Matt. 27:33-44; Luke 23:33-43; John 19:17-25. Matthew changes Mark's account only slightly, substituting "gall" for myrrh, skipping Mark's "it was the third hour when they crucified him," but adding a quote from Ps. 22:8 to the taunting. Also notice Matthew twice inserts "Son of God" (Matt. 27:40, 43). Luke rearranges the passage and introduces material on the two criminals. Luke also provides the great words, "Father, forgive them; for they do not know what they are doing," although the sentence is not found in many principal manuscripts. Luke also changes Mark's myrrh, an anaesthetic, by substituting vinegar [to conform to Ps. 69:21], rewrites some of the taunts, adding specific reference to the taunts of the soldiers, and skips any mention of destroying the temple (Mark 15:29). All three accounts mention dicing for Christ's clothing in order to confirm the prophecy in Ps. 22:18.

[69] See Hengel (*Crucifixion,* chaps. 4, 5, and 8), who supplies Latin documentation as well as some fairly gruesome descriptions drawn from the period. The fact that Christ died a slave's death is not without theological meaning, particularly in view of the "Christ Hymn" in Philippians 2.

[70] M. A. Tolbert (*Sowing,* 279-80) offers an analysis of the chiastic pattern in Mark's crucifixion narrative. I represent her analysis, with some modification, as follows:

A The soldiers mock Jesus as a king (vv. 16-20)
B 1. Bystander is co-opted to carry the cross (vv. 21-22)
   2.   Christ offered wine (v. 23)
   3.   Christ crucified (v. 24a)
   4.   Garments divided (v. 24b)
C 3d hour reference (vv. 25-27)
   Mockery by all (vv. 29-32)
C' 6th to 9th hour reference (v. 33)
   Jesus' cry to God (v. 34)
B' 1. Bystander thinks Jesus is calling Elijah (v. 35)
   2.   Christ offered vinegar (v. 36)
   3.   Christ dies with great cry (v. 37)
   4.   Temple curtain torn (v. 38)
A' The centurion says Christ is Son of God (v. 39)

Jews?" (15:2); and the taunt about Jesus claiming to be Christ echoes the high priest's question, "Are you the Christ, the Son of the Blessed One?" (14:61). Even the odd detail about the robbers ("one on his right and one on his left") echoes the ambition of the sons of Zebedee, who wanted to be enthroned with Jesus. Thus the story of Jesus' death is orchestrated like a symphony in which themes played before return, join, and produce a final coda. As a whole the passage recalls words from the Wisdom of Solomon (2:17-20):

> Let us see if his words are true,
> and let us test what will happen at the end of his life;
> for if the righteous man is God's child, [God] will help him,
> and will deliver him from the hand of his adversaries.

> Let us test him with insult and torture,
> so that we may find out how gentle he is,
> and make trial of his forbearance.

> Let us condemn him to a shameful death,
> for, according to what he says, he will be protected.

But the idea of testing in order to "see and believe" is unthinkable to Mark (8:11-12).

Notice the repetitions of "come down" and "save yourself."[71] The taunters want Christ to come down to their level, a level determined by self-preservation. But in the garden Christ prayed that God's will be done, and not his own; thus Jesus will not respond. Does the phrase "Others he saved, but he can't save himself" express Christian conviction when reversed? Certainly Christ has saved many "others."

The passage is overloaded with allusiveness and is therefore difficult to preach. Perhaps we can begin with the demands "come down" and "save yourself," for, after all, they articulate the way we live, the way of the human world. More, they voice a peculiar understanding of God, a God who is used as a bail-out for human distress. But instead, we should affirm Christ's obedience: "Not what I want, but what you want." Then we can begin to see the unseen movement of God's saving purpose brought about through the cross.

The Two Criminals (§248; Luke 23:32-33, 39-43)

The story of the two thieves, found only in Luke, is generally regarded as a pious legend. Legend or not, it has been preached for centuries and

---

[71] For discussion of the repeated "down," see Tolbert, *Sowing,* 282.

illustrates Christ's forgiving prayer, "Father, forgive them; for they do not know what they are doing," in Luke 23:34.

> ³²Two others, criminals, were led off with him to be executed. ³³When they came to the place called The Skull, there they crucified him along with the criminals, one on the right and the other on the left. . . .
> ³⁹One of the hanging criminals kept insulting him, "Aren't you the Christ? Save yourself and us!" ⁴⁰But the other, rebuking him, said, "Don't you even fear God, since you're under the same sentence? ⁴¹We are justly punished—we are getting what we deserve for what we did; but this man has done nothing crooked." ⁴²And he said, "Jesus, remember me when you come into your kingdom." ⁴³And he said to him, "Truly, I'm telling you, today you will be with me in paradise."

The story demonstrates two different responses to Christ, and also underscores a favorite theological theme, namely, the forgiveness of sins. Some scholars suppose that Luke has constructed three tauntings— by the rulers, the soldiers, and the criminals—to parallel his temptation story at the beginning of Christ's ministry (Luke 4:1-13). More likely, mention of the criminals demonstrates a fulfillment of Isaiah 53:12:

> He poured out himself to death,
> and was numbered with the transgressors;
> yet he bore the sin of many,
> and made intercession for the transgressors.

Of course, Luke is also showing Christ proclaiming "release to the captives," as was promised in his sermon at Nazareth (Luke 4:18).

The first criminal taunts Christ, but with a degree of self-interest: "Aren't you the Christ? Save yourself and us!" But if Christ is to "seek out and to save the lost" (Luke 19:10), he cannot indulge in self-preservation. The other criminal, named Dysmas in an apocryphal writing,[72] interrupts the taunting: "Don't you even fear God, since you're under the same sentence?" The implication is that (1) they will soon face the judgment of God, and (2) as cursed people "hung on a tree," they are "under God's curse" (Deut. 21:23). He goes on to affirm Christ's innocence and to admit his own guilt: "We are getting what we deserve" (see 2 Macc. 7:18). Twice Pilate testified to Jesus' innocence; now a third testimony is given to confirm Luke's portrait of Christ as the righteous martyr.

The criminal suddenly echoes Psalm 106:4; he says, "Jesus, remember me when you come into your kingdom."[73] Only here is Jesus

---

[72] See the Gospel of Nicodemus or the Acts of Pilate (10.2), in *The Apocryphal New Testament,* trans. M. R. James (1924; reprint, Oxford: Clarendon Press, 1972), 104.

[73] There are a number of textual variants for the words. For discussion see Fitzmyer, *The Gospel according to Luke,* 1510.

addressed by his proper name, Jesus, no doubt recalling the angel's words to Mary in Luke's first chapter: "And you will name him Jesus. He will be great, and will be called the Son of the Most High" (1:31-32).

Jesus' reply is much debated: "Today you will be with me in paradise." Two words are troubling: *today* and *paradise*. The word *paradise* is Persian in origin. Twice it appears in the late writings of the Hebrew scriptures, Nehemiah 2:8 and Ecclesiastes 2:5, where it designates a park or enclosed garden. The word is used in the LXX, however, to translate Genesis 2:8 (a "garden" in Eden), Genesis 13:10 (the "garden" of the Lord), and Ezekiel 31:8 (the "garden" of God). The word appears frequently in apocalyptic writings in a similar way.[74] In the Christian scriptures, the word is used by Paul to refer to visions (2 Cor. 12:4) and in Revelation 2:7: "To everyone who conquers, I will give permission to eat from the tree of life that is in the paradise of God." Thus, paradise seems to be employed as a metaphor and not as the literal location of a Persian pleasure garden. Because of the connection with Eden, we can assume that paradise symbolizes a restored relationship with God. Of course, the important words in Jesus' promise are "with me."

The word *today* is more difficult. Does the word guarantee an immediate resurrection? Probably not. The word is used often in Luke (2:11; 4:21; 5:26; 13:32; 19:5, 9; 22:34, 61) to designate decisive time, a time of judgment or of salvation. So it is used by Luke much in the same way as in Paul's cry: "See, now is the acceptable time; see, now is the day of salvation" (2 Cor. 6:2). Clearly, it is not used to designate a specific twenty-four-hour period.

So the passage locates Christ with outcasts. All through his Gospel, Luke has pictured Jesus going to the injured, the rejected, the condemned, the lost; now he dies with outcast crooks. And he dies as a righteous martyr whose death converts a criminal. Earlier Jesus had prayed, "Father, forgive them." Here he tosses mercy to a repentant, dying criminal. More, he opens the kingdom to a socially rejected man: "Today," he says, "you will be with me."

Death on the Cross (§250; Mark 15:33-39)

The account of Christ's death may be the most awesome passage in the Christian scriptures.[75] Certainly it leaves would-be preachers almost wordless:

---

[74] For example, Ps. Sol. 14:3; 1 Enoch 60:8; Test. Levi 18:10.
[75] Other versions: Matt. 27:45-56; Luke 23:44-49; John 19:28-30. Matthew follows

33When it was noon, there was darkness all over the earth until three o'clock. 34At three o'clock, Jesus cried out with a loud voice, "Eloi, Eloi, lema sabachthani?," which translates, "My God, my God, why have you forsaken me?" 35Those who were standing by listening said, "Look, he calls Elijah!" 36Then someone ran up and, soaking a sponge with vinegar, put it on a stick and gave him a drink, saying, "Stop! Let's see if Elijah comes to take him down." 37But Jesus, letting out a great shout, died. 38And the veil of the temple was split in two from top to bottom. 39The centurion, who stood facing him, watching as he died, said, "Truly, this man was a Son of God."

The passage bristles with difficult questions: (1) What exactly is Christ's final cry? Is it the shout of a man forsaken or, as it quotes a Psalm, is it an expression of pious faith? (2) Why does the sky go dark and the temple curtain get torn in two? (3) What do the centurion's last words confess — "*a* Son of God" or "*the* Son of God"? Most of the questions send us scurrying toward Mark's theology; they are not historical queries. The passage is awesome. We will work through it carefully.

The Book of Amos (8:9, 10b) contains a prophecy about the Day of the Lord:

> On that day, says the Lord God,
>   I will make the sun go down at noon,
>   and darken the earth in broad daylight.
> I will make it like the mourning for an only son,
>   and the end of it like a bitter day.

So Mark darkens the whole earth at noon. To Mark, the crucifixion is judgment; it is truly the Day of the Lord and the end of the age. Also he is echoing Jesus' apocalyptic discourse in which a verse from Isaiah (13:10) predicts that "the sun will be darkened" (Mark 13:24). Darkening the sky is a sensitive literary convention; able writers have the sky weep in tragic moments, or storm when there is madness.

Now what of the cry of dereliction ("My God, my God, why have you forsaken me?")? Mark translates the cry from a Hebraized Aramaic, "Eloi, Eloi, lema sabachthani?"[76] Many scholars suppose that Mark has placed words from Psalm 22:1 on Jesus' lips. According to the

---

Mark closely, but adds a section mentioning an earthquake and the opening of tombs and the dead wandering Jerusalem (Matt. 27:51b-53). Luke moves the rending of the temple curtain toward the start of the account and he drops the cry of dereliction along with the vinegar and references to Elijah. But Luke puts a final commendation on Jesus' lips (v. 46). Further, instead of "Truly, this man was a son of God," Luke has the centurion praising God and testifying to Christ's innocence. John covers the death of Christ in two verses that will be studied later. I have reserved Mark 15:40-41 for discussion in the next section.

[76] Because of breath sounds, "eloi" would scarcely sound much like "Elijah." Thus, Matthew alters the text, using Hebrew, which brings the sounds much closer together.

Midrashim, the Psalm is the cry of a righteous sufferer who, sub-sequently, gives way to sheer praise for deliverance.[77] Was the earliest tradition merely a great shout from the cross for which later Christians supplied a text?[78] But many others, as far back as the early Christian interpreters, have read the words of Jesus as an expression of God-forsakenness. And, certainly in Mark's context, the words surely express desolation. Christ has been dropped by his family, refused by his hometown, deserted by his disciples, accused by religious leaders, condemned by the crowds, mocked by soldiers, and taunted by the criminals with whom he is executed. The howling taunts have risen to a crescendo. The cry of dereliction fits the context: "My God, my God, why have you forsaken me?"[79] Of course, as always, Mark is remarkably subtle because, although the prayer voices God-forsakenness, it is a prayer and it will be answered.

Popular legends with regard to Elijah support the notion behind "Look, he calls Elijah!" According to Malachi 4:5, Elijah, who had ascended into heaven (2 Kings 2:11), would return as a precursor of the Messiah: "Lo, I will send you the prophet Elijah before the great and terrible day of the Lord comes." Further, popularly, Elijah was believed to come to the aid of the righteous in times of trouble. But the statement "Let's see if Elijah comes to take him down" is cynical ridicule. The offer of vinegar is also abuse, although fulfilling Psalm 69:21.

Suddenly "the veil of the temple was split in two from top to bottom" (v. 38). There has been much debate over which "veil" is intended;[80] there was a curtain separating the Holy Place from the Holy of Holies and another, larger curtain separating the temple from the courtyard. Does Mark symbolize the opening of the Holy of Holies, or a free access to the holy temple for outsiders? Almost certainly, the Holy of Holies is opened for Christ to enter and, of course, for followers as well (Heb. 6:19-20). The word I have translated "split" (*eschisthē*, from the verb *schizō*) is used here and only once before in Mark, when the heavens are "split" by a descending dove at Jesus' baptism (*schizomenous*) (Mark 1:10).

Again, there has been debate over the centurion's verdict: "Truly,

---

[77] Oddly enough the apocryphal Gospel of Peter has instead, "My power, my power, why have you left me?"

[78] So argued H. Braun, *Jesus of Nazareth: The Man and His Time,* trans. E. R. Kalin (Philadelphia: Fortress Press, 1979), 35.

[79] For an especially fine discussion of the cry, see Tolbert, *Sowing,* 284-88.

[80] For a summary of positions, see Taylor, *The Gospel according to St. Mark,* 596-97.

this man was a Son of God." Grammatically, as well as on the basis of manuscript evidence, the text may be translated either "*a* Son of God" or "*the* Son of God." Mark may be as subtle as ever, having the centurion say "a Son of God" while readers, familiar with the Gospel's first words ("The beginning of the good news of Jesus Christ, the Son of God") can supply the definite article.

We have said the passage is awesome; it is. Preachers should take the terrible cry seriously, particularly in a terrifying world where there may be little shared sense of God's presence. Luther likened the cry of dereliction to a "descent into hell," and surely he was right. On the cross, Jesus is absolutely alienated, which is ultimate suffering. Nevertheless, his cry splits the ages, and the heavens open for him and for us. No wonder the centurion voices our confession of faith.

Women Witnesses and Jesus' Burial
(§§250-51; Mark 15:40-47)

Mark supplies an epilogue,[81] written in measured Greek, that introduces new characters, a group of women and Joseph of Arimathea.[82]

> [40]Now there were also women looking on at a distance; among them were Mary Magdalene and Mary, the mother of James the younger and Joses, and Salome, [41]who had followed him and served him when he was in Galilee, and many others who had come up to Jerusalem with him.
>
> [42]As evening came, since it was Preparation, that is the day before the Sabbath, [43]Joseph of Arimathea, a respected member of council, who himself was looking for God's new order, courageously went to Pilate and asked for Jesus' body. [44]Pilate was surprised that he was already dead and, calling in the centurion, asked him how long ago he died. [45]When he heard from the centurion, he gave the corpse to Joseph. [46]Having bought some linen cloth, [Joseph] took him down and wrapped him in the linen and laid him in a tomb that had been cut out of rock. He rolled a stone against the door of the tomb. [47]Mary Magdalene and Mary the mother of Joses were watching where he was laid.

Mention of the women is somewhat abrupt. They are said to be

---

[81] For a perceptive study of the epilogue, see Tolbert, *Sowing*, 288–93.

[82] Other versions: Matt. 27:55-61; Luke 23:48-56; John 1:38-42. Matthew establishes the women as followers from Galilee, and changes Salome into the mother of the sons of Zebedee. Otherwise Matthew abbreviates Mark's story, dropping mention of the Preparation as well as the dialogue between Pilate and the centurion. Luke skips the list of women's names and designs a quite different conclusion to resonate with his previous description of the crowd on the way to the cross (Luke 23:27-32). Luke also exonerates Joseph of Arimathea from decisions of the Sanhedrin; he "had not agreed to their plan and action." Luke has the women preparing spices for Christ's body and then resting on the Sabbath day.

women "who had followed him and served [*diēkonoun*] him when he was in Galilee." Mark gives their names. Thus in a way they are likened to disciples, but whereas the disciples have betrayed, denied, and deserted Jesus, they are on hand, although "looking on at a distance." They are faithful witnesses who will see Christ's death, burial, and opened tomb. Some scholars suggest that their story certifies Christ's real death and his actual burial in a particular tomb. But in Mark's drama they arrive on the scene offering some future hope of faithfulness in spite of Christ's forsaken death.

In v. 42, Mark identifies the day as Friday — with evening approaching. Although Romans had been known to leave crucified corpses hanging, in Jewish society bodies were buried promptly, particularly in view of a coming Sabbath.[83] Who was Joseph of Arimathea? He is identified as a "respected member of council, who himself was looking for God's new order." He was thus a member in good standing of the Sanhedrin. The phrase "looking for God's new order" does not necessarily mean he was a disciple or that he became a disciple; it may mean he was a devout Jew, perhaps a Pharisee, who longed for God's righteous rule. As a pious Jew, he could fulfill the law by burying the corpse of a criminal. He is named either because he subsequently became Christian or, more likely, to identify the location of Christ's tomb.

Mark reports a brief dialogue between Pilate and a centurion, in which Pilate appears to be surprised that Jesus is already dead. When he is assured that he is really dead, he awards the corpse to Joseph of Arimathea. Joseph has purchased a linen cloth to wrap the body — like the linen shift worn by the young man who fled the Garden of Gethsemane. He then places the body in a tomb hewn out of rock, and closes the cave-tomb with a stone. The description of the tomb may be designed to match Isaiah 22:16.

As a closure to the account, once more we hear of the women ("Mary Magdalene and Mary the mother of Joses") watching. Again, they are faithful witnesses, although ultimately they too will disappoint us — "Going out, they ran from the tomb for they were beside themselves and shaking. No one said anything; they were afraid for . . ." (Mark 16:8).

The epilogue Mark provides introduces people who "follow and

---

[83] Josephus reports, "The Jews used to take so much care of the [interment] of men, that they took down those that were condemned, and buried them before the going down of the sun" (*History of the Jewish Wars* 4.5.2).

serve." The women function as faithful witnesses. Joseph of Arimathea appears as a faithful man who provides for Christ's burial according to the law. So, although Jesus has been destroyed by faithless, rebel people who have turned from God's will, there are a few, a remnant of sorts, who serve and follow.

THE GOSPEL OF JOHN

The Gospel of John is a peculiar book. Most scholars suppose that the book was assembled from some early sources — perhaps a passion narrative and a "book of signs" — and then rewritten and rewritten and rewritten over the years by a floating Christian community before it was finally edited sometime after 110 c.e.[84] The language of the Gospel seems to range from the style of Jewish wisdom literature to proto-Gnostic forms. In John we find symbolic stories, mystery dialogues, signs, "I am" speeches, sermons, and so on. As a Gospel it is a far cry from the story of Christ found in the Synoptics. If the authors of John were familiar with Synoptic materials, they seem to have constructed a meditative/symbolic Gospel that, in effect, interprets the Synoptic tradition for a very different theological mind.[85]

One of the baffling problems in the Gospel is arrangement. The Gospel sharply departs from Synoptic chronology and rearranges materials to fit a "festival structure" or, perhaps, a journeying structure. One does not chase history too much when reading the Gospel of John. Fortunately for preachers there are a number of splendid, if somewhat imposing, commentaries on John, works by C. K. Barrett, Rudolf Bultmann, Raymond E. Brown, Ernst Haenchen, R. H. Lightfoot, Barnabas Lindars, Rudolf Schnackenburg, Fernando Segovia, and others.[86] In addition there are more specialized works on the types of

---

[84] See R. E. Brown, *The Community of the Beloved Disciple* (New York: Paulist Press, 1979). For another perspective, see M. Hengel, *The Johannine Question* (Philadelphia: Trinity Press International, 1990).

[85] Those wishing to study the relationship of John to Synoptic texts may turn to H. F. D. Sparks, *The Johannine Synopsis of the Gospels* (New York: Harper & Row, 1974).

[86] C. K. Barrett, *The Gospel according to St. John: An Introduction with Commentary and Notes on the Greek Text,* 2d ed. (Philadelphia: Westminster Press, 1978); R. E. Brown, *The Gospel according to John: Introduction, Translation, and Notes,* 2 vols. (Garden City, N.Y.: Doubleday, 1966, 1970); R. Bultmann, *The Gospel of John: A Commentary,* trans. G. R. Beasley-Murray (Philadelphia: Westminster Press, 1971); C. H. Dodd, *The Interpretation of the Fourth Gospel* (Cambridge: Cambridge University Press, 1953); idem, *Historical Tradition in the Fourth Gospel* (Cambridge: Cambridge University Press, 1965); E. Haenchen, *John 1: A Commentary on the Gospel of John Chapters 1–6,* and *John 2: A*

literature, on parts of the book, on arrangement, symbolism, and goodness knows what else. Robert Kysar provides a useful survey of scholarship.[87] Ministers who seek to interpret the Gospel of John for contemporary congregations will need to acquire a basic library to assist them.

The Gospel of John requires a special hermeneutic. Every passage is overloaded with symbolic allusiveness. In any passage we can expect (1) references to the Hebrew scriptures; (2) allusions to previous passages and passages yet to come (watch out for the vocabulary, particularly the verbs); (3) some reference to Christ's "hour" — that is, to the great death/resurrection/ascension/gift of the Spirit event; (4) a structural design that is theologically and rhetorically significant; and, above all, (5) in-group allusions to life in the new community of the Word and the Spirit that has resulted from Christ's coming. Thus the texture of any passage is thickly woven but expressed in deceptively simple Greek. So how should the Gospel be read? Basically, every passage refers to us, to our life together in faith now. Living together in the Spirit we look back spotting the ironies and wonders of Jesus Christ, but always recognizing the hints and symbols that refer to our common experience in the new community; the Gospel is marvelously contemporary.

The story of the passion is radically rearranged in the Gospel of John. Some episodes, such as the Lord's Supper, have disappeared; other episodes, such as Christ's garden prayer, have been woven into discourse material. Chapters 18 and 19 contain a series of pericopes leading to the death and burial. Yet the Gospel of John is in our lectionaries and is often preached during Holy Week services. Therefore, we will discuss several passages. For each passage, we will supply a few selected bibliographic references that may be available in a minister's

---

Commentary on the Gospel of John Chapters 7–21, trans. R. W. Funk (Philadelphia: Fortress Press, 1984); E. C. Hoskyns, *The Fourth Gospel,* ed. F. N. Davey, 2d ed. (London: Faber and Faber, 1967); R. H. Lightfoot, *St. John's Gospel,* ed. C. F. Evans (Oxford: Clarendon Press, 1956); B. Lindars, *The Gospel of John* (London: Marshall, Morgan & Scott, 1972); J. Marsh, *The Gospel of St. John* (Baltimore: Pelican Books, 1968); R. Schnackenburg, *The Gospel according to St. John,* 3 vols. (New York: Seabury Press, 1980, 1982); F. Segovia, *The Farewell of the Lord: The Johannine Call to Abide* (Minneapolis: Fortress Press, 1991).

[87] For an overview, see R. Kysar, *The Fourth Evangelist and His Gospel: An Examination of Contemporary Scholarship* (Minneapolis: Augsburg, 1975); idem, "Community and Gospel: Vectors in Fourth Gospel Criticism," *Interpretation* 31, no. 4 (October 1977), 355–66.

well-stocked library. Such a list is scarcely intended to be comprehensive, but merely notes some helpful source materials.

As in our other exegetical sections, translations, although seeking to represent the text, also attempt to render the *koine* into a more colloquial language.

We must note a glaring omission: There will be no discussion of Christ's "priestly prayer" in chapter 17 or the several discourses in chapters 14–16. Just as Mark 13 is a crucial preface to Mark's passion narrative, so the Johannine discourses are absolutely necessary to a proper reading of John's story.[88] Nevertheless, although of absolute importance, such material is excluded from discussion by reason of my limited competence and by limited space.

In the Synoptic Gospels, following Mark, the passion story is prefaced by Christ's apocalyptic "sermon." In John, there is no apocalyptic discourse. Instead, the raising of Lazarus is a preface to the passion. So John constructs a huge irony: It is Christ's life-giving power that triggers his ultimate death.

Priests and Scribes Plot to Kill Jesus (John 11:47-53)

In the Synoptic Gospels, two stories begin the passion: The priests and scribes plot Jesus' death and, at the same time, a woman anoints Christ in Bethany; the stories stand in a deliberate antithesis. The Gospel of John adopts the same pattern although with a different theology. Look at the story of the chief priests and Caiaphas:[89]

> [45]Many of the Jews who had come to visit Mary and who saw what [Jesus] did, believed in him. [46]But some of them went off to the Pharisees and reported what Jesus had done. [47]So the chief priests and the Pharisees gathered the Sanhedrin together. "Now what are we going to do?" they said. "This man is performing many signs. [48]If we leave him alone, everyone will believe in him; then the Romans will come and take both this holy place of ours and the nation." [49]But one of them, Caiaphas, who was high priest that year, said to them: "You're not thinking! [50]Isn't it better for us that one man die [for the people] than for the whole nation to perish?" [51]He did not say this on his own, but, as high priest that year, he prophesied that

---

[88] Readers are directed to a careful study of the discourses by Segovia, *The Farewell of the Word.*

[89] Sources: Brown, *Gospel,* 1:438–44; C. H. Dodd, "The Prophecy of Caiaphas: John 11, 47–53," in *More New Testament Studies* (Grand Rapids, Mich: William B. Eerdmans, 1968), 58–68; P. D. Duke, *Irony in the Fourth Gospel* (Atlanta: John Knox Press, 1985), 86–88; Haenchen, *John 2,* 74–81; Schnackenburg, *Gospel,* 2:346–51.

Jesus was about to die for the nation [52]—and not for the nation alone, but also to gather the scattered children of God into one. [53]So from that day on, they plotted to kill him.

Here we have a "pronouncement story" that features an epigrammatic word from Caiaphas. The saying in v. 50 is obviously ironic. Inadvertently, Caiaphas has told the truth. For Caiaphas, it is a word of political expediency from a seasoned religious compromiser; for us it is the truth of the gospel message.

Notice that vv. 45-47 follow on the raising of Lazarus. As with all Jesus' great signs, many believe, while others disbelieve and, what is more, do so in action; they go off and report to the Pharisees. So news of the raising of Lazarus triggers an official reaction—the life-giver will be destroyed. According to John a rump meeting of the Sanhedrin is called: "Now what are we going to do?" they ask in a panic. At a time when messianic pretenders could threaten social stability, they fear that Jesus could draw a large-scale public following—"Look, the world has gone after him" (12:19). If it appears that the Israelites are restless, the Romans might move in on the land, destroying the temple precincts and the nation's well-being. Obviously members of the Sanhedrin have thumbed through some early-day Émile Durkheim, for they seem to believe that religion is central to a settled society.

Then, according to the story, Caiaphas, the high priest, stands up and speaks. Caiaphas was high priest from 18 to 36 C.E., a lengthy tenure that testifies to his political savvy. Possibly he is quoting a well-known adage, for there are parallels to the saying in rabbinic as well as pagan literature.[90] In effect he argues for expediency: "Isn't it better for us that one man die . . . than for the whole nation to perish?" Please notice that his advice is eminently practical and, in fact, astonishingly modern. He voices our common mind for, again and again, we defend policy on the basis of numbers—the good of the whole (i.e., the economy, the democracy, the "national interest") is more important than a few personal tragedies. When preaching the passage, we must recognize our own thinking in Caiaphas's practical advice and not portray him as a snide villain.

In a way, Caiaphas was prophetic: Eventually the temple was destroyed and the land overrun by military force. But for Christians, Caiaphas was more profoundly prophetic than he knew. By Christ's self-giving death, the human world "may not perish, but may have

---

[90] See Haenchen, *John 2,* 79, who cites material from Billerbeck and from Windisch.

eternal life." So, there are all kinds of irony in the passage. Perhaps the ultimate irony, the kind of irony that is full of glad laughter, is that while rational Caiaphas was arguing for the expediency of Christ's death, God was at work to accomplish the reconciliation of "the scattered children" through Caiaphas's unwitting plans. Apparently God can plot too.

The Anointing at Bethany (John 12:1-8)

John's story of the anointing at Bethany[91] is not too much different from the episode in Mark:

> [1]Six days before the Passover, Jesus came to Bethany, where Lazarus lived, whom Jesus raised from the dead. [2]They gave a dinner party for him there; Martha served while Lazarus was with those at table. [3]Then Mary took a pound of perfume, expensive pure nard, and poured it on Jesus' feet, wiping it off with her hair. And the house was filled with the fragrance of the perfume. [4]One of the disciples, Judas Iscariot, who was about to betray him, protested: [5]"Why wasn't this perfume sold for ten thousand dollars and the money given to the poor?" [6]He did not say this because he cared anything for the poor, but because he was a thief and kept his hand in the purse where money was put. [7]"Let her alone," said Jesus. "She has kept the perfume for the day of my burial. [8]You will always have the poor with you, but you will not always have me."

Because the anointing at Bethany appears in all four Gospels, scholars have had a field day tracing the evolving tradition from Mark's "royal anointing" by an anonymous woman, to Luke's scandalous anointing by a shady lady in the house of Simon, to John's account that includes Mary, Martha, and Lazarus as well as pointing a finger at the dismaying Judas.

John fixes the cost of the perfume at three hundred denarii, which, if each coin was worth around thirty-five dollars, was a sizeable sum — more than ten thousand dollars. And John has the woman, whom he identifies as Mary, pour the perfume on Jesus' feet, wiping them with her loosened hair. By first-century standards of decorum, she was not only impulsively extravagant but somewhat scandalous; proper women did not flaunt their hair in public. But, apparently, Mary is not too concerned about standards of decorum. Notice that, as in the Lukan tale of Mary and Martha, Martha is conventionally serving while an "uppity" Mary honors the Lord.

---

[91] Sources: J. D. M. Derrett, *Law in the New Testament* (London: Darton, Longman & Todd, 1970), 266–75; Haenchen, *John 2,* 82–89; Lindars, *Gospel,* 412–19; Schnackenburg, *Gospel,* 2:365–73.

Of course the odd detail is that, like Luke, John has Mary anointing Jesus' feet, feet which would be stretched out while Jesus reclined at table. Thus the symbol of a kingly anointing, which was a Markan emphasis, has disappeared. Why feet? Probably John is preparing for the soon to come footwashing scene. If Jesus urges his disciples to serve one another by washing feet in a demonstration of humility and servant love (13:14-15), Mary has already qualified as a faithful, self-giving disciple. She loves extravagantly.

Instead of murmuring onlookers, John reduces the reaction to Judas's complaint: "Why wasn't this perfume sold . . . and the money given to the poor?" Judas sounds like a moralist sans theology, a tedious breed. But, no, John drops in a parenthetic explanation: Judas does not give a hang for the poor, he says, but likes money and was in fact dipping into the group money cache. In John, Judas is a chronic liar who always has an ulterior motive.

Jesus' defense of Mary ("Let her alone. She has kept the perfume for the day of my burial") should be interpreted with care. Although some translators have read the verse, "Let her alone so that she can keep the [the rest of the] perfume for the day of my burial," such an interpretation is unlikely. Later, Nicodemus will show up with a hundred pounds of embalming spices (19:39). No, Mary's act is an expression of love for the Christ who, dying, will be lifted up. Jesus is using the phrase "the day" in a broad sense to mean the entire time, which has already begun, of his passion, death, resurrection, and ascension.

As with Mark, we must never read "You will always have the poor with you" as a basis for either benign neglect or unchecked religious extravagance. While he is present, Mary rightly honors Jesus, who "has come from the Father." When he is gone from us, then, in his Spirit, we can pour out our lives for the poor.

The Triumphant Entry (John 12:9-19)

The Gospel of John tells of several trips to Jerusalem.[92] Here is John's account of the "triumphant entry," which he locates after the story of the anointing and before Jesus' agonized prayer to the Father.[93]

---

[92] Material on the triumphant entry has been drawn from a previous publication, see D. G. Buttrick, *Proclamation 4 — Pentecost 3* (Philadelphia: Fortress Press, 1989), 62-63.

[93] Sources: Brown, *Gospel,* 1:455-64; W. R. Farmer, "The Palm Branches in John 12, 13," *Journal of Theological Studies,* n.s., 3 (1952): 62-66; Lindars, *Gospel,* 420-26; Schnackenburg, *Gospel,* 2:373-80.

⁹A great crowd of Jews found out where Jesus was and came, not only because of Jesus, but to see Lazarus whom he had raised from the dead. ¹⁰So the high priests plotted to kill Lazarus as well, ¹¹since many of the Jews came because of him, and believed in Jesus.

¹²On the next day, a big crowd attending the feast heard that Jesus was coming into Jerusalem. ¹³[They] took palm branches and went out to meet him, shouting, "Hosanna. Blessed is he who comes in the name of the Lord, even the king of Israel." ¹⁴Jesus, having found a young donkey, sat on it; for it is written:

¹⁵"Fear not, daughter of Zion.
Look, your king is coming,
riding on a donkey's colt."

¹⁶The disciples did not understand all these things at first, but when Jesus was glorified, then they remembered that the [scripture verses] were written about him and happened to him. ¹⁷Now the crowd that had been with him when he called Lazarus from the tomb and raised him from the dead, spread the news. ¹⁸That is why the crowd went to meet him, because they had heard that he had done a miracle. ¹⁹So the Pharisees said among themselves: "See, nothing works, the world has gone after him."

The structure of the passage is interesting: We have a prologue in vv. 9-11 and an epilogue in vv. 17-19. In between we have a story of Jesus' entry into Jerusalem, woven out of quotations from the Hebrew scriptures (vv. 12-15). The story is followed by an "editorial note" in v. 16. Although Jesus is addressed as a king in the passage, John supplies a very different definition of kingship.

Notice the peculiar character of John's account of the triumphant entry compared to what we find in the Synoptic Gospels. In the Synoptics, the story is climactic and is followed by Jesus' cleansing of the temple. In John, there have been prior visits to Jerusalem and thus, in this passage, there is no disruption of the temple. Instead, the crowd has been stirred by news of the raising of Lazarus, causing chief priests to plot death because "many of the Jews were deserting and were believing in Jesus" (v. 11).

Waving palms, the crowd comes out to greet Jesus. As there is little evidence for palm trees in Jerusalem, the reference is symbolic. Palms were a symbol of national liberation (see 1 Macc. 13:51 and 2 Macc. 10:7). So, Jesus is being greeted with hosannas as a political leader. To underline the symbol, John adds the phrase "even the king of Israel" to the familiar quote from Psalm 118, "Blessed is he who comes in the name of the Lord!"

Then John redefines Jesus' messianic role. He offers an abridged quote from Zechariah 9:9: "Fear not, daughter of Zion / Look, your king is coming, / sitting on an ass's colt." Significantly, John drops "triumphant and victorious is he" from the quotation in Zechariah. (He also deletes the word *humble,* which appears in Zechariah; humility is not the point here.) The important idea that John is promoting is to be found in the context of Zechariah's prophecy. The king will *not* come armed, riding in a war chariot, but as a peacegiver to the whole world (Zech. 9:10).

Verse 16 suddenly forces a reader (along with the disciples) to reflect on the story while recalling the cross/resurrection/ascension event that has created the new community of the Spirit in which we live. We realize that Jesus is not a power Messiah who can ride a crest of rampant nationalism, but rather is one who gives new life (vv. 9, 17) and peace (v. 15) to the world. As the Pharisees observe: "The world has gone after him."

A sermon on the passage may well begin with the cries of the crowd; they thought they had found a liberator. Here comes a Savior with clout who could make them great. But, hold on, he comes looking like a fool perched on a donkey. He is not waving from the turret of a tank in the midst of a ticker-tape parade. No, he comes weaponless on a farm animal. Of course, his entry into Jerusalem was nothing compared to the cross. He dies without force or fury, clinging to faith and forgiving his killers. Maybe he is, after all, a different kind of liberator. Power in our world waves death and tramples the powerless. He gives peace and, yes, life. Look, we are called to follow the fool "king" on a donkey, and to hail his coming, so that someday the whole world will follow him into a life of peace.

A Promise and a Prayer (John 12:20-36)

Immediately after Jesus enters Jerusalem, we get a strange discourse prompted by visiting Greeks.[94] John has no scene in the Garden of Gethsemane, but he does have a version of the great prayer in the middle of a discourse.

20Now there were some Greeks among those who were going up to worship at the festival. 21They approached Philip, who was from Bethsaida in Galilee, and asked him, "Sir, we want to see Jesus." 22Philip went and told Andrew, and Andrew and Philip went and told Jesus.

23Jesus answered them, saying, "The hour has come for Humanity's Child to be glorified. 24Truly, truly, I'm telling you, when a grain of wheat falls into the ground,

---

94 Sources: Barrett, *Gospel,* 350–58; Brown, *Gospel,* 1:465–80; Dodd, *Historical Tradition,* 338–43, 366–69; Lindars, *Gospel,* 426–36; Schnackenburg, *Gospel,* 2:380-97; F. Segovia, "'Peace I Leave with You, My Peace I Give to You,' Discipleship in the Fourth Gospel," in *Discipleship in the New Testament,* ed. F. Segovia (Philadelphia: Fortress Press, 1985).

unless it dies, it stays a single seed; but if it dies, it bears much fruit. [25]Whoever loves life will lose it; and whoever hates life in this world will have life eternal. [26]Whoever serves me must follow me; where I am, my server will be there as well. Whoever serves me, my Father will honor.

[27]"Now is my soul shaken: What shall I say? — Father, save me from this hour? But I have come for this hour — [28]Father, glorify your name!" Then a voice came out of the sky: "I have glorified it; and will glorify it again." [29]The crowd standing by listening said it was thunder. Others said, "An Angel talked to him." [30]Jesus answered, saying, "The voice happened not for me, but for you. [31]Now is the judgment of this world; now the ruler of this world will be thrown out. [32]And I, if I am lifted up from the earth, I will draw all people to me." [33]He said this to show what kind of death he was soon to die.

[34]The crowd answered him: "We learned from the law that the Christ will remain forever. How come you say, Humanity's Child must be lifted up? Who is this Humanity's Child?" [35]Jesus said to them, "For a little while the light will be with you; walk around while you have the light, before darkness overtakes you. Those walking in the darkness don't know where they're going. [36]While you have the light, believe in the light, so you may be children of light."

The passage begins with the arrival of Greeks who were evidently "God-fearers," that is Gentiles who were Jewish proselytes, and who came as pilgrims to the festival. To John they represent the Gentile world that eventually will be drawn to Christ. They want to see Jesus, and so approach Philip, who is from Galilee, a territory bordering on pagan districts. More important, the mention of Philip and Andrew recalls the first chapter of the Gospel of John where disciples are invited to "come and see." Here Greeks come to see Jesus and are thus potential disciples. But, although the passage begins with a covey of Greeks, almost instantly they disappear.

In v. 23 Jesus begins a discourse, somewhat reminiscent of Mark 8:34-38.[95] Initially he refers to "the hour," meaning the hour of his death and glorification.[96] He then produces a little parable about a grain of wheat that must die in order to produce "much fruit." The grain of wheat analogy is found in rabbinic literature and, of course, is also used in 1 Corinthians 15:37. Here, however, the parable is given a missionary emphasis: If a seed does not die it remains "single," but if it dies, it multiplies. The death of Christ will result in many — including Gentiles such as "the Greeks" — being drawn as disciples into faith. No wonder the discourse turns to a discussion of discipleship:

---

[95] Verses 24-26, which R. Brown regards as an insertion disrupting a natural sequence from v. 23 to v. 27, contain a number of Synoptic parallels: Matt. 10:39; 16:25; Mark 8:35; Luke 9:24; 17:33.

[96] On John's understanding of exaltation and glorification, see an excursus in Schnackenburg, *Gospel,* 2:398–410.

Disciples must willingly lose life in order to gain life. John's use of "love" and "hate" is deliberately extreme, underscoring the radical commitment involved. Nevertheless, those who risk their lives, their livelihood, and their possessions to be servants (*diakonos*) of Christ will be honored by God.

Suddenly the passage turns into a kind of soliloquy and we get John's version of Jesus' prayer in Gethsemane. "Father, glorify your name!" is obviously equivalent to Mark's "Nevertheless, not what I want, but what you want." It also seems to echo our Lord's Prayer: "Make holy your name." The voice from the sky affirms God's sovereign will and ratifies Jesus' obedience. Some hear thunder (1 Sam. 12:17-18; Ps. 29:3-9), while others suppose an angel has spoken (John 1:51). Then the discourse turns to the effects of Christ's forthcoming death, resurrection, and ascension: Evil ("the ruler of this world") will be thrown down and Christ will be lifted up, drawing all people into faith.[97] The use of "all" stresses a universal call to salvation.

The crowd's question is somewhat peculiar: They claim that they have learned from scripture that the Messiah ("Christ") will "remain forever."[98] Therefore they are confused by the mention of being "lifted up." How can an everlasting Christ be crucified? In reply, Jesus speaks of light and darkness, echoing the prologue to the Gospel (1:4-9) as well as other light/darkness speeches (8:12; 9:4; 11:9-10). So Jesus calls the crowd to believe in him while he is present with them. The reference to "children of light" implies a contrast with "children of darkness" who have been taken in by "the ruler of this world" (see Luke 16:8; 1 Thess. 5:5; Eph. 5:8). The same term is found in Qumran literature where the "sons" of light and darkness are repeatedly contrasted.

The passage is extremely difficult to preach in part because of the introductory mention of the Greeks who want to see Jesus. A solution might be to begin with the images of darkness that assuredly describe our age. Where is "light"? We see the Christ who lived for God's glory and whose death, like a grain of wheat, has multiplied believers. But to follow Christ will mean we lose our worldly lives. Yet, in doing so, we do become children of light.

---

[97] Some manuscripts read "thrown down" and others "thrown out." In either case, there is a contrast with "lifted up."

[98] While there is no text that specifically says that "Messiah" or "Son of Man" will reign forever, Isa. 9:6ff. and Ezek. 37:26 seem to refer to such a messianic rule. Of course, Dan. 7:13-14 refers to the rule of the Son of Man: "His dominion is an everlasting dominion that shall not pass away."

The Footwashing (John 13:1-17)

The footwashing scene has been preached during Holy Week for centuries.[99] The passage is difficult because it contains visual description, a "mystery dialogue" between Peter and Jesus, and finally instruction for disciples.

[1]Before the feast of the Passover, Jesus knew the hour had come for him to leave this world and go to the Father. Yet he loved his own who were in the world and he loved them to the end. [2]Even as supper took place, the devil had already primed the heart of Judas, son of Simon, to betray him. [3]Knowing that the Father had put all things into his hands, and that he had come from God and was going to God, [4]Jesus got up from the supper table and laid aside his clothes. He picked up a towel and tied it around his waist. [5]After pouring some water into a basin, he began to wash his disciples' feet, drying them with the towel from around his waist.

[6]When he got to Peter, Peter said to him, "Lord, you're not going to wash my feet are you?" [7]Jesus answered him, saying, "You don't realize what I'm doing now, but later you will understand." [8]Peter replied, "No, Sir, you'll never wash my feet, not now, not ever!" "If I do not wash you," said Jesus, "you will have no share in my life." [9]Then Simon Peter said, "Lord, don't just wash my feet, but my hands and face as well." [10]Jesus told him, "A man who's taken a bath doesn't need to wash; he's clean clear through. You are clean, but not all of you." [11]For he knew who was betraying him, so he said, "Not all of you are clean."

[12]After he had washed their feet, put his clothes back on, and returned to his place at table, Jesus said to them, "Do you understand what I have done for you? [13]You call me Teacher and Lord, and you're right, for I am. [14]If, therefore, I, your Lord and Teacher, wash your feet, you ought to wash one another's feet too. [15]I have given you an example: As I have done, so you must do. [16]Truly, truly, I tell you, a slave is not greater than the boss, and a messenger greater than the sender. [17]If you know all these things, blessed are you if you do them."

The passage has occasioned much scholarly debate. The Synoptic Gospels picture Jesus preparing for a Passover meal with disciples, and represent his words at table that, in the life of the church, have become the "Words of Institution." In the Gospel of John, the meal in chapter 13 is emphatically not a Passover, but an ordinary dinner (*deipnon*), and the dating of the event is quite different.[100] Moreover John includes no traditional "Words of Institution." Obviously John is familiar with eucharistic celebration; the discussion in chapter 6 almost certainly has reference to the Lord's Supper. Why then has the Last Supper disappeared from his passion narrative and been replaced with the

---

[99] Sources: Barrett, *Gospel,* 363–74; Brown, *Gospel,* 2:548–80; Bultmann, *Gospel,* 461–79; Haenchen, *John 2,* 102–14; Lindars, *Gospel,* 441–53; Schnackenburg, *Gospel,* 3:6–47; F. Segovia, "John 13:1-20, the Footwashing in the Johannine Tradition," *Zeitschrift für die Neutestamentliche Wissenschaft* (New York: Walter de Gruyer, 1982).

[100] On the problem of dating, see the summary discussion in Brown, *Gospel,* 2:555–56. Although Brown rejects the notion of an Essene calendar for the Gospel, I find the suggestion more likely.

footwashing? There have been all kinds of answers. Bultmann suggested that the final prayer in chapter 17 is out of place and should be relocated at table, replacing the usual words of institution.[101] Other scholars claim that the omission is deliberate either because the ritual was a secret (*disciplina arcani*) or because of a somewhat antisacramental tendency within the Gospel.[102] Still others suppose that John assumes familiarity with the meal and, therefore, need not specifically mention the Last Supper.[103] Still others believe that John has supplied the footwashing as a theological meditation on the true meaning of the supper. Literature puzzling the problem enlarges yearly.[104]

The passage begins by underscoring Jesus' knowledge and his love. He knows his hour is at hand and he knows that soon he will be "going to God." But he loves his own and loves them "to the end" (*eis telos*), a phrase that implies both duration and complete fulfillment. At the same time, Judas has been primed to betray Jesus. Thus, the scene is set.

In Jesus' world people usually washed their own dusty feet—Jewish slaves were not required to do so—but, as a form of deferential honor, students might wash a rabbi's feet or dutiful children the feet of a parent. Here Jesus does the menial, but honorary, task. The phrase "laid aside his clothes" employs a verb (*tithēsin*) also used of Jesus' laying down his life. Like the anointing at Bethany, Jesus wipes (*ekmassein*) the feet of his disciples. Some preachers see the event as a living illustration of the so-called Christ Hymn in Philippians 2.

Now John introduces what I have termed a "mystery dialogue." These dialogues—there are several in John—function on the basis of double entendre with the persons in a conversation functioning on different "wave lengths," each pursuing a different subject matter. So, although they converse, clearly Jesus has one set of meanings and Peter another; no wonder Peter seems so incredibly obtuse. Jesus is speaking of his "hour" and the great salvation his life, death, resurrection, and ascension will achieve. Peter rather obviously is not tuned in to the same meanings. The mystery dialogues work wonderfully because we who overhear the conversation live on the far side of the great Christ event and can understand.

The conversation begins with Peter's demur: "Lord, you're not going

---

[101] Bultmann, *Gospel,* 459–60, 485–87.
[102] So argues Barrett, *Gospel,* 42, 71.
[103] So argues Hoskyns, *Fourth Gospel,* and, to some degree, Lindars, *Gospel.*
[104] For summaries of positions, see Lindars, *Gospel,* 441–46, and Schnackenburg, *Gospel,* 3:7–15, 42–47.

188 The Passion of Jesus Christ

to wash my feet are you?" In effect, Peter is appalled, saying, *you* wash *me?* Proper positions have been reversed; a disciple should honor his teacher, not vice versa. Jesus' answer points toward the future. After the cross, after Christ has ascended and the Spirit is given, then Peter will grasp the meaning of his Lord's self-abasement. Peter responds emphatically: "You'll never wash my feet, not now, not ever!" In a way, Peter is saying, "No, you will never die for me." Jesus answers with a steely firmness, "If I do not wash you, you will have no share in my life." Jesus might as well be saying, "If you do not accept my death for you, you will not receive the Life — capital *L* — I give." Whereupon Peter becomes superreligious, requesting a complete wash job: "Don't just wash my feet, but my hands and face as well." Jesus responds, stressing the once and for all character of his atoning death. Although the back and forth mystery dialogue is difficult to preach, it is a stunning display of theological insight.

Is there a hidden reference to baptism in the discussion of washing and, therefore, a triple entendre? Once more scholars are sharply divided.[105] Perhaps the best answer is a both/and answer. In Pauline thought, baptism is into the death and resurrection of Jesus Christ — by going under water we are in a sense buried with Christ, and rising from the water we are cleansed for new life. Clearly, the footwashing is related to Christ's self-giving death, in which he lays aside his life and, thereby, lifts us to God. But does not baptism have much the same reference? The verb in v. 10, "taken a bath" (*louein*), is used of baptism in the Christian scriptures.

Now the passage turns into instruction.[106] In doing so, it seems to echo some Synoptic texts (Matt. 10:24; Luke 11:28). Note the term for messenger in v. 16 (*apostolos*), which possibly is a deliberate reference to apostolic leadership.

Most preachers when they build a sermon on the passage put together the visual picture of the footwashing (vv. 3-5) with the instruction in vv. 12-16, and thus skip the seemingly complex mystery dialogue. The practice is unfortunate. Instead the scene of the footwashing can serve as a vivid introduction to a sermon. The scene is dramatic: Jesus

---

[105] For example, C. H. Dodd, C. K. Barrett, and R. E. Brown suppose there is some reference to baptism here, while R. Bultmann, J. D. G. Dunn, and others reject the notion.

[106] Some scholars, among them Bultmann and Brown, believe that two interpretations (the dialogue and the teaching), one earlier and one later, have been pieced together in the passage. Those who so argue suppose that the teaching (vv. 10-16) is the earlier material.

removes his clothes, ties a long scarflike towel around his waist, and bends to scrape road dirt from the disciples' feet. But the main moves of the sermon can be derived from the shifts in dialogue between Peter and Jesus. Finally, the sermon can move on to a call to discipleship based on the instruction given in vv. 12-16.

The Betrayer at Table (John 13:18-30)

The account of Judas at table continues immediately,[107] as follows:

> 18"I am not talking about all of you—I know whom I have chosen. But scripture must be fulfilled: 'He who eats bread with me has raised his heel against me.' 19I'm telling you this now before it happens, so that, when it happens, you may believe [who] I AM. 20Truly, truly, I tell you, whoever welcomes anyone I send, welcomes me; and whoever welcomes me, welcomes the one who sent me."
>
> 21Having spoken, Jesus was shaken in spirit, and announced, "Truly, truly, I'm telling you, one of you will betray me." 22The disciples looked at one another, wondering whom he was talking about. 23One of his disciples, the one whom Jesus' loved, was relaxed close beside Jesus. 24Peter nodded to him and said, "Find out who he's talking about." 25While relaxed close to Jesus, the disciple whom Jesus loved said to him: "Lord, who is it?" 26Jesus answered, "The one to whom I give a piece of bread after I've dipped it." So, when he dipped the piece of bread, he gave it to Judas, Son of Simon Iscariot. 27And, after he took the bread, then Satan entered him. So Jesus said to him, "What you're going to do, do quickly." 28But no one at table knew what he was talking about. 29Some thought that, since Judas had the common purse, Jesus was telling him to buy what was needed for the feast or that he should give something to the poor. 30Then, after receiving the piece of bread, at once he went out. And it was night.

Verses 18-20 are transitional, conjoining the footwashing and the episode of the betrayer at table. The shift begins with v. 18: "I am not talking about all of you—I know whom I have chosen." Some scholars suppose that Jesus is saying that he knows his *true* disciples (i.e., excluding Judas), but such an interpretation is unlikely in view of John 6:70: "Did I not choose you, the twelve? Yet one of you is a devil." More likely is the idea that Christ knows those whom he has selected, and knows them well. In the same verse we get a scripture citation from Psalm 41:9, which reads: "Even my bosom friend in whom I trusted, / who ate of my bread, has lifted the heel against me." Either "lifted his heel against me" refers to a sneaky kick or it may describe some Semitic form of insult. In any event, Hebrew notions of hospitality are violated; eating together is a pledge and a communion. The verse that follows,

---

107 Sources: Brown, *Gospel,* 2:548-80; Bultmann, *Gospel,* 479-86; Lindars, *Gospel,* 454-59; Schnackenburg, *Gospel,* 3:6-47.

v. 19, may echo Isaiah 48:5, but it clearly ends with "I AM."[108] "I AM" is, of course, the divine name, and its use by John seems to indicate Jesus' oneness with God and his status as Word of God become flesh. Notice that v. 20 seems to follow v. 16, leading some scholars to suppose that vv. 18-19 are an editorial insertion.

If we compare John's portrayal of Judas at table with Christ with the accounts in the Synoptics we sense a very different picture. In the Synoptics, the disciples ask, "Surely, not I?" But in John there is no doubt of the betrayer, for he is identified by Jesus as Judas. In a note, Raymond Brown describes a likely seating arrangement—a central table with the company horseshoed around on the sides. He supposes that Jesus is seated in the middle of the center table with the "loved disciple" on his right and Judas, the group treasurer, on his left.[109] But who knows? We have previously discussed the mysterious "loved disciple."[110] Scholarly suggestions have included John, John Mark, Lazarus, the author of the Gospel, and even Paul. But the figure is strangely anonymous and therefore may be an idealized disciple; we cannot know with any certainty.[111] But almost always we get the "loved disciple" and Peter in tandem. Here Peter nods and the "loved disciple," who is leaning on Jesus' chest, pops the question: "Lord, who is it?" Jesus says that it will be one who dips bread with him—again, a terrible breach of unity.

After Judas eats the bread, Satan enters him and the betrayal is fixed. "What you're going to do, do quickly," Jesus says, and the story ends dramatically with the single phrase, "And it was night."

Please notice that John indicates Jesus' foreknowledge of his betrayal. Such foreknowledge is not magic, but an indication that Jesus and the Father are one. Thus, Jesus knows that God's purpose is being fulfilled, namely the salvation of the world. So although Satan may betray Christ through Judas, God is greater and God's will will be done, even through satanic agencies.

But, on a deeper level, the dipping of bread is not merely a signal, a pointing finger identifying Judas; it is an astonishing act of grace— Jesus Christ feeds the one who will betray him. So although God is

---

[108] On the "I AM" sayings in John, see Brown, *Gospel,* 1:533–38, and Schnackenburg, *Gospel,* 2:79–89.

[109] Brown, 2:574.

[110] See p. 82 above.

[111] For a summary discussion, see Schnackenburg, *Gospel,* 3:375–88.

moving through all things, even the betrayal, the love of God is also expressed in and through all things — even in the dark.

The Arrest (John 18:1-11)

Although John does not picture Jesus at prayer in the Garden of Gethsemane, he does supply a dramatic scene in which Jesus is betrayed and taken prisoner:[112]

> [1]Having so spoken, Jesus went out with his disciples across the Kidron valley to a garden where he and his disciples gathered. [2]Now Judas, who was betraying him, also knew the place because Jesus often met there with his disciples. [3]So Judas took a detachment of soldiers and police from the chief priests and Pharisees with lanterns and torches and weapons. [4]Then Jesus, knowing all the things that were going to happen, went out and said to them, "Whom are you looking for?" [5]They answered him, "Jesus the Nazarene." He told them, "I AM [he]." Now Judas, his betrayer, stood with them. [6]When he said to them, "I AM," they pulled back and fell to the ground. [7]So, again, he asked them, "Whom are you looking for?" And they said, "Jesus the Nazarene." [8]Jesus replied, "I told you that I AM [he]; if you are looking for me, let these go." [9]This [he spoke] to fulfill the word he had said: "Those you have given me, I have lost none of them." [10]Then Simon Peter, who had a sword, drew it and struck the high priest's slave, cutting off his right ear — the name of the slave was Malchus. [11]So Jesus said to Peter, "Put the sword into its sheath; shall I not drink the cup that has been given to me by the Father?"

The story of the arrest in John is different from the accounts found in the Synoptic Gospels. At the outset, please notice that John has no garden prayer, no sleeping disciples, no kiss of betrayal, and no disciples hightailing it from the garden to save their own skins. We do get the odd story of someone slicing an ear from the high priest's slave (Mark 14:47), but in John the incident is elaborated; Peter is the one with the sword and the slave's name is given, Malchus. Otherwise, John's story is unique and shaped by Johannine theology.

There are deliberate exaggerations. According to John, Judas arrives in the garden leading a troop of Roman soldiers. They are described as a "cohort" (in Greek a *speira*), which would be six-hundred strong; along with them is a detachment of temple police. Thus John has around seven or eight hundred armed troops to arrest one defenseless Jesus. They arrive in the darkness and, as children of darkness, must bring along lanterns and torches in order to see. Although the account is historically doubtful, it is symbolically stunning and full of deliberate

---

[112] Sources: Barrett, *Gospel,* 430-36; Brown, *Gospel,* 2:803-18; Bultmann, *Gospel,* 637-41; Duke, *Irony,* 109-11; Schnackenburg, *Gospel,* 3:221-27.

irony. Here the Romans and the Jews come together with power as a "world" against Jesus.

Jesus comes forward and asks, "Whom are you looking for?" "Jesus the Nazarene," they reply. Whereupon Jesus says, "I AM." Although many translators supply the implied "I am he," the text has only the significant "I AM" (*egō eimi*). Remember that when Jesus told of his forthcoming betrayal at table, he said, "I'm telling you this now before it happens, so that, when it happens, you may believe I AM" (13:19). The words "I AM" are the divine name, which is, of course, why the troops pull back and fall to the ground; as Bultmann observes, "the Redeemer is speaking."[113] Notice that a word from Jesus is able to confound the huge contingent of soldiers and police. Some scholars believe that the scene is designed as a fulfillment of Psalm 27:2-3 (and perhaps Psalm 35:4): "My adversaries and foes — / they shall stumble and fall" (27:2b).

Then Jesus, after repeating the dialogue, asks that his disciples may go: "If you are looking for me, let these go." So instead of running away, the disciples are set free by Jesus. According to John, Jesus spoke to fulfill his own words: "Those you have given me, I have lost none of them." The citation is somewhat imprecise as we can find no such words of Jesus previously spoken within the Gospel. But then John is not always exact, and he is probably alluding to John 6:39; 10:28-29; or 17:12. In chapter 10, Jesus identifies himself as the Good Shepherd who will lay down his life for his sheep; here in the garden he does so.

The episode in which Peter pulls out a sword against a small army is slightly ludicrous. Is the cut-off ear a symbol of the high priest's inability to hear? Perhaps. Symbolic subtleties are John's specialty. In any event, Jesus stops Peter sharply: "Put the sword into its sheath; shall I not drink the cup given to me by the Father?" Although the cup metaphor is used several times in Mark, here in John it is employed for the first time. The cup is the bitter cup of suffering and death.

Ironies in the passage are quite wonderful and should pique preaching excitement. Here, in the dark, we have a whopping troop of soldiers and police arriving with weapons to subdue one defenseless Jesus. But the word of God, "I AM," drops them in their tracks. Who is the "I AM"? He is the one who saves his disciples and, in obedience, will faithfully drink the cup.

---

[113] Bultmann, *Gospel*, 639.

The Appearance before Annas; Peter's Denial (John 18:12-27)

John deliberately patches two scenes together so the contrast between Jesus' testimony and Peter's denial will stand out clearly.[114] We shall discuss the two episodes separately, although commenting from the one text:

> [12]Then the troops, their officer, and the Jewish police tied him up [13]and led him first to Annas, Caiaphas's father-in-law, who was high priest that year. [14]Now Caiaphas was the one who had advised the Jews that it is expedient for one man to die on behalf of the people.
>
> [15]Simon Peter and another disciple followed Jesus. Since that disciple was well-known to the high priest, he went with Jesus into the high priest's courtyard, [16]while Peter stood outside at the door. The other disciple who was known to the high priest spoke to the woman doorkeeper and let Peter in. [17]Then the woman doorkeeper said to Peter, "Aren't you also this man's disciple?" "Not me," was the answer. [18]Now the slaves and the police were standing by a coal fire they had made, warming themselves because it was cold. Peter was standing with them warming himself.
>
> [19]Then the high priest questioned Jesus about his disciples and his teaching. [20]Jesus answered him, "I have spoken to the world openly; I always taught in the synagogue or in the temple where all Jews gather; I said nothing in secret. [21]Why are you questioning me? Question those who heard me speak. They know what things I said." [22]While he was speaking, one of the police standing by slugged Jesus, saying, "Do you talk back to a high priest that way?" [23]Jesus answered him, "If I spoke wrong, then testify to the wrong; but if I spoke well, why are you beating me up?" [24]So Annas tied him up and sent him to Caiaphas.
>
> [25]Now Simon Peter was standing, warming himself. They said to him, "Aren't you one of his disciples?" "I am not," was his denial. [26]Then a servant of the high priest, whose relative had an ear cut off by Peter, said, "Didn't I see you with him in the garden?" [27]Again, Peter denied it, and at once a rooster was crowing.

Scholars have struggled to bring John's account of a trial before Annas into accord with the Synoptic reports.[115] Mark has a night meeting of the Sanhedrin with a high priest presiding; Matthew mentions Caiaphas by name; and Luke has a nighttime interrogation by Caiaphas followed by a morning meeting of the Sanhedrin. None of the Synoptics mentions Annas, who would have been an ex-high priest at the time. John has once more rearranged the tradition. He has already described a meeting of the Sanhedrin in 10:22-39, which may have been influenced by the Synoptic tradition. Now he has another trial that is very different in character and may even be a Johannine creation.

---

[114] Sources: Brown, *Gospel,* 2:819-42; Bultmann, *Gospel,* 641-48; Duke, *Irony,* 85-100; Lindars, *Gospel,* 544-52; Schnackenburg, *Gospel,* 3:227-40.

[115] For summaries of the discussion, see Lindars, *Gospel,* 544-47, and Brown, *Gospel,* 2:820-21, 828-36. The question of the actual shape of the historical event may not be crucial for preachers.

The trial before Annas begins with the high priest asking about Jesus' "disciples and his teaching." Jesus responds, "I have spoken to the world openly. . . . I said nothing in secret." The latter phrase may be drawn from Isaiah 45:19 or, perhaps, 48:16, which reads: "Draw near to me, hear this! / From the beginning I have not spoken in secret." Jesus then says, "Why are you questioning me? Question those who heard me speak." In so speaking he may be asking for a fair trial with two witnesses, but it is more likely that John is suggesting that the best testimony to Christ is from the hearers of his word. Suddenly a soldier cuffs Jesus for sassing the high priest, perhaps an allusion to Exodus 22:28: "You shall not revile God, or curse a leader of your people." And Jesus' reply may ask, In what way have I cursed a leader? "If I spoke wrongly, then testify to the wrong; but if I spoke well, why are you beating me up?" Obviously the trial is getting nowhere, so Annas has Jesus tied up and dispatched to Caiaphas. Of course John's underlying purpose in presenting the preliminary trial is to contrast Jesus' openness and outspoken courage with Peter's crass denials.

Peter's denial has been predicted at the end of chapter 13:

> [36]Simon Peter said to him, "Lord, where are you going?" Jesus answered, "Where I'm going, you can't follow me now, but you will follow later." [37]"Lord, why can't I follow you yet?" Peter said. "I will lay down my life for you." [38]Jesus answered, "Will you lay down your life for me? Truly, truly, I tell you, the rooster will not crow until you've denied me three times."

Now Peter shows up following Jesus along with "another disciple." Is the odd reference to another disciple actually to the "loved disciple," who so often is mentioned in tandem with Peter? Probably not.[116] Whoever "another disciple" is, he is well-known (*gnostos*) to the high priest and,[117] therefore, is admitted to the courtyard, while Peter is on the outside looking in. Using a little influence, the other disciple persuades the woman doorkeeper to allow Peter to enter. The woman presses a question: "Aren't you also this man's disciple?" Peter's answer is abrupt: "Not me" (*ouk eimi*), which some scholars suppose may contrast with Christ's "I AM" (*egō eimi*), although they may be squeezing too much from the text. Notice that, after the denial, Peter stands *with* the police. Twice more Peter is questioned, the last time by a relative of the slave whose ear was sliced off: "Didn't I see you with him in the garden?" After Peter's final denial, a rooster is heard crowing.

---

[116] So says Lindars and Schnackenburg, although Brown is less certain.

[117] Bultmann (*Gospel*, 645) notes that *gnostos* implies "on friendly terms with," rather more than a nodding acquaintance; thus I have translated the word as "well-known."

John's interweaving of the two stories is a clue for preachers. Although Peter follows Jesus, he does not follow all the way; he is unwilling to lay down his life. Instead, Peter denies his Lord and thus aligns himself unwittingly with the police. So although Peter goes free, he has failed terribly. By contrast Jesus is tied up and abused for the truth; yet Jesus is open and acknowledges his message. Indirectly the passage is a call to brave, not-counting-the-cost discipleship. Preached, the passage should speak to all of us who are embarrassed to admit our ties to Jesus Christ.

The Trial before Pilate
(John 18:28—19:16a)

John has drawn together the scourging, the choice of Barabbas, and the interrogation by Pilate into one long trial scene in which Pilate becomes a central figure who goes in and out of the governor's residence (praetorium) as he deals with the Jewish leaders, the crowd, and Jesus. John tells the story in seven scenes.[118] We shall study the passage episode by episode.

The scene takes place outside, as Pilate engages Jewish leaders and the milling crowd, and inside, as Pilate interrogates Jesus. As several scholars have noted, the scenes seem to be arranged in a chiastic pattern.[119] John's account of the trial differs from the Synoptic stories; for example, he has the scourging take place while the trial is proceeding, which is historically doubtful. John also adds a preface dealing

---

[118] Sources: Barrett, *Gospel,* 442–54; Brown, *Gospel,* 2:843–96; Bultmann, *Gospel,* 651–66; Dodd, *Historical Tradition,* 96–120; Duke, *Irony,* 106–7, 126–37; Haenchen, *John 2,* 175–88; Lindars, *Gospel,* 552–73; Schnackenburg, *Gospel,* 3:241–67.

[119] Essentially, Brown (*Gospel,* 2:859) diagrams the episodes in the following manner:

1. Outside (18:28-32) Jews demand death	7. Outside (19:12-16a) Jews obtain death sentence
2. Inside (18:33-38a) Dialogue with Jesus: Kingship	6. Inside (19:9-11) Dialogue with Jesus: Power
3. Outside (18:38b-40) Pilate says not guilty; Barabbas	5. Outside (19:4-8) Pilate says not guilty; "Look—the man!"

4. Elsewhere (19:1-3)
The Scourging

with Jewish law's prohibition of the imposition of capital punishment by the Sanhedrin; again, this material may or may not be accurate. But obviously John has designed the trial scene to include two theological dialogues between Jesus and Pilate. He has also brought the whole trial to an ironic conclusion in which the chief priests, who earlier had worried over defilement, finally announce: "We have no king but Caesar!"

Episode 1

28It was early when they led Jesus from Caiaphas to the praetorium. To avoid defilement, so they could eat the Passover, they did not go into the praetorium. 29So Pilate came out to them, saying, "What charge are you bringing against this man?" 30They answered him, saying, "If this man wasn't doing evil, we wouldn't have brought him to you." 31Then Pilate said, "You take him, and judge him according to your own law." "But it's not legal for us to put anyone to death," said the Jews, 32fulfilling the words of Jesus when he spoke of the death he would die.

Notice that at the beginning of the trial, the chief priests are scrupulous: They are concerned with defilement; they defend Jesus' arrest; and they show a pious concern for the letter of the law. Scholars have debated whether in fact the Sanhedrin could conduct an execution; the debate is unresolved.[120] But John suggests that they had to secure a Roman sentence in order for Jesus to be "lifted up" in crucifixion. Earlier, in chapter 12, Jesus had spoken of his coming death:

31"Now is the judgment of this world; now the ruler of this world will be thrown out. 32And I, if I am lifted up from the earth, I will draw all people to me." 33He said this to show what kind of death he was soon to die.

John 18:28-32 displays subtle forms of disrespect. Pilate points to Jesus as "this man," almost as if he were saying, "this Jew." In turn, the Jewish leaders, forced to co-opt Pilate, but still scornful, answer: "If this man wasn't doing evil, we wouldn't have brought him to you." They want Jesus to be strung up on a Roman cross; still scrupulous, they say execution is "not legal for us." So here we have leaders ironically maintaining purity while, at the same time, conniving to have Jesus crucified. All the while, Jesus not only has anticipated crucifixion but knows, "If I am lifted up from the earth, I will draw all people to me."

Episode 2

33Going back into the praetorium, Pilate called in Jesus and said to him, "You are King of the Jews?" 34Jesus answered, "Are you speaking on your own or have others

---

120 See Barrett, *Gospel,* 445–46, for a brief summary of the debate.

been telling you about me?" [35]Pilate answered, "No, I'm not a Jew, am I? Your people and the chief priests turned you over to me. What did you do?" [36]"My kingdom is not of this world. If my kingdom were of this world, my police would be fighting so that I wouldn't be turned over to the Jews; but no, my kingdom is not here." [37]So Pilate said to him, "You're not really a king are you?" Jesus answered, "You're [the one] saying that I am a king. I have been born and come into the world as a witness to the truth. Everyone who is of the truth hears my voice." [38]To him, Pilate said, "What is truth?"

Pilate goes back into the praetorium. Throughout the trial the movement in and out of the praetorium creates a drama occurring on two stages at once: the outside drama of Pilate and the Jewish groups and the inside drama of Pilate and Jesus. Pilate opens the dialogue by asking, "You are king of the Jews?" The same question shows up in the Synoptic tradition.[121] Jesus answers by turning the trial around — suddenly Pilate is on trial. Is he genuinely asking about Jesus or simply echoing an accusation? Pilate's answer is emphatic. He is definitely *not* a Jew, and thus he has no interest in a "king of the Jews." Then Pilate asks about Jesus' crime, "What did you do?" Whereupon, Jesus replies contrasting his kingdom with the kingdoms of earth. If his kingdom were of this world, he would have police fighting to protect him. But he has no worldly power precisely because his kingdom is of a different order. Please note: Jesus is not contrasting a heavenly kingdom or an invisible kingdom with the power politics of earthly nations. Rather the contrast is between two spheres with entirely different modus operandi. The worldly political spheres operate with the power of deadly force — our defense budgets enlarge and our armies multiply. But, instead, Jesus gives life and persuades by the word of truth, serving the purposes of God in the power of the Spirit of love.

In effect Pilate answers by saying, "So you're not really a king, are you?" Notice Pilate defines kingship in terms of power; without such obvious power, there is no kingship. Then Jesus replies, observing that Pilate is the one who has brought up the subject of kingship. Instead, Jesus defines himself quite differently as a "witness to the truth," adding that "everyone who is of the truth hears my voice." By "hears" he means to understand and believe. Pilate's answer ("What is truth?") may or may not be cynical. Certainly it indicates that Pilate is not "of the truth," but rather is thinking in an entirely different way. The real question for Pilate is not truth, but who has the power, the political

---

[121] A few scholars translate the verse, "*You* are king of the Jews?" rather than, "Are you king of the Jews?" The first alternative might imply either incredulity or a touch of scorn.

leverage; truth is either secondary or irrelevant. His comment defines the trial itself. Is the truth about Jesus relevant? Or is political expediency the dominant concern?

The irony of the passage is that although Jesus stands on trial before Pilate, under God, it is Pilate who is tried and found wanting. The final question, "What is truth?," may be addressed to us who visualize the scene, and who live in two spheres at once—in a world where power rules and, as Christians, in Christ's new order of life and love and light. In a sense, we too are on trial. Preachers must not draw a contrast between the physical, here-and-now world and some unseen, "spiritual," heavenly realm—a never-never land of dreamy religion. No, the real contrast is between realms: In the ways of the world, "my police would be fighting"; but in God's ways, the seemingly impotent power of self-giving, nonviolent love is sufficient. Caught in such a contrast, we must ask with seriousness, What is truth? What is reality? Our answer to the questions will shape the lives we live.

Episode 3

> 38bHaving spoken, he went out to the Jews again and told them, "I don't find him guilty. 39But, according to your custom, I should set one of your prisoners free at Passover. Do you want me to release the king of the Jews for you?" 40They shouted back, "Not this one, but Barabbas!" Now Barabbas was a robber.

A brief scene concludes the first half of the dramatic trial. Pilate goes out to the Jews again and, perhaps impressed by Jesus, says point-blank, "I don't find him guilty." So, although Pilate seems to know the truth, he abdicates his decision and appeals to public opinion. In an age when pollsters seem to determine political choice, we can understand the impulse.

There is no evidence that some prisoner was regularly released at Passover time; however, such an act of clemency during a holy season is not intrinsically impossible.[122] But questions of historicity are perhaps beside the point; Pilate cops out and hands his decision over to popular vote: "Do you want me to release the king of the Jews for you?" Just why the question is so phrased is a little baffling, for it scarcely seems impartial. In any event, the crowd noises a reply: "Not this one, but Barabbas!" The last phrase of the scene is full of irony: "Now Barabbas was a robber" (*lēstēs*). John has used the word *robber*

---

[122] See Barrett, *Gospel,* 448, and Brown, *Gospel,* 2:856–57, 870–72, for discussion of the issues.

earlier in a discussion of the Good Shepherd: "Very truly, I tell you, anyone who does not enter the sheepfold by the gate but climbs in by another way is a thief and a bandit" [*lēstēs*]" (John 10:1). "All who came before me are thieves and bandits [*lēstēs*]; but the sheep did not listen to them" (John 10:8). So, ironically, the crowd chooses Barabbas, a true insurrectionist, and votes to condemn the Good Shepherd, Jesus, to death.

The passage may be difficult to preach to Americans who have all but deified democratic process. We truly seem to believe that the will of the majority, democratically achieved, is a guarantee of divine rightness. But here is a case of "democracy in action" gone awry. The bandits of the era were strongly supported by the populace because of their disdain for the Roman occupation; the bandits were regarded as patriots. Is it possible that democracy also is governed by patriotic self-interests? John's blunt last words—"Now Barabbas was a robber"—do raise the question. In a sinful, rebellious world, democracy can be sinful too.

Episode 4

[1]Then Pilate took Jesus and had him scourged. [2]And the soldiers, twisting together a crown of thorns, put it on his head and threw a purple robe around him, [3]and kept coming up to him, saying, "Hail, King of the Jews!" Then they slugged him.

The fourth section of the trial narrative is sort of an entr'acte. The scene fulfills prophecy, for Isaiah 50:6 reads:

> I gave my back to those who struck me,
>   and my cheeks to those who pulled out the beard;
> I did not hide my face
>   from insult and spitting.

The crown of thorns may have been a wreath of thorns. Some Roman coins pictured emperors wearing a radiant wreath. The color of the robe, purple, is an imperial color. The greeting, "Hail," mimics "Ave Caesar." The Synoptics locate the scourging prior to crucifixion, but John has moved it into the middle of his trial scenes. A German scholar, Josef Blank, argues that John's trial is a bizarre parody of a "King's Epiphany."[123] After a man is declared king, the monarch is robed and crowned, and then brought before the people. Although the

---

[123] Discussed by Duke, *Irony*, 132.

suggestion is uncertain, it does explain why John has relocated the scourging.

The brief passage is ironic. Although the soldiers mock Jesus as a king with a tilt of twisted thorns and a purple robe, in reality Jesus is God's royal child who will be "lifted up" in risen glory. John has predicted that all people, and specifically the Gentiles, will be drawn to Christ; here Gentile soldiers bow unwittingly before their Lord.

Episode 5

> [4]Again, Pilate went out and said to them, "Look, I'm bringing him out to you, so you'll understand I don't find him guilty." [5]Then Jesus came out wearing a crown of thorns and a purple robe. And [Pilate] said to them, "Look—the man." [6]When the chief priests and the police saw him, they shouted, "Crucify! Crucify!" To them, Pilate said, "You take him and crucify, for I don't find him guilty of any crime." [7]The Jews answered him, "We have law, and according to the law, he should die—he passed himself off as God's Son." [8]When Pilate heard what was said, he was more afraid.

The scene begins with Pilate's second declaration of Jesus' innocence (see v. 18:38: "I don't find him guilty"). Although Pilate finds Jesus innocent, displaying weakness, he does not stop the proceedings. Instead, with Jesus standing by him with a crown of thorns and a royal robe of purple, he says: "Look — the man." The words are difficult to interpret and, therefore, have occasioned much scholarly discussion.[124] Is Pilate's remark disparaging (i.e., "Look at the pathetic fellow")? Or is it a statement of admiration (i.e., "Look, here is a real man")? Or is the phrase "the man" an eschatological title similar to "Humanity's Child" (Aramaic, *bar nāšā'* = man, or Son of Man)? Because John has repeatedly put appropriate confessional material on the lips of unwitting Pilate, here again we may have a kind of double entendre. Although Pilate may be disparaging, in fact he announces Jesus' messianic status.[125] A citation from the prophet Zechariah may be relevant: "Take the silver and gold and *make a crown, and set it on the head* of the high priest Joshua son of Jehozadak; say to him: Thus says the Lord of hosts: *Here is a man* whose name is Branch: for he shall branch out in his place, and he shall build the temple of the Lord" (6:11-12; emphasis added). Perhaps Pilate, without knowing, has announced the appearance of "Humanity's Child," promised in chapter 12.

In response to Pilate's announcement, the chief priests and police

---

[124] For a survey of some options, see Brown, *Gospel,* 2:876; also, Schnackenburg, *Gospel,* 3:256-57.

[125] So argues W. A. Meeks, *The Prophet King: Moses Traditions and the Johannine Christology,* Supplements to *Novum Testamentum* 14 (Leiden: E. J. Brill, 1967), 70-71.

shout out, "Crucify! Crucify!" Perhaps exasperated, Pilate snaps back, "You take him and crucify," knowing full well that the Jewish leaders cannot do so. Then Pilate adds a third declaration of Jesus' innocence: "I don't find him guilty of any crime." An answer comes, "We have law, and according to the law, he should die — he passed himself off as God's Son." Apparently the priests are alluding to Leviticus 24:16: "One who blasphemes the name of the Lord shall be put to death." If Jesus claims to be God's Son, he claims divinity. And Pilate is more afraid than ever. Does John imagine that a superstitious Pilate fears God or that Pilate fears the mounting pressure compelling him to act? As for the accusation, John expects his readers to recall an earlier discussion in chapter 10:

> "The Father and I are one." The Jews took up stones again to stone him. Jesus replied, "I have shown you many good works from the Father. For which of these are you going to stone me?" The Jews answered, "It is not for a good work that we are going to stone you, but for blasphemy, because you, although only a human being, are making yourself God." Jesus answered, "Is it not written in your law, 'I said, you are gods'? If those to whom the word of God came were called 'gods' — and the scripture cannot be annulled — can you say that the one whom the Father has sanctified and sent into the world is blaspheming because I said, 'I am God's Son'?"

Surely the very dramatic passage is the stuff of preaching. We are called to look at the man Jesus, decked in thorns and wrapped in a mock royal robe. We are shown his abased humanity. But we are also asked to look with eyes of faith, knowing that he has come from God and, soon, will return to God, having completed God's saving work. At the same time, we must see entrenched religion — and these days all religion is entrenched — as well as poll-taking politics coming together to reject God's chosen envoy. Said Pilate: "Look — the man." A sermon must help us to look, look deeply, and see both our own involvements and God's astonishing patience — indeed, God's saving, patient love.

Episode 6

⁹Going back into the praetorium, he said to Jesus, "Where do you come from?" Jesus did not give him an answer. ¹⁰"Why don't you answer me?" Pilate said to him. "Don't you know that I have power to set you free or to crucify you?" ¹¹Jesus answered him, "You have no power over me, unless it's been given you from above. The one who handed me over to you has done the greater sin."

Once more Pilate turns back into the praetorium for a second, brief dialogue with Jesus. Instead of asking "What did you do?" Pilate asks the loaded question, "Where do you come from?" The question has been asked before (7:27-29; 8:14; 9:29-34). So we are meant to recall that Jesus comes from God. Of course, Pilate may be asking a jurisdictional question as he still tries to duck responsibility. But again, unknowingly, Pilate asks *the* question.

Then, even more exasperated by Jesus' silence, Pilate loses his "cool," "Why don't you answer me? Don't you know that I have power to set you free or to crucify you?" Jesus had kept silent; how could he tell Pilate where he was from? Now, Jesus speaks: "You have no power over me, unless it's been given you from above." Of course, to Pilate Jesus' words may sound like a recognition of his authority conferred by the divine Caesar, but Christian hearers of the Gospel know what Jesus is really saying. Here is Pilate boasting of power, when, actually, he faces Christ, who represents the power and authority of God. Suddenly we are meant to sense God's purpose working through the terrible events of the passion, permitting and yet ordaining human decisions. Once more there is a contrast between supposed earthly political power and the overarching power of the God of love, which to human beings may seem to be impotency.

Jesus' final one-liner is peculiar; it seems to exonerate Pilate. Yet the verb "handed over" (*paradous*), which can also be translated "betrayed," has occurred throughout the passion narrative: Judas hands Jesus over, and Annas hands Jesus over, and Caiaphas hands Jesus over. There is a chain of betrayal running through the story. So who exactly is Jesus speaking of here? Is he referring to Judas, or Caiaphas, or more generally to "the Jews"? Perhaps—as a bolder if somewhat singular guess—he is referring to satanic power, the power of humanity in the grips of evil rebellion. Such a surmise would fit Johannine theology.

The second dialogue within the praetorium parallels the first dialogue; both discuss the question of power. But here, in the second dialogue, Christ discloses the true source of power, namely the God of love.

Episode 7

¹²After that, Pilate tried to let him go, but the Jews shouted, "If you let this man go, you're no Friend of Caesar. Anyone who claims he's a king speaks against Caesar." ¹³Hearing what they said, Pilate brought Jesus out and sat him on a judge's seat in the place called Stone Pavement, in Hebrew, Gabbatha. ¹⁴Now it was about noon on the Preparation for the Passover, and he said to the Jews, "Look—your king!" ¹⁵So they shouted, "Take him away! Take and crucify him!" "Shall I crucify your

king?" Pilate said to them. The chief priests replied, "We have no king but Caesar." [16]So he handed him over to them to be crucified.

The climactic episode of the trial is filled with knotty questions and appalling ironies. Here is Pilate, who wants to release Jesus, dodging decision until it is too late. "If you let this man go, you're no Friend of Caesar," shout the Jews. Is the term "Friend of Caesar" an official title for an imperial representative such as Pilate? Probably.[126] So the crowd appeals to the source of Pilate's authority, Caesar. If he should let Jesus off, then he has betrayed his responsibility to Caesar. For if Jesus has claimed kingship, he is clearly anti-Caesar.

In response to the accusation, Pilate brings Jesus out and either sits him on a judge's bench or seats himself on the bench with Jesus standing before him. The Greek text allows for either interpretation. Naturally, scholars are sharply divided.[127] The issue can be answered only by a guess at John's theological purpose. Is John picturing a final decisive judgment being made by Pilate, or is Pilate engaging in a final, brilliant act of ridicule? With considerable trepidation, I have opted for the latter position: Pilate has deliberately put Jesus on the judge's bench, judging the crowd of Jews. Thus he evades a decision until his hand is finally forced. The place is described as the "Stone Pavement" (*lithostrotos*), which John says is "Gabbatha" in Hebrew — the word is actually Aramaic and may mean "raised up place." Again there is much discussion over where such a place might have been, particularly with the discovery of an elaborate stone mosaic on the site of the fortress of Antonia.[128]

Suddenly John intrudes upon his story to mention the time and the day; it is "about noon on the Preparation for the Passover" — a time when traditionally the priests slaughtered the Passover lambs. Is John alluding to the slaughter of lambs or is he picking up some other more obscure reference?[129] Pilate says, "Look — your king!" Once more he is taunting his Jewish audience and yet telling theological truth. The two phrases, "Look — the man" and "Look — your king," express a christology. The crowd responds, "Take him away!" "Shall I crucify your

---

[126] Although see the discussion in Brown, *Gospel,* 2:579.

[127] See Brown, *Gospel,* 2:880–81. Most scholars opt for historical accuracy and so picture Pilate seated on the *bema*. The apocryphal Gospel of Peter, 7, has, "And they clothed him with purple, and set him on the seat of judgment, saying, 'Judge righteously, king of Israel.'" Justin in *1 Apology,* 35, also knows of a similar tradition.

[128] Brown, *Gospel,* 2:881–82.

[129] Schnackenburg, *Gospel,* 3:264–65.

king?" Pilate answers. Finally, in an act of appalling apostasy, the chief
priests reply, "We have no king but Caesar." So, although they have
accused Jesus of blasphemy, they end up speaking a terrible blasphemy
themselves, for they have denied the kingship of God. Soon the great
hymn for Passover, the Greater Hallel, would be sung: "From everlasting to everlasting thou art God; beside thee we have no king,
redeemer, or savior, no liberator, deliverer, provider. None who takes
pity in every time of distress or trouble. *We have no king but thee.*"[130] The
trial is done. And John ends his account with a brief conclusion: "So
he handed him over [*paredōken*] to them to be crucified." Pilate, out of
indecision and fear, is now linked in the chain of betrayal.

A word about constant reference to "the Jews": Preachers must guard
against an implicit anti-Semitism. Although John does lay blame on the
Jews and, to some extent, exonerates Pilate,[131] we must be cautious.
Clearly, John's repeated use of "handed over" implicates all of us, all
sinful humanity satanically opposed to God's will. So, in preaching the
passages in the trial story, we must set events into the wide context of
humanity's sin, lest inadvertently we fan flames of hostile anti-Semitism.

The Crucifixion (John 19:16b-30)

John tells the story of the crucifixion with unusual restraint.[132] The
account unfolds in four brief episodes—the account of the title over the
cross, the division of clothing, the mention of Jesus' mother, and,
finally, Jesus' last words.

16bSo they took Jesus away. 17Carrying his own cross, he went out to the place
called Skull, which in Hebrew is Golgotha. 18There they crucified him, and with him
two others, one on either side, with Jesus in the middle. 19Pilate had a sign written
and put on the cross, and it read: JESUS THE NAZOREAN, THE KING OF THE
JEWS. 20Many Jews read the sign, which was written in Hebrew, Latin, and Greek,
because the place where he was crucified was near the city. 21The chief priests of
the Jews said to Pilate, "Don't write 'king of the Jews,' but 'This man said, I am king
of the Jews.'" 22Pilate replied, "What I've written, I've written."
23Then, when they crucified Jesus, soldiers took his clothes and divvied them up
into four parts, giving each soldier a share, except for the robe. The robe was woven
without a seam from top to bottom. 24So they said to one another, "Let's not tear it,

---

130 The text as cited by Duke, *Irony*, 135; emphasis added.
131 For a study of John's problems with "the Jews," see the essays in J. L. Martyn,
History and Theology in the Fourth Gospel, 2d ed. (Nashville: Abingdon, 1968).
132 Sources: Barrett, *Gospel*, 455-60; Brown, *Gospel*, 2:897-931; Dodd, *Historical
Tradition*, 121-35; Lindars, *Gospel*, 573-83; Minear, *John: The Martyr's Gospel* (New
York: The Pilgrim Press, 1985), 143-52; Schnackenburg, *Gospel*, 3:265-85.

but let's draw lots to decide whose it will be." Thus the scripture was fulfilled: "They tore my clothes and drew lots for my robe." So that is what the soldiers did.

²⁵Near the cross of Jesus was his mother; his mother's sister; Mary, the wife of Clopas; and Mary Magdalene. ²⁶Seeing his mother standing by the disciple whom he loved, Jesus said to his mother, "Woman, see your son." ²⁷Then he said to the disciple, "See, your mother." And from that hour, the disciple took her into his own home.

²⁸Afterwards, Jesus, knowing that everything was completed, to fully carry out the scriptures, said, "I'm thirsty." ²⁹There was a jar full of vinegar. So they put a sponge full of vinegar on hyssop and held it up to his mouth. ³⁰After he took the vinegar, Jesus said, "It is finished." Then he bowed his head and handed over his Spirit.

The crucifixion in John is told with surprising brevity. Much is left out that is found in the Synoptic Gospels: There is no Simon of Cyrene, no taunting, no darkness, no terrible cry of abandonment. But there are additions and elaborations: The story of the sign Pilate puts on the cross, mention of Christ's seamless robe, and, of course, the episode involving Jesus' mother. Throughout the narrative Christ seems to act deliberately, like an actor interpreting a role. He does the will of God.

The entire story is woven from fulfillments of scripture — particularly of the "passion Psalms," 22 and 69. So mention of others crucified with him fulfills Isaiah 53:12; the division of clothing, Psalm 22:18; the offer of vinegar, Psalm 69:21; the words "I am thirsty," Psalms 22:15, 69:3, 21; and the women watching, Psalm 38:11. Then, in v. 28, John changes his usual word for "fulfill" (*plēroun*); the text has "to fully carry out [*teleioun*] the scriptures" — implying that now all the necessary prophecies have been realized.

Jesus took up "his own cross." The phrasing recalls the Synoptic call for disciples to "take up their own cross and come after me." Historically, criminals carried only the crossbeam, the *patibulum,* because vertical stakes were already in place. Jesus climbs to the "Skull-Place" (in Aramaic, Golgotha), so named no doubt because of its shape.[133] Pilate has had a sign put on the cross: "JESUS THE NAZOREAN, THE KING OF THE JEWS." Such signs were thought to be a deterrent to future crime. Once more, what Pilate has done as a jibe is, in fact, theologically true. Of course the sign is offensive to Jewish leaders, who insist that it be rewritten: "This man said, I am king of the Jews." But Pilate with magnificent disdain announces, "What I've written, I've written." Does mention of the languages — "Hebrew, Latin, and Greek" — prefigure the universal outreach of the gospel? Probably.

Four soldiers usually carried out crucifixion. And, as was customary,

---

[133] Barrett, *Gospel,* 456.

they split up a condemned man's clothing. Psalm 22:18 reads: "They divide my clothes among themselves, / and for my clothing they cast lots." John has turned the parallelism of the Psalm verse into two different actions, dividing up and drawing lots. Scholars have puzzled over the mention of a seamless robe. Does it symbolize the unity Christ brings, much in the same way as does the net that does not tear in chapter 21? Again, perhaps.

The brief episode involving Jesus' mother has led to all kinds of sermonic mawkishness on the subject of "mother love." The passage has also led to scholarly debates, frequently between Protestants and Catholics.[134] Mary does play a significant role in the Gospel of John; along with the "loved disciple," she welcomes Jesus' ministry, demonstrating both faithfulness and insight. Rudolf Bultmann has argued that Mary represents a Jewish Christianity that overcame the scandal of the cross, whereas the loved disciple stands for Gentile Christianity.[135] But his position has won few adherents. Other scholars have suggested that Mary is a new Eve, a mother for Christian generations. Still others have supposed that the repetition ("Woman, see your son. . . . See, your mother") is a biblical adoption formula.[136] What we can say with some assurance is that vv. 26-27 point toward a new-order community in which we are intimately related to one another as children of God, a bond in the Spirit that transcends traditional familial loyalties: "From that hour, the disciple took her into his own home" (i.e., kinship). Therefore, oddly enough, the text may point clear beyond our sentimental notions of "mother love."

The last episode underscores finality; see the verbs "completed," "fully carry out," "finished." The vinegar in the jar was a not unpleasant, sour wine and, therefore, should not be read as a torment. Scholars have worried over the reference to hyssop, noting that the branches of a hyssop bush could not support a sponge. Has there been a scribal error, writing *hyssōpō* (hyssop) for *hyssō* (spear)? Or is the mention of hyssop symbolic? (Hyssop, instead of blood, was used to mark doorways in Passover ritual.) Or should the text read "and hyssop," referring to a common flavoring of wine with hyssop? Answer: Who knows? What is important in the episode is its final verse: "Jesus

---

[134] For discussion, see Brown, *Gospel,* 2:922-27; Schnackenburg, *Gospel,* 3:274-82; and also R. E. Brown et al., eds., *Mary in the New Testament* (Philadelphia: Fortress Press, 1978), 179-218.

[135] Bultmann, *Gospel,* 673.

[136] Barrett, *Gospel,* 459.

said, 'It is finished.' Then he bowed his head and handed over [*paredōken*] his Spirit." "Finished" surely means that Jesus' work of salvation is complete and he may now return to the Father from whom he has come. The use of "handed over" is peculiar. All through the passion narrative, Jesus is "handed over"; now he hands over his Spirit to God, a Spirit that will be given to his disciples. Are we suddenly to see all the "handing over" as part of God's purpose?

In the Christian preaching tradition, the four episodes of the crucifixion scene are frequently shaped into separate sermons, a practice that is probably wise. Of course, the themes that run through all episodes can be remarked: (1) The work of Christ is a fulfillment of scripture and, thus, of God's eternal purpose; (2) the work of Christ will result in a universal gospel (v. 20), a united church (v. 23b), new communal relationships (vv. 26-27), as well as life in the Spirit of Christ (v. 30); (3) the work of Christ is the saving work of the Father's love. Now, it is complete!

The Pierced Side (John 19:31-37)

Some scholars suppose that the story of the pierced side, which employs some non-Johannine vocabulary, comes from some extra source that John incorporates, and to which v. 35 was added by a final editor. The story is full of puzzles.[137]

> [31]Since it was the Preparation, and bodies should not remain on the cross during the Sabbath, because the Sabbath was a special day, the Jews asked Pilate to have the legs broken and the bodies removed. [32]So the soldiers came and broke the legs of first one and then the other of those crucified with him. [33]When they came to Jesus, they saw he was already dead, so they did not break his legs; [34]but one of the soldiers stabbed him in the side with his spear. Suddenly out came blood and water. [35]The one who saw all this is a witness to the truth, and he knows what he says is true, so you may believe. [36]Everything happened so the scriptures would be fulfilled: "Not a bone of his shall be broken." [37]Again, another scripture says: "They shall gaze on him whom they have pierced."

According to Deuteronomy 21:22-23, bodies of those executed for capital crimes must be buried on the same day. There was a double urgency because of the approaching Sabbath and the Passover (which is not mentioned). So the Jews ask Pilate to finish off Jesus quickly; leg-breaking with an iron club did speed death. The soldiers, presumably

---

[137] Sources: Brown, *Gospel,* 2:932-38, 944-56; Bultmann, *Gospel,* 675-79; Lindars, *Gospel,* 583-91; Schnackenburg, *Gospel,* 3:285-94.

those who had mocked him and, later, diced for his clothes, show up to carry out the procedure. They break the legs of first one criminal and then the other, but when they get to Jesus they find he is already dead. So one of the soldiers stabs Jesus in the side with a spear, perhaps to strike his heart, assuring death. Suddenly there is a flow of blood and water.

We could dismiss the reference to blood and water as a primitive medical description (referring to blood and body fluids), except that v. 35, which immediately follows, calls attention to the unusual significance of the flow. Not surprisingly scholars have debated the symbolic meaning of blood and water, some arguing for an allusion to the sacraments, eucharist and baptism, others finding clues within the Gospel to a more general theological meaning, still others searching for texts in the Hebrew scriptures.[138] Given some tendency in the Gospel toward reserve with regard to sacramental practice, an allusion to baptism and the Lord's Supper seems unlikely. There could be an allusion to Moses in Exodus 4:9, which reads: "If they will not believe even these two signs or heed you, you shall take some water from the Nile and pour it on the dry ground; and the water that you shall take from the Nile will become blood on the dry ground." But, again, the story of Moses does not quite fit the context in John. The significance of the flow of blood and water may draw on previous texts in John itself, as for example 7:37b-38: "Let anyone who is thirsty come to me, and let the one who believes in me drink. As the scripture has said, 'Out of the believer's heart shall flow rivers of living water.'"[139] Certainly John has used symbols of blood (chap. 6) and water (chap. 4) previously. If we draw on previous symbolic references to blood and water, we can suppose that John regards the self-giving death of Christ (blood) as conferring new life (water). Such an interpretation is supported by 1 John 5:6-8 (1 John being a letter that also comes from the Johannine "school"): "This is the one who came by water and blood, Jesus Christ, not with the water only but with the water and the blood. And the Spirit is the one that testifies, for the Spirit is truth. There are three that testify: the Spirit and the water and the blood, and these three agree." In John 19:35, the editor intrudes on the story to say that the episode is true and is told so that hearers may believe. Similar intrusions occur in 20:30-31 and 21:24-25.

---

[138] For a summary of some positions, see Brown, *Gospel,* 2:944–52.

[139] It is difficult to know what scripture is cited; see Lindars, *Gospel,* 299–300.

Finally, the passage concludes linking the story to the fulfillment of scripture. Two texts are cited, neither with accuracy. The first, "Not a bone of his shall be broken," could be an allusion to Exodus 12:46 (also Num. 9:12) in which we are advised regarding the Passover lamb—"you shall not break any of its bones." Or, the verse could refer to Psalm 34:20: "[God] keeps all their bones; not one of them will be broken." Although the Psalm text is probable, an allusion to the Passover lamb would not be inappropriate. The second citation is less uncertain; Zechariah 12:10 reads: "And I will pour out a spirit of compassion and supplication on the house of David and the inhabitants of Jerusalem, so that, when they look on the one whom they have pierced, they shall mourn for him, as one mourns for an only child, and weep bitterly over him, as one weeps over a firstborn."

The only way the passage can be preached is to go for a theological structure of meaning. Here is the world trying to make sure that Christ, in the words of the poet Ferlinghetti, "just hang there on His Tree . . . real dead."[140] But although the world has murdered Christ, from his wounds new life has flowed into our common lives, like living water. Christ is our Paschal Lamb. Now we gaze at the cross with both remorse—we are sinners—and wondering gratitude: "Love so amazing, so divine, demands . . . our all."

The Burial (John 19:38-42)

The Synoptics tell of Jesus' burial, and John follows the tradition.[141] He does, however, introduce the figure of Nicodemus into the story.

> 38Now, afterwards, Joseph of Arimathea, who, afraid of the Jews, was a secret disciple of Jesus, asked Pilate if he could take Jesus' body. Pilate permitted it. So he came and took his body. 39Nicodemus, the one who had first visited him at night, also came along bringing a mixture of myrrh and aloe, around one hundred pounds. 40They took the body of Jesus and wrapped it in linen with the spices as is customary with burial among the Jews. 41Now there was a garden where he was crucified, and a new tomb within the garden where no one had as yet been buried. 42Because it was the Jewish Preparation, and the tomb was near, they put Jesus there.

John tells of two people tending to the burial of Jesus, Joseph of Arimathea and Nicodemus. John does not mention that Joseph is a

---

[140] Lawrence Ferlinghetti, *A Coney Island of the Mind* (New York: New Directions, 1958), 16.

[141] Sources: Brown, *Gospel,* 2:938-44, 956-60; Bultmann, *Gospel,* 679-80; Lindars, *Gospel,* 591-94; Schnackenburg, *Gospel,* 3:295-99.

member of the Sanhedrin, as does Mark, but the tradition may have influenced the addition of Nicodemus to the story. Both men, then, are covert disciples. Previously, John has had a dim view of such persons: "Nevertheless many, even of the authorities, believed in him. But because of the Pharisees they did not confess it, for fear that they would be put out of the synagogue; for they loved human glory more than the glory that comes from God" (John 12:42-43). But here, John apparently regards Joseph's asking for Jesus' body as a risky public avowal. Nicodemus, "the one who had first visited him at night" (see John 3:1-12), has evidently also come out of the Sanhedrin closet.

Now John details the embalming and burying of Jesus. That there are differences in the time schedule and the embalming between John and the Synoptics has occasioned no little discussion.[142] But John has his own reasons for his story. One detail is quite astonishing, namely the amount of myrrh and aloe that Nicodemus brought along—one hundred pounds (*litras*) of spices, more than could possibly be needed in a normal burial. Evidently, the spices are to be scattered within layers of linen wrapping. Raymond Brown suggests that the large amount of spices matches royal burials and, therefore, John is providing kingly symbolism.[143] Perhaps the proleptic anointing at Bethany—"She has kept the perfume for the day of my burial" (12:7)—is now fulfilled in royal excess. King Asa's burial is described in 2 Chronicles 16:14: "They buried him in the tomb that he had hewn out for himself in the city of David. They laid him on a bier that had been filled with various kinds of spices prepared by the perfumer's art." Some other scholars, Paul Duke and Wayne Meeks among them, believe that the huge amount of spices displays a failure to understand that Jesus is being "lifted up."[144] The two closet disciples have come only part way into faith, not unlike Mary Magdalene in the subsequent twentieth chapter.

Maybe the story of the burial shows us two halfway disciples who, presumably, will find faith and come out of the darkness with the light of Easter Day.

John alone describes the burial place as a garden. Christ is laid out in a new tomb. John does not mention the stone rolled into the doorway of the tomb. His final verse, which begins "Because it was the Jewish day of Preparation," leaves us waiting for a new dawn.

---

[142] For a review of problems, see Brown, *Gospel,* 2:957–58.

[143] Ibid., 960.

[144] See Duke, *Irony,* 110; he cites W. A. Meeks, "The Man from Heaven in Johannine Sectarianism," *Journal of Biblical Literature* 41 (1972): 55.

The Promise
of Salvation

IN ONE OF Robert Penn Warren's novels, a Greek by the name of Nick Papadoupalous attends an outdoor revival meeting. He listens to the singing—"Rock of Ages, cleft for me"—and he hears Brother Sumpter preaching a hot gospel message. Nick is startled when he sees a peg-legged drunk bawling over his sins: "O God, the things I done." And he is even more shocked when staid Old Man Duckett cries out, "I feel the breath of Jesus," and then faints in the grass. "God, in Thy mercy, this man is saved," Brother Sumpter announces. "Saved," thought Nick Papadoupalous, "saved from what?"[1]

For centuries, Christian preaching has announced salvation.[2] Because of the death and resurrection of Jesus Christ, we are being "saved." But what on earth does "salvation" mean and how can the passion of Christ—something that happened around 28 C.E.—have much to do with our twentieth-century lives? Like Nick Papadoupalous, let us ask questions: Saved from what? How?

Unoriginal Sin

Let us begin where we are: We live in a sin*ful* world. In our world God is an absence and mutuality is an inescapable discomfort. Most of

---

[1] R. P. Warren, *The Cave* (New York: Random House, 1959), 266–73.

[2] This chapter was written before the publication of E. Farley's theological anthropology, *Good and Evil: Interpreting a Human Condition* (Minneapolis: Fortress Press, 1990), which is surely the most perceptive work on sin and salvation to be published in recent years.

211

us bumble through our lives without much thought of God. God exists at the fringes of contemporary life as a memory from childhood or as ritual left over from the religious past, ritual that is still mumbled at significant occasions such as births, deaths, or marriages.[3] God is a social anachronism — along with other old-fashioned notions like "conscience" and "destiny." As for neighborliness, true neighborliness is rare. We live with one another like friendly aliens, not understanding but trying to imitate others around us. Meanwhile the social systems and the transsocial attitudes we revere hold us captive. Our paychecks flow from a military-industrial complex founded on death. Our "free" enterprise has produced homeless families who wander our streets. Social institutions — our corporations, schools, churches, governments, judiciary, and so on — seem to be chronically sinstruck. Although newborn babies may appear to possess a degree of innocence, because they are "centered" selves driven by desire, they are vulnerable to the "social disease" of sin.[4] Guided by all those nifty courses in "Parenting," we teach our children to adapt and fit into the world. Unfortunately, the world is sin*ful*.

We have begun with the world so as to underscore the complex nature of salvation. If God is to redeem us, not only must persons be liberated from internal, psychological coercions,[5] but the social order itself must somehow be transformed. Perhaps prejudice can be eased by a change of heart, but racism is built into our society — racism is tacitly accepted in politics, education, commerce, and religion. In our world not only are children contaminated early by prejudice, but the born-again are regularly reinfected, for we are all trapped in social structures of sin. No wonder that when Paul speaks of the redemptive work of Christ, he looks for the taming of transsocial "powers that be": "Then comes the end, when [Christ] hands over the kingdom to God the Father, after he has destroyed every ruler and every authority and

---

[3] The genius of Woody Allen's film *Crimes and Misdemeanors* is that it depicts the residual presence of God in an absent-minded world. God is the memory of a conversation overheard during a Seder, a memory triggered by the return visit to a childhood home. Or God is an anxious sense of anachronistic guilt to be eased by social adaptation. Or God is the recitation of an ancient Hebrew text in a marriage service. Otherwise, the film is filled with a terrifying sense of divine absence.

[4] For a penetrating study of sin as disease and salvation as healing, see D. Gowan, "Salvation as Healing," *Ex Auditu* 5 (1989): 1–19.

[5] See E. Farley, "Psychopathology and Human Evil: Toward a Theory of Differentiation," in *Crosscurrents in Phenomenology,* ed. R. Bruzina and B. Wilshire (The Hague: Nijhoff, 1978).

power. For he must reign until he has put all his enemies under his feet. The last enemy to be destroyed is death. For 'God has put all things in subjection under his feet'" (1 Cor. 15:24-27). Salvation is not a one-by-one miracle in which converted Jesus people are somehow bracketed off from the world and guaranteed fancy motel reservations in heaven. No. Salvation is emphatically social. The contaminating power of the past will be nullified, and God's new order will arrive. Of course, salvation is connected with a notion of resurrection; the Bible looks for a "new heaven and a new earth" and a new redeemed humanity.

Most images of salvation in scripture are social. In the Bible, *Zion* is a large word indeed.[6] Yes, someday human nature will be redeemed: People will have new, law-engraved hearts; they will "know the Lord" and live as forgiven children in free and easy covenantal obedience (Jer. 31:31-34). But the social order will also be revamped: Nations will study peace, and nature will be miraculously fruitful. The lion and the lamb will nuzzle; children and serpents will play together; weapons will be beaten into farm machinery; poor people will see free justice; and all humanity will gleefully feast on the mountain of the Lord (Isa. 2:1-4; 11:4, 6-9; 25:6). In Christian scriptures, images of salvation are equally broad. Do not the Beatitudes speak of the poor and of peace-makers and of those who thirst for social righteousness? As for the final vision that fills the back pages of the Book of Revelation, it is the *city* of God, a new society filled with light and life and the Lamb enthroned. Salvation must be world-sized or not at all.

We begin by acknowledging our sin*ful* universe.

Salvation — A Chameleon Doctrine

Salvation is not a fixed, biblical doctrine. *Salvation* is a word that changes meaning in every age. In every age we diagnose the human predicament quite differently; configurations of evil have a different shape and therefore dreams of redemption are equally different. Yes, there do seem to be perennial problems: We grow old and die and we would rather not; we are spooked by fears of nonbeing from birth; we struggle to balance license and law in responsible freedom; we seek to serve neighbors, but are constrained by self-interest. There are perennial unmet social goals as well — fairness, peace, freedom, and "the pursuit of happiness." All such matters are not only viewed

---

[6] See D. Gowan, *Eschatology in the Old Testament* (Philadelphia: Fortress Press, 1986).

differently in different eras, but are also weighed quite differently. Has any earlier age had to reckon with nuclear warheads or stealth bombers? Has any other culture had to calculate the power and/or irresponsibility of multinational corporations? Did our primitive ancestors worry over the greenhouse effect or how to dispose of their radioactive waste? Our images of reconciled humanity are very different from those dreamed in the first century, or in medieval Europe, or even beside Walden Pond. Salvation is an everchanging doctrine.[7]

Now we must be cautious: Images of salvation are not utopian. They are not the products of so-called futurists. While utopian dreams may well depict a perfect future, such thinking is generated by the prides of present achievement, as, for example, computer science or space technology. Utopian thinking is "Future Shock" stuff.[8] Although sometimes it may feature apocalyptic fantasies of good and evil, ultimately it lacks a sophisticated awareness of sin. Utopian thinking is heady with human accomplishment. Back in 1939, the New York World's Fair featured a walk-through world of tomorrow. You sauntered a quaint, Victorian, gas-lit street; passed through a time tunnel; and emerged in a twenty-first-century dream city, with glass skyscrapers and bubblelike cars. During the first week after the exhibit opened, someone was mugged in the city of the future. There is a kind of excited, overconfident naiveté about utopian fantasies. Built on incautious pride, utopian thinking can too easily tumble into the Orwellian nightmare. Instead, true images of salvation are formed from our awareness of sin and from a grasp of God's purposes for humanity, purposes that have been revealed by religious tradition. Although an understanding of God's purpose (e.g., the Great Commandment) will give notions of salvation a certain constancy of vision, our experience of bondage alters from age to age. Salvation is a chameleon doctrine.

Of course we do not merely reverse patterns of sin in order to sketch salvation. No, there are experiences of wholeness, of social and personal well-being, in the midst of our brokenness. Such experiences are "on file" in memory; they are like secret, solemn promises of something more. Although we should shy away from trying to base a doctrine of salvation on primal experiences of pleasure and pain, or infant recollections of separation and unity, we must admit that there is more to life

---

[7] See P. S. Fiddes, *Past Event and Present Salvation* (Louisville: Westminster/John Knox Press, 1989), 3–13.

[8] A. Toffler, *Future Shock* (New York: Bantam Books, 1970).

than is conveyed by the three-letter word *sin*.[9] In the midst of life, are there not brief moments of something like harmony? The cheerful, if somewhat untidy, experience of sexual oneness; the happiness of working together on some common task; the tenderness of shared frailty in the presence of the dying; the arm-swinging enjoyment of a bright spring day; the still oneness some folk find in the penumbral hush of a forest glade — all such experiences seem to pledge a wider "shalom." Their common character is a kind of unselfconscious, childlike at-one-ment with ourselves, our neighbors, the good earth, and, perhaps, sometimes with God. Experiences of wholeness are also different in different ages. But, like Dante's Beatrician smile, they beckon us toward a more profound reconciliation than we know.[10]

Previously we mentioned biblical metaphors for atonement — Christ as sacrifice, Christ as ransom, Christ as conqueror.[11] These metaphors try to make sense out of Christ's death on the cross. Obviously, they also relate to first-century experiences of sin and salvation. But, as we have suggested, biblical metaphors are dated: slavery has been abolished; animal sacrifice is no longer normal in our religious rituals; and military imagery may not be appropriate to the helpless agony of Christ's dying. Because every age experiences sin and salvation differently, new metaphors must be generated. We can trace such images through Christian history: salvation as the restoration of a primal "image of God" (Greek); as satisfaction for an insult to feudal honor (Anselm); as a transforming demonstration of love (Abelard); as undeserved judicial release (Reformers); as psychological wholeness via transference (modern); and so on. While such metaphors are helpful and do connect the cross to actual experiences, they cannot be turned into theological explanation without becoming contradictory — for example, Does God offer God as a sacrifice to satisfy God? Such hand-me-down images are still preached, but they may not be terribly compelling in our very different modern world. What preachers can do is to unpack traditional metaphors to see what kinds of experiences they once conveyed and, thus informed, seek contemporary images to conjoin the *now* of our lives to the *then* of the cross.

---

[9] For a discussion of salvation that is grounded in the pleasure/pain dichotomy, see E. Schillebeeckx, *Christ: The Experience of Jesus as Lord* (New York: Seabury Press, 1980), pt. 4.

[10] See C. Williams, *The Figure of Beatrice* (London: Faber and Faber, 1943), 31–35.

[11] For discussion, see R. H. Culpepper, *Interpreting the Atonement* (Grand Rapids, Mich.: William B. Eerdmans, 1966).

A Three-Letter Word

Let us turn to the three-letter word found on perfume bottles and in homiletic discourse, the word *sin*. There are as many metaphors for sin as for salvation. Sin is described as a sickness; as dumb-sheep waywardness; as estrangement; as "missing the mark"; as contamination; as lawbreaking; as rebellion; as alienation; as idolatry; and so on. No doubt all such metaphors are apt. But is there any way that we can get at the basic character of sin? Yes. If what God intends for humanity is well summarized in the Great Commandment—to love God with heart, mind, and soul, and to love neighbors as our own (selves?)[12]—then presumably sin is the opposite. Whatever sin may be and however sin arose, its essential character must be opposition to God's good purposes for humanity, namely, love. Although we quote the Great Commandment from the Bible—patching together the Shema from Deuteronomy 6:4 with a verse from Leviticus 19:18—the command is as old as creation. God created all things in love for love. Therefore, if we refuse the commandment to love God and neighbors, we violate creation and defy the eternal purposes of God.

How on earth did sin happen? We can explore the myth of Eden or read of tumbledown angels, but the "how" of sin is an inexplicable mystery. Three key words may help us to understand: *creature, freedom,* and *desire.*

The word *creature* points to a certain on-our-ownness that characterizes human life. We are created in relationship to God, and yet we are somehow separate. The famous doctrine of creation *ex nihilo* implies that we are not extensions of God—creation is not "God's body"—but rather have some degree of independent, not-God existence. God is not oppressively present to us or within us; we are not sparks struck from divinity. We are human beings with a kind of independent dignity that, although conferred by God-love, is emphatically ours. Moreover, as creatures we are strangely centered selves; in consciousness, we see the world as all around us. Thus it may be constitutionally difficult for us to realize the centrality of God or the separate but equally centered concerns of our neighbors. Of course, as creatures, we are decidedly

<hr/>

[12] D. N. Freedman has argued against translating the Great Commandment as "You shall love your neighbor as your self." Rather, Freedman suggests that a proper reading of the phrase from Leviticus 19 could be, "You shall love your neighbor as your own [kin]." See Freedman's article, "The Hebrew Old Testament and the Ministry Today: An Exegetical Study of Leviticus 19:18b," *Perspective* (Pittsburgh Theological Seminary), 5, no. 1 (March 1964): 9–14.

limited. We are emphatically not God. Therefore we cannot know God as God knows us. Knowledge of God comes to us as a passed-along rumor, a strangely indistinct and indirect option. So our creatureliness, with its wonderful *ex nihilo* independence, may actually inhibit the love of God and neighbors.

The word *freedom* is much bandied about in America. But how free are we human beings? We all seem to possess an inner sense of personal freedom, but in actual fact we are very limited. We do not choose our birth — where, when, or with whom. We cannot choose our death — the mortality rate still runs around 100 percent. And, obviously, we are not free to leap out of time and space whenever we wish. All of us are victims and/or beneficiaries of selective opportunity — the places we have lived, the color of our skin, our sexual orientation, the language we have learned, the schools we have attended, the cash our parents did or did not have, and so on. So in many ways we are *un*free, hedged by all kinds of limiting factors. Yet, with respect to relationship we must have some degree of freedom. God has created us for love: Can love be love without freedom? Although we are structurally with others and before God, evidently we can refuse love. Our freedom, real freedom, is in and for relationship.

Finally, there is the word *desire*. Did not William Blake picture humanity as a little person standing beside a ladder that stretched into the sky, looking up, and saying, "I want, I want"?[13] Our lives are motivated by wants. Newborn babies are entirely focused by their hungers, although later they may learn to enjoy the coos and kisses of relationship as well. Our young years may be determined by a so-called pleasure principle. We hunger and thirst, have sexual promptings, require rest, crave companionship, enjoy play, and so on. Such creaturely desires are splendidly human and, in fact, keep us alive. But there are other, less splendid wants. Driven by a shadowy fear of non-being, we struggle to realize and secure ourselves. Such desire is understandable. In consciousness, we continually transcend ourselves — in daydreams we traverse time, leap space, and enjoy a kind of immortality. Unfortunately, we are fairly fragile, embodied creatures who are emphatically mortal, with brief time and limited space. So in all of us there is a desire to live beyond the limits of our finitude. Such desire is not bad; it has improved health care and prompted most technological advances. But, at the same time, the desire to secure ourselves

---

[13] R. Garnett, *William Blake: Painter and Poet* (London: Seeley & Co., 1895), 28.

may have demonic consequences. If we wish to live beyond our finitude, we must reckon with God, who defines our finitude, and with neighbors, whose desires are as extensive as ours.

How did sin happen? Put three words together—creature, freedom, desire—and perhaps we can muddle a meaning. Somehow creaturely desire within free relatedness led humanity to reject God-love and the familial bond with neighbors. What is sin? Sin is a terrible reversal of the Great Commandment.

On Being a Full-time Liar

We have defined sin. Sin is the opposite of the Great Commandment and, thus, a refusal of love. But sin's modus operandi is falsity. In the astonishing myth of Eden, where the snake does not have all the lines, we read:

> Now the serpent was more crafty than any other wild animal that the Lord God had made. He said to the woman, "Did God say, 'You shall not eat from any tree in the garden'?" The woman said to the serpent, "We may eat of the fruit of the trees in the garden; but God said, 'You shall not eat of the fruit of the tree that is in the middle of the garden, nor shall you touch it, or you shall die.'" But the serpent said to the woman, "You will not die; for God knows that when you eat of it your eyes will be opened, and you will be like God, knowing good and evil." (Gen. 3:1-5)

Sin, according to the myth, begins with the serpent giving lie to the word of God. Sin is falsity.

As creatures, we are related to God and to one another within the lushness of a lovely world. The form of our relatedness is defined modestly by creaturely limitations. We may desire to know like God, but we cannot, and if we try to do so, our knowledge will become perverse and morally skewed. Likewise, we may desire to relate to neighbors as if we were God, with imagined divine control, but of course we cannot, and if we attempt to do so, human harmony will be disrupted. For how can we be like God when we are not God and, at the same time, live before God? And how can we relate to neighbors as if we were God when we are in fact two-legged human like everyone else? Our only solution is falsity. We must deny the presence of God, the familial character of neighbors, and even our own true related-to-God selves. We must embrace falsity full-time, which, of course, we do.

The Burden of Idolatry

We are created *ex nihilo* — related to God and yet with a kind of separate creaturely independence. Perhaps because we are centered selves, inevitably we seek to displace God. But if we cannot live apart from God, what can we do? We can (1) live as if God were not, or (2) manufacture a false god to displace the true God. Chronically, we do both.

Living as if God were not comes easy. After all, we are creatures and, therefore, cannot know God in any direct, unmediated way. God comes to us as a culturally transmitted "rumor," and rumors are chancy at best. Moreover, God's providential care is modest; God's energy in nature is as unassuming as silent sudden buds in springtime, and God's guidance in our affairs is hidden in the complex pattern of motive and memory, dreaming and impulse that constitutes the causal field of most human events. God is seldom featured on front pages. Thus, we can manage to anesthetize what Tillich termed our "ultimate concern," devote ourselves to short-term proximate matters, and get by without recourse to the ancient "God-hypothesis." We can puzzle the mysteries of the stock market, baseball statistics, or the internal combustion engine instead of brooding on the ways of God. Many of us, including many decent, sensitive, and generous people, do so. What is more, we will work hard with neighbors to preserve a whole world of proximate meanings. Anything as determined as the falsity of sin requires a society.

Idolatry, however, is a more systematic solution. False gods can obscure the presence of the true God, who interfaces with creation and with whom we are related inevitably as creatures. No wonder the Hebrew Bible lists a first commandment that forbids all forms of idolatry: "You shall have no other gods before me" (Exod. 20:3). Now, having a false god is not a matter of personal choice, as many preachers suppose. By definition, gods are social, and thus false gods have a correlate — namely, organized false religion. False gods are a corporate achievement, a social projection in which quite inadvertently we can participate. Individuals do not construct golden calves all by themselves. Real idolatries are culturally constructed and are related to particular social groupings. So if we wish to live in falsity, we will probably be drawn into a false religion that ritually bows before a false god. Many preachers rail against the idolatry of "things," but things (good gifts of God?) are seldom our false gods. The most successful false gods are those connected with the worthy aims and values esteemed by society — patriotism, family life, morality, hard work, technology, and so on. False religions, like any religion, will develop ritual, symbols, special days, initiations, feastings, rules, and moral codes. For example, we can think of flags, Fourth of July parades, school children reciting a Pledge of Allegiance, not to mention patriotic slogans, posters, personal testimony, and the like. Large corporations may foster a kind of religious loyalty with logos, slogans, competitive rewards, as well as requisite behavioral patterns.[14] When biblical writers fret over "principalities and powers," they may be spotting systems of socially organized false religion.

We should mention that idolatry invades all of life, even our Christianity. "You nitwit Galatians!" writes Paul, "Who cast a spell over you?" (Gal. 3:1). Paul has discovered that the Galatians, who had been set free in Christ, are reverting to an idolatrous religion of spiritual exercises, rituals, required "days of obligation," and the burdens of false religious law. Social forms of Christianity are always an admixture of faith and idolatry, whether they be Bible-fondling fundamentalism or open-to-the-world religious liberalism. Of course, these days, denominational hoopla is *always* a false religion, even when it is Christian or promoted with episcopal enthusiasm.

There are problems with maintaining a false God. Long ago Reinhold Niebuhr described how the true God, to whom we are truly related, will be experienced as a terrible threat to those who live in falsity and in false religious idolatry. Sin will know God not as love but as a kind of ontic anxiety — a chronic fear felt at the fringes of consciousness. Such anxiety, of course, can drive us to intensify our devotion to false gods. If we live in idolatry, God will be experienced as our enemy.

Our Enemy, the Neighbor

In sin, neighbors are a constant annoyance; they frustrate our desire to be "like God." "Hell," as one of Jean-Paul Sartre's characters complains, "is other people."[15] "Other people" are a problem: (1) they remind us of our own finite humanity; (2) they get in the way of our self-securing desires; and, on occasion, (3) they can threaten us with both love and true religion. If we wish to secure our own lives, others are a constant embarrassment, for not only do they keep getting in our way, but they are witnesses to our interdependence; life is designed for

---

[14] See A. Harrington, *Life in the Crystal Palace* (New York: Alfred A. Knopf, 1959), 188–209.

[15] J.-P. Sartre, *No Exit and Three Other Plays* (New York: Vintage Books, 1955), 47.

mutuality — we live by exchanges. How can we possess ourselves when they are around? So, as a result, we view others not as sisters and brothers in a common humanity, but as competitors. Obviously capitalism, based on a notion of free competition, is grounded in sin.

Socially, the problem of the "others" gives rise to corporate "we" and "they" thinking. We form alliances to further our own agendas and block the access of others. In effect, we secure our corporate selves by demoting "them." Within such social groupings we develop in-group language, behavioral styles, and commandments that are designed to approve and/or exclude others. Frequently we give our groups a kind a sacral status. Our cause is righteous, and we can demonstrate allegiance to a false god by opposing an unrighteous "them." In recent history, did not a somewhat senile American president speak of the USSR in apocalyptic terms as an "evil empire"? Since then, a similar rhetoric has been applied to Saddam Hussein in order to justify a rallying of American forces in Saudi Arabia. Modern societies ripped by contending pluralisms are surely a witness to sin.

Our refusal of neighbors takes many forms: "benign neglect," social thoughtlessness (i.e., "They all look the same to me"), social stereotypes (i.e., "welfare cheats"), racism, sexism, homophobic stereotypes, and so on. We tag others with racial or ethnic labels in order to deny our common humanity. And we design forms of social exclusion — clubs, guilds, castes, and so on — to obscure our familial relatedness. But beneath all such strategies is what we have previously described as a "killer instinct." The fact is, we do *not* love our neighbors.

We Have Met the Enemy, and They Are Us

In our falsity, we have an embarrassing problem — our true selves. If, as creatures, we are related to God and to our neighbors, what on earth are we to do with our true selves? In sin, we are trying to live within a false self-image. To do so, we will have to suppress, deny, or displace our true self-before-God. Thus, in all of us, there are bound to be structures of self-hatred and self-suppression, which have been charted by Freud and other perceptive analysts. Self-destruction, which can take many different forms, will characterize our lives. The problem is not within the self alone; it has social dimensions. Catering to human self-destruction can be big business. We can cite well-advertised health hazards, everything from environmental pollution to substance abuse. We behave quite murderously toward ourselves.

The social dimension of self-annihilation is more pervasive than we know. If we are truly related to God, then we are "justified" by God's love. To maintain our false selves we will have to find other forms of justification that, almost always, will involve social approval. If we are approved within some social group, then perhaps we can approve ourselves — that is, our false selves. Thus, we are driven to secure social approval at the same time as we attempt to smother our true self-before-God. In our world, social approval is earned by being some-body, having something, or getting somewhere. Is not the multibillion dollar advertising industry in America based on hawking social approval?

Sin is the ultimate source of self-hatred. To protect the falsity in which we live, we must deny or destroy our true self-before-God. Thus, sin is essentially suicidal — "The wages of sin is death" (Rom. 6:23).

Christ Our Substitute

Through Christian history there have been many notions of atone-ment. Some seem to be "objective" in the sense that God has done something in Jesus Christ so as to permanently alter the historic structures of human existence (e.g., "There was no other good enough / To pay the price of sin; / He only could unlock the gate / Of heaven, and let us in."[16] Other theories are said to be "subjective" in that they appear to stress the effect of Christ's self-sacrificing death on our sensi-bilities — "Love so amazing, so divine, / Demands my soul, my life, my all."[17] The sharp distinction between objective and subjective theories of atonement is less than helpful. Yes, we do have to explain how a par-ticular death back in the first century is related to human experiences of redemptive life that, in fact, still occur today. But contrasts between external event and internal emotional effect are quite unnecessary; both occur in human consciousness.

Obviously, the cross exposes patterns of human sinfulness. The pas-sion narrative in any of the Gospels is a terrifying story of betrayal, desertion, denial, conspiracy, religious defensiveness, sick patriotism, and downright blood lust. Gathered at the cross are human beings in

---

[16] "There Is a Green Hill Far Away," by C. F. Humphreys, was published in 1848. Humphreys was influenced by the High Church Oxford movement.

[17] The last two lines of the hymn "When I Survey the Wondrous Cross," by The Reverend I. Watts. The hymn was included in a collection of communion hymns, *Hymns and Spiritual Songs,* published in 1707.

their protective social alliances displaying huge rage toward one who may be viewed as true God, true neighbor, and true self-before-God. The reason the theme of falseness runs through the passion narratives is not because Christ was crucified by a clatch of thoroughgoing rogues as contrasted with "good people," but because the cross was erected by the falsity of sin. Thus, we are told of false witnesses, false accusations, false trials, and the like. We watch as truth is twisted or suppressed. For in the passion stories, human beings are protecting their false religion, false political idolatry, as well as socially promoted false self-images. To study the passion narratives in the Gospels is to explore the social nuances of sin.

We have argued that sin will attempt to destroy our true self-before-God. Obviously Jesus is represented in the Gospels as a true self-before-God, as one who prays "Abba" on a full-time basis. Is he not labeled Son of God? Because he is among us as a true self-before-God, he threatens the false images in which we live — in particular, the false-self-before-false-god we construct so carefully. Therefore, it is not surprising that we human beings would rise up and crucify him.

Likewise, Jesus Christ comes to us as our true neighbor. The creeds affirm that he is "truly human," God's child, and thus our true sister/brother. Please notice: Jesus refuses to relate to anyone on a "we/they" basis. He eats and drinks with "sinners," reaches out in compassion toward Gentiles, befriends racketeers such as Zacchaeus, heals outcasts, and affirms oneness with common sinful humanity. He urges us not only to love neighbors, which is difficult enough, but to love enemies as well. Again and again, he refuses power over others in favor of a servant's role. So he is of course a terrible embarrassment to a world driven by competitive disdain toward neighbors, a world given to labeling (e.g., "sinners," "Gentiles," etc.) in order to deny relatedness. Christ is crucified because he troubles a "we/they" society that is deliberately designed to dehumanize neighbors.

Finally, Jesus Christ comes as God-with-us. Obviously he himself lives toward God. But, more, he speaks for God quite deliberately, so that his words are God's address to us. Thus he represents the true God we have refused to love and in fact deny. We have said that the true God will be experienced as a threat to falsity and idolatrous false religion. Therefore, it is not surprising that Jesus is rejected by religious leaders, who brand him a blasphemer. We do not suggest that Jewish faith is false religion, or is any more false than Christian congregations in America today. No, all religious communities within our sinful world are admixtures of revelation and falsity; they are all given to self-preservation, triumphalism, exclusiveness, and the like. Any religion, including our own Christianity, can, like the cursed fig tree (Mark 11:12-14), be attractive yet fruitless. And any religion can seek to secure itself socially by condemning the truth. Jesus Christ, true God-with-us, was crucified not only by the sovereign political power of Rome but also by organized religion. The true God is always a threat to the falsity of political dominance and religious authority.

We are arguing that the cross exposes sin. In sin, we seek to deny true God, true neighbor, and our true self-before-God. In Jesus Christ, we do so. Thus, in a way, we can say that Christ has taken our place. Our sin should destroy us, our faith, and our human community. Instead, we crucify Jesus Christ who, strange to say, seems to bear the force of our self-destruction. On the cross, Christ becomes our substitute.

Living in the Mercy

Although Christ's once-and-for-all death and resurrection are locked up in past-tense history, the preaching of Christ continues. News of the resurrection comes to us regularly not only on Easter Day but throughout the year by way of liturgy, the pulpit, and religious education. Likewise, the dark mystery of the cross is held before us in Christian art and countless sermons. Thus we should not feel shortchanged by time—born too late for true salvation. Most early Christians were not eyewitnesses to the crucifixion or the glory of Easter Day. News of Christ came to them the same way that it comes to us—by word of mouth. No wonder that both Luther and Calvin called preaching the "word of God," for Christ comes to us through the human spoken words of preaching. Bluntly, although the tomb was sealed, the word of the gospel is alive and addresses us now.

What is more, Christ comes to us as forgiveness. The church has been commissioned to announce the mercy of God. Luke is explicit: "Repentance and forgiveness of sins is to be proclaimed in his name to all nations" (Luke 24:47). Likewise, in the Gospel of John, the risen Christ sends his disciples out into the world with absolution for sin: "'As the Father has sent me, so I send you.' When he had said this, he breathed on them and said to them, 'Receive the Holy Spirit. If you forgive the sins of any, they are forgiven them; if you retain the sins of any, they are retained'" (John 20:21-22). According to the Gospel of John, the preaching of forgiveness *is* forgiveness. A God of mercy

stands behind the words we speak; they are guaranteed. We all live on
the wrong side of the crucifixion; our sin has been exposed by the cross.
But the word of the risen Christ still comes to us as an absolution—we
are forgiven.

God's mercy is declared in the resurrection *and* death of Jesus Christ.
The resurrection enables us to read forgiveness back into the story of
the crucifixion. Without resurrection, Jesus' words, "Father, forgive
them," would never have been added to the Lukan story. If the risen
Christ returned to his chosen disciples, disciples who denied and
deserted him, can we not suppose a "for them" impulse to his dying?
So Christ's remarkable patience on the cross is not merely a stoic
bravery, but self-giving love. While we are crucifying Christ, he is willingly dying for us. Paul's famous words may be heightened: "While we
were being sinners, Christ died for us!" (Rom. 5:8). God's radical love
cannot be split into neat distinctions; God hates sin but loves sinners.
No. What we do *is* us. In the midst of our sinning—hoist the cross,
throw the spear—God's suffering mercy is toward us.

Moreover, in the cross and resurrection, we see the outright futility
of sin. In one way, sin is absolutely impotent. It is a falsity, and how
can falsity have any status in reality? But in another way, sin seems
fierce and fearfully destructive. Sin sets out to destroy neighbors, the
self-before-God, and even the true God. Yet in the resurrection, Christ
returns and, in so doing, testifies to God's indestructible love. The
destructive death-power of sin has no ultimate power beside the resili-
ency of God's sustaining faithful love. So although sin may be terrible,
God's covenantal faithfulness is greater. In the resurrection, the constancy of God is displayed. Resurrection "eucharists" are a remarkable
symbol.[18] The risen Christ and the disciples eat and drink together.
Previously, in the Gospel story, Jesus has been eating and drinking
with sinners, has provided loaves for a hungry crowd, and has broken
bread with the unreliable disciples before his death. Now, after human
sinfulness has done its worst, here is risen Christ still breaking bread
with those he loves—those who have in fact betrayed and denied him.
In eucharist, we sinners recall the passion and the cross and know that

[18] O. Cullmann has discussed the connection between resurrection and eucharistic
worship in his "The Meaning of the Lord's Supper in Primitive Christianity," in *Essays
on the Lord's Supper,* trans. J. G. Davies (Richmond, Va.: John Knox Press, 1958), 5–16.
We seem to have resurrection eucharists in Luke 24:28-31 and 24:41-43, as well as in
John 20:19-23 and 21:1-14. There are similar references in apocryphal Christian
writings such as the Acts of John (106–10) and the Acts of Thomas (27, 49–50, 133).
There are also representations in early Christian art.

we are all sinners. Yet we do so in the midst of a meal with the risen Christ. God has made a free, unconditional covenant with humanity, and the resurrection testifies to the faithfulness of God. The God who *is* mercy is ever faithful. Therefore, sin is ultimately powerless.

The mercy of God is unconditional and very wide. In scripture's story, resurrection follows a terrible crucifixion. We have already asserted that the cross has exposed worldwide patterns of sin. The cross displays sin's awful, destructive power and its universal character. At the cross, we see humanity in its social shape — government, religion, judiciary, democracy — crucifying true God, true neighbor, and true self-before-God. But, although the cross depicts universal social sinfulness, the resurrection surely testifies to God's love for the whole sinful world. God's mercy is not merely therapy for a few individuals beset by guilt because of their inadvertent involvement in the cross. No. In Christ's death and resurrection a whole world is assured of God's pardon. We sing the familiar hymn "There's a Wideness in God's Mercy,"[19] and for centuries have debated the question, How wide is wide? The church is not always generous in dispensing the mercy of God. But God is. God does not dole out mercy like cookies only for good, repentant children. God's mercy is not conditioned by our response. God *is* mercy. So, wide is wider than we guess. In the cross and resurrection, all humanity has been given God's Declaration of Pardon.

Of course, the cross and the resurrection are in history. Thus, to us they happened before we were born. As a result, there is a sense in which mercy is always prior to our sins; we are forgiven before we confess and indeed before we ask for mercy. But, as they are in history, the cross and resurrection absolve all history. Must we not suppose that in the strange web of causality *all* human history led Christ to his cross? But, likewise, because the cross and resurrection are effective in history, mercy flows through time and is now the context of history. Such claims do not ultimately rest on the historic character of the cross and resurrection, but rather on the character of God, who is mercy and is mercy from everlasting to everlasting. Nevertheless, how can history be redeemed unless human history is also absolved?

Now we all live in the mercy, and some of us know it! Our calling is to live in mercy:

---

[19] Written in 1854 by F. W. Farber, a High Church Anglican cleric who had become Roman Catholic in 1846.

As God's chosen ones, holy and beloved, clothe yourselves with compassion, kindness, humility, meekness, and patience. Bear with one another and, if anyone has a complaint against another, forgive each other; just as the Lord has forgiven you, so you also must forgive. Above all, clothe yourselves with love, which binds everything together in perfect harmony. (Col. 3:12-14)

In Christian worship from the first century until today, there has been some sort of act of reconciliation, usually a kiss of peace. Recalling God's unmerited mercy, in the kiss of peace, we absolve one another, enacting the good news. "In Jesus Christ," we say, "we are forgiven." So we look into each other's eyes without illusions; we are sinners all. Yet we embrace each other *in* the mercy, the wide, wide mercy of God.

Mercy and the World's New Beginning

The meaning of Christ's death and resurrection is more than a declaration of pardon. Yes, although sinners, we are justified "as is" by the free, unmerited mercy of God. We are emphatically accepted on no other basis than God's own prodigious love; we do live in the wideness of God's mercy. Nevertheless, mercy alone is not salvation.

Without any hope for social renewal the notion of forgiveness is a disaster. Although our guilt might be eased on a regular basis, sin's destructiveness would be undaunted. Thus, Christian faith would be reduced to a daily therapeutic fix of good feelings for chronically guilty folk — cheap grace at its worst. The message of justification without any real hope for social sanctification is a little like a get-well-quick card mailed to a hospice. Unless society can be changed, unless new humanity is possible, forgiveness is nothing more than a religious placebo.

But the resurrection texts do declare that, with Christ risen, a new-Adam era has begun. We are therefore not only forgiven sinners, but forgiven sinners in the midst of a being-redeemed world. No wonder that Paul can declare, "Now is the day of salvation" (2 Cor. 6:2). The same power of God that raised up Jesus is at work in the world bringing renewal to humanity. The end-term promises of God are not only certain, but they are already beginning to happen among us. So the good news that the church is commissioned to declare is not only mercy for our sin, but an invitation to join the new humanity, God's new order in the midst of a broken, sinful world. The gospel is not merely the promise of inward rehabilitation — you can be a new you. Rather the gospel is news of a new order under the risen Christ: Come join God's coming new world.

Now it would be nice to say that the church is God's coming new world. Unfortunately, the church is emphatically not the kingdom of God that Jesus proclaimed. Nevertheless, the church as it is animated by the Spirit is meant to be a sign of the new order in an old-order world. In the words of Matthew, we are supposed to be "salt of the earth" and "light of the world" (Matt. 5:13-15). But these days in America, when you cannot tell the Christians from anyone else without a score card, the church seems to have lost it saltiness and dimmed its light. When the whole sense of a promised new order is absent, ecclesiology is bound to be deformed. Without any connection to the new humanity, baptism is reduced to a church membership ritual and eucharist becomes a togetherness rite. Although the church is not God's new order, it is meant to be a hint of the new order now and, more, a training school for new-order people. Rightly, we declare the good news — the promise of God's new order, forgiven and free — and then in our common baptized life demonstrate an inclusive bread-breaking love for all the world to see. What is the good news? We are being saved in a being-saved world.

Atonement Now

The problem for us is a "how" problem. Granted that once upon a time Christ died and was raised, that divine absolution has been declared, *how* does saving mercy reach out of the past to our lives? C. S. Lewis phrased the question nicely: "What I couldn't see was how the life and death of Someone Else (whoever he was) 2000 years ago could help us here and now."[20] What is the bridge that can cross the ages? How can the cross be saving for us twenty centuries later? Answer to the question has divided the church, often separating Catholics and Protestants, both of whom are still struggling to get over that substantial upset we call the Reformation.

For Protestants, the bridge between the ages is preaching and faith. The gospel of the cross and resurrection is preached and, if there is faith and repentance, salvation is activated and becomes potent in our modern lives. Thus, God's saving grace seems to be conditioned by

---

[20] Walter Hooper, ed., *They Stand Together: The Letters of C. S. Lewis to Arthur Greaves, 1914-1963* (New York: Macmillan, 1979), 427.

right preaching and a right response of believing repentance. Of course, the Protestant tradition insists that right preaching happens by God's grace as does the right response of faith. The problem with the scheme is that salvation can become an inward, personal event without social connection. In the revival tradition, converted faith is an individual heart miracle that triggers God's saving power, sans church and sans neighbor. No wonder we get "dream preachers" who shout, "Believe in Jeeeesus and be saved!"[21] And no wonder Catholics regard such theology as a fideist heresy, which no doubt it is.

For Catholics, the connection is the church with sacraments. The death and resurrection of Jesus reconstituted a discipleship under the leadership of the risen Christ. And the risen Christ breathed his Holy Spirit into the community. So what bridges time? Why, the church, the body of Christ. The church brings us the saving power of Christ via preaching and the sacraments. The Catholic position has virtue, the virtue of embodiment. Catholics affirm a social reality to match our social sinfulness. But the problem with such theology is that, inevitably, the church is equated with Christ. Triumphalism, a most unbecoming heresy, can be a chronic problem.

To Protestants, the Catholic position tends toward idolatry and false religion. To Catholics, the Protestant position smacks of disembodied Docetism, immodest pulpits, and a false, amorphous faith.

Earlier we argued that resurrection texts contain brief confessional statements, "creedlets," along with allusions to the common life of the Christian community, such as to preaching, the Lord's Supper, forgiving, and the like. So although the church is not Christ, and in fact is always an admixture of falsity and being saved, nevertheless it confesses Christ's faith and continues Christ's own work by preaching, teaching, healing, prophetically witnessing, breaking bread, and so on. Thus, the risen Christ continues to save *through* the broken body of the church. Salvation does not have an ecclesial trademark: God is the source of the church's life and message, and is the saving power that flows through the foolishness of the church. So, as Paul insists: "Let the one who boasts, boast in the Lord" (1 Cor. 1:31).

As for faith, disembodied faith is no faith. Surely faith is more than a quick baptismal dive into Pat Boone's swimming pool! Faith that responds to Christ's death and resurrection is faith that is socially embodied; it is faith of a new humanity in the midst of our broken

---

[21] The phrase "dream preachers" is from Luther.

world. We hear the gospel through the preaching of the church, and we respond with a believing repentance that can shape a new social reality. Perhaps we can embody faith and seek to run from triumphalism at the same time. Obviously, in view of the broken character of the church, we cannot suppose that the church *is* God's new order, or even that the sacraments and preaching are preserved from sinful distortion. But in and through our brokenness, grace is at work, the saving grace of our Lord Jesus Christ, crucified and risen. As for the church being the body of Christ, we must avoid a language of identity; the term "body of Christ" refers to an eschatological reality that we see dimly, perhaps sacramentally. The church, in its brokenness, is a promise of what sometimes we refer to as "the communion of saints."

Saving mercy comes to us from a community and calls us into a community. If sin is socially shaped so is our being saved. And the church is, as Calvin supposed, a kind of kindergarten in which we practice new-order life in the midst of our brokenness. Were it not for the unseen, unfelt working of the Holy Spirit, the church would be unbearable. Like all human social groupings, the church also is shot through with falsity and, emphatically, with false religion. Remember, sin is a social disease and churches live within society, although with the shared Holy Spirit ever at work. Ministers are often disillusioned by the church, just as the laity are often disillusioned by the ministry. But in and through the church, the saving message is spoken in stumbling words, and bread is broken by trembling hands, and we are, to our astonishment, being saved — now.

The Power of a Saving Symbol

Of course the real bridge across the years is God, the eternal God. God, who was working with saving power through Jesus Christ, is with us with saving power now. Moreover, the eternal God has been a saving power since creation. Such a God is the God of Abraham and Sarah, of Isaac and Jacob, of Hebrew prophets and Hebrew priests. So, when the Book of Acts, speaking of Jesus Christ, announces, "There is salvation in no one else," it cannot mean that there was no salvation before the arrival of the historical Jesus. To so argue would be to elevate the historical figure of Jesus Christ and depose the God he proclaimed. Ultimately such a claim would deny the Trinity.[22] No, Acts

---

[22] The Trinity includes three persons: God, the Eternal Word, and the Holy Spirit. To suggest that there was no salvation before Jesus Christ is to deny the second person of the Trinity, the Eternal Word.

must mean that there is no salvation except through the power of God revealed in the life and death and resurrection of Jesus Christ. The God disclosed in Jesus Christ is none other than the creator, the sustainer of all life, and the God of Sarah, Abraham, and the Hebrew prophets. The eternal God bridges all time and space.

So we must insist that from the creation God has intended free communion with humanity, a communion that is singularly embodied in Jesus Christ. Therefore, from the beginning God has had in mind what we call "salvation," namely, the social realization of the Great Commandment — a whole wide world living in the holy courtesies of exchanged love. No wonder that in the first chapters of Colossians and Ephesians we come across exalted hymns linking creation and Christ — "all things have been created through him and for him" (Col. 1:16) and "[God] chose us in Christ before the foundation of the world to be holy and blameless before [God] in love" (Eph. 1:4). Thus, we must never preach salvation as an emergency tactic brought about by Eve and Adam's unfortunate apple munching. To preach in such a manner implies that salvation is a project forced upon God by our sin, which had God stymied until God, suddenly inspired, dreamed up the idea of the cross. No, we declare that all along God has intended a oneness (at-one-ment) with humanity: "I will be their God and they will be my children" (Rev. 21:7). It is true that under the conditions of sin, the oneness God intended ended in a crucifixion. Yet, at the same time, through crucifixion God's original purpose will be realized.

So all along, through generation after generation, with saving power God has been seeking compassionate oneness with a free, created *ex nihilo* humanity. God is still seeking oneness with humanity. But now, in a way, God has come closer to humanity through the living symbol, Jesus Christ. Rather obviously, we cannot know Christ in his humanity, even though we know he was a human being as are we all. Now Christ comes to us through song, story, and stained glass, in sermons and Sunday school lessons, prayers and pictures — he arrives as a word and forms in common consciousness as a symbolic figure. As symbol, he mediates truth; he is true God-with-us, our true and loving neighbor, and our true humanity before God. (No wonder we can call Christ "God-with-us" and, at the same time, speak of him praying to God.) Through Christ's symbolic ministry, we can struggle against falsity and be reconciled with ourselves, our neighbors, and with God.

Some rather conservative Christians may squirm over the word *symbol*. We are using the term to express the reality of Christ's saving power in our lives today. To argue that Christ has become a symbol in consciousness is not to deny the reality of Christ, but to affirm the mode of Christ's real saving power. Scripture scholars and church historians can trace the elevation of Christ's life and death and resurrection, first in the cosmic structures of Paul's apocalyptic theology, and then in the titles Christ was given in the Gospels, and then in subsequent liturgical practice and theological reflection until, finally, the church affirmed a creed that declared Jesus Christ was "truly God" and "truly human."[23] Theological liberalism may have pointed to a disparity between the historical, human Jesus and the symbolic Christ of the creeds. We are not doing so. No, instead we are suggesting that Christ has become a saving symbol by God's own design. The mode of Christ's saving power is as a symbol in social consciousness.

The Widening Images of Salvation

If we flip Bible pages we can trace a widening vision of salvation — from the promised land, to perfect kingship, to a restoration after exile, to the image of Zion. All such images of salvation rest on the notion of covenant; they all involve God and God's wayward, often captive, people. Certainly, images of salvation are not merely religious. They include justice and peace and freedom and some degree of economic well-being. They are emphatically social; directly or indirectly they are all looking for a new order of God. So although the Bible begins in a garden, it ends in an urban promise, a holy city descending from God. Please note: salvation is not a return to Edenic innocence. We will not be saved by dropping our fig leaves or leaving incurious apples to rot on the Tree of the Knowledge of Good and Evil. No, salvation must mean a transformation of selves *and* of social structures rather than some kind of reversion to infant naiveté. Salvation is the redemption of history and not an obliteration of history by circling back to a once-upon-a-time primal innocence.

But how can society be saved by a person, even the symbolic person of Jesus Christ? A Protestant pattern of personal, one-by-one salvation via individual conversions will not suffice. We need to recognize the church as a social reality, a collectivity among many collectivities. Although the church may well be corrupt and inevitably compromised, it can speak the gospel. In a sophisticated multimedia world, the church has an amplified voice that can speak as a social organization to social

---

[23] See discussion of the famous formula of Chalcedon (451) in J. H. Leith, ed., *Creeds of the Churches* (Garden City, N.Y.: Doubleday, 1963), 34–36.

organizations. The church can address the state, the economic community, the entertainment industry, and the like. When individual Christians, usually those of the political right wing, deplore the church's social pronouncements, they do not understand the necessity of the church's witness to the corporate world. Without a doubt, the church's denominational fragmentation weakens its social voice. Nevertheless, the church as an institution must preach the gospel to social institutions.

As a social symbol, Jesus Christ can reach beyond the church. Certainly many of the cultural representations of Jesus Christ are distorted or even mildly heretical. *The Last Temptation of Christ,* filled with Kazantzakis's own Bergsonian *élan vital;* Ignazio Silone's *Bread and Wine,* portraying a Marxist Christ; more recently, the satiric christology of A. J. Langguth's *Jesus Christs;* and even Monty Python's brazenly amusing *Life of Brian (of Nazareth)*—all these works have distressed conservative Christians because they are disrespectful or not true to scripture.[24] And of course, they are not true to scripture. They reflect different ways in which Christ is understood, received, or rejected. In so doing, they all present the symbolic Jesus Christ to culture. Even the dreadful kitsch TV religious spectaculars that are seen during the Easter or Christmas season contribute to a cultural image of Christ. From the earliest centuries, when Christ showed up in sculpture as a young Adonis, to the present day, there have been many, many cultural manifestations of Christ. Medieval artists portrayed him as a knight or a mystic. In the nineteenth century he showed up as an innocent "natural" teacher. In every age, the figure of Christ participates in artistic images of heroism and of agony, all of which are cheerful distortions of the biblical record. So the figure of Christ enters into social consciousness and, as a social symbol, has saving power.[25]

When the Bible tells of principalities and powers, such texts may refer to social customs and social attitudes that we project and that then

---

[24] N. Kazantzakis, *The Last Temptation of Christ,* trans. P. A. Bien (New York: Simon and Schuster, 1960); I. Silone, *Bread and Wine,* trans. G. David and E. Mosbacher (New York: Harper & Bros., 1937); A. J. Langguth, *Jesus Christs* (New York: Ballantine Books, 1968); Monty Python, *The Life of Brian (of Nazareth)* (New York: Grossett & Dunlap, 1979). For discussion, see T. Ziolkowski, *Fictional Transfigurations of Jesus* (Princeton, N.J.: Princeton University Press, 1972).

[25] On different cultural representations of Christ, see J. Pelikan, *Jesus through the Centuries: His Place in the History of Culture* (New Haven: Yale University Press, 1985); G. S. Sloyan, *The Jesus Tradition: Images of Jesus in the West* (Mystic, Conn.: Twenty-Third Publications, 1986); E. Malatesta, ed., *Jesus in Christian Devotion and Contemplation* (St. Meinrad, Ind.: Abbey Press, 1974); and G. H. Tavard, *Images of the Christ: An Enquiry into Christology* (New York: University Press of America, 1982).

turn and dominate us, our behavioral patterns, and our ways of thinking. The principalities and powers are inadvertent human creations that, given a kind of sacred status, can coerce us. According to the Christian scriptures, Christ has stripped the principalities and powers of their sacred aura and has shown them up as no-powers. Certainly, the principalities and powers were involved in the crucifixion; fixed tradition and conventional wisdoms were clearly on display. But in his humanity Christ resisted the powers, and in his resurrection he demonstrated their impotence. Paul anticipates that eventually Christ will tame all the social powers in God's great salvation.

The Mystery and the Passion

Christian eschatology seems to be trapped in the once-was or the yet-to-be, in the past tense or the future perfect. We look back at the crucial event of the cross as a once-was act of salvation or we gaze far into the future toward a someday consummation. Both ways of thinking leave us in between where, like the two tramps in Beckett's *Waiting for Godot*, we wait for God to the neglect of our oppressed neighbors.[26] But, as we have already noted, the apostle Paul sings a different song: "*Now* is the day of salvation," he cries.

Perhaps the figure of Christ, the cross and the Easter glory disclose the mysterious saving power of God that is ever at work in and through the human world. Suppose God is one who does not dominate history but, in suffering, self-giving love, seeks to transform us all. And suppose God's power is *now.* We live now in a world already being saved by God's unassuming grace. Suppose that the world, our world, is shot through with trajectories of grace that are, even now, moving toward God's purpose. Perhaps in the midst of our decaying, polluted city of earth we are meant to catch sight of the gleaming turrets of the new Jerusalem. Like a double exposure, one picture impressed on another, we can see both the sinful world and the shapes of God's new creation all at once.

If we are being saved, the whole wide world of us being saved in the bright mercy of God, then we can live with a certain sprightliness, disrupting each other's busyness with the profound conversations of love. We can seek to shape all our moments into an embodiment of the Great Commandment. Above all, we can meet each other in the grace of the Lord Jesus Christ, our true neighbor, God-with-us, and the hidden true self we all shall be.

---

[26] S. Beckett, *Waiting for Godot* (New York: Grove Press, 1954).

Indexes _____

MAJOR PASSAGES DISCUSSED

RESURRECTION PASSAGES

235

SYNOPTIC PASSION PASSAGES

JOHANNINE PASSION PASSAGES

REFERENCES TO ANCIENT SOURCES

SUBJECTS